SALES TECHNI

SALES

TECHNIQUE AND MANAGEMENT

Geoff Lancaster
MSc, DMS, FCIM, MBIM, MInstPS
Universities of Hull and
Newcastle-upon-Tyne

David Jobber
BA(Econ), MSc, PhD
University of Bradford Management Centre

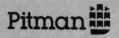

Pitman Publishing
128 Long Acre, London WC2E 9AN

A Division of Longman Group (UK) Limited

©Macdonald & Evans Ltd 1985
 Longman Group UK Ltd 1990

First edition published by Macdonald & Evans in 1985
Reprinted by Pitman 1988
Second edition published in 1990

A CIP catalogue record for this book is available
from the British Library.

ISBN 0-273-03190-2

Printed in Great Britain by The Bath Press, Avon

Contents

List of Illustrations

List of Tables

Foreword

The selling and sales management function has not received the attention
it deserves from British universities and polytechnics. One reason for this
is the paucity of suitable textbooks for undergraduate and postgraduate
teaching. This book blends applied theory with the down-to-earth realities
of the selling function, and provides a comprehensive coverage of the
topic in a readable way. I believe this textbook will find favour among
academics and may even stimulate a more in-depth treatment of the
subject on marketing and business studies courses.

At the end of each chapter the authors provide mini-case studies and
practical exercises to aid teachers in designing tutorial and seminar
material, and students in exploring their understanding of the material
to be found in the chapters. Typical examination questions are also
included to supplement the case studies.

The practitioner, likewise, cannot fail to learn something from this
book. The practicalities and problems of selling and sales management
are explored in detail, and methods which have proved successful in the
real world are explained lucidly.

Both Geoff Lancaster and David Jobber are experienced teachers of
sales and marketing, and it is this training which has enabled them to
produce an outstanding book.

1990   PROFESSOR PETER DOYLE
                                        University of Warwick

Preface

The text covers what must still be the most important element of the marketing mix for most students and practitioners. With a move away from the selling function towards more esoteric areas of marketing over the past few years, this vital aspect of marketing has been somewhat neglected. However, in the end it has to be face-to-face contact that eventually wins the order, and this text therefore explains and documents the selling and sales management process from both the theoretical and practical viewpoints.

More precisely, the text is split into five logical parts: Sales Perspective, Sales Technique, Sales Environment, Sales Management and Sales Control. Sales Perspective examines selling in its historical role and then views its place within marketing and a marketing organisation. Different types of buyers are also analysed in order to help us achieve an understanding of their thinking and organise our selling effort accordingly. Sales Technique is essentially practical and covers preparation for selling, the personal selling process and sales responsibilities. Sales Environment looks at the institutions through which sales are made; this covers channels, including industrial, commercial and public authority selling followed by selling for resale. International Selling is an increasingly important area in view of the ever increasing 'internationalisation' of business and this merits a separate chapter. Sales Management covers recruitment, selection, motivation and training, in addition to how we must organise and compensate salesmen from a managerial standpoint. Finally, Sales Control covers sales budgets and explains how this is the starting point for business planning. Sales forecasting is also covered in this final section, and a guide is given to the techniques of forecasting and why it is strictly a responsibility of sales management and not finance.

Each chapter concludes with a mini-case study and practical exercises, together with formal practice questions typical of those the student will encounter in the examination room.

Since the first edition was written, many developments have taken place in the field of public relations. Today it is seen as a complementary activity to marketing in general, and to selling in particular. With this in mind, a new section has been included on public relations.

The text will be invaluable to those students studying for the examinations of the Chartered Institute of Marketing, the Communication, Advertising and Marketing Education Foundation, the London Chamber of Commerce and Industry higher stage selling and sales management subject, marketing specialisms on Higher National Certificate and Diploma in Business Studies, first degrees with a marketing input, and postgraduate courses like the Diploma in Management Studies and Masters of Business Administration that have a marketing input. In addition, the text emphasises the practical as well as the theoretical, and it will be of invaluable assistance to salespersons in the field as well as to sales management.

The authors wish to thank Mr R. Edwards, sales training manager, ICI Pharmaceuticals, for permission to reproduce his role playing exercise. We would also like to thank John A. Saunders and Tong Hon-Chung for permission to reproduce the material on selling to Japan, together with the publishers MCB University Press Ltd, Toller Lane, Bradford.

1990   GL
                                                                              DJ

PART ONE
Sales Perspective

1 Development and Role of Selling in Marketing

1.1 BACKGROUND

Perhaps no other area of business activity gives rise to as much discussion within and between those directly involved and the so-called man in the street as the activity known as selling. This is not surprising when one considers that so many people derive their livelihood, either directly or indirectly, from selling. Even those who have no direct involvement in selling come into contact with it in their roles as consumers. Perhaps, because of this familiarity, many people have strong, and often misplaced, views about selling and sales people. Surprisingly, many of these misconceptions are held by people who have spent their working lives in selling; some of this might be due to the well-known saying of 'not being able to see the wood for the trees'.

It is important to recognise that selling and sales management, although closely related, are not the same and we shall start in this chapter by examining the nature and role of selling and sales management in the contemporary organisation and exploring some of the more common myths and misconceptions.

We shall also look at the developing role of selling, because, like other business functions, it is required to adapt and change. Perhaps one of the most important and far reaching of these business changes has been the adoption of the concept and practice of marketing, due to changes in the business environment. Because of the importance of this development to the sales function, we shall examine the place of marketing within the firm and the place of selling within marketing.

1.2 NATURE AND ROLE OF SELLING

The simplest way to think of the nature and role of selling (or salesmanship as it is sometimes termed) is that its function is to make a sale. This seemingly obvious statement disguises what is often a very complex process, involving the use of a whole set of principles, techniques and substantial personal skills, and covering a wide range of different types of selling task. Later in the chapter we will establish a more precise meaning for the term selling, but first we will examine the reasons for the intense interest in this area of business activity.

The literature of selling abounds with texts, ranging from the more conceptual approaches to the simplistic 'how it is done' approach. Companies also spend large sums of money training their sales personnel in the art of selling. The reason for all this attention to personal selling is simple: in most companies sales personnel are the single most important link with the customer. The best designed and planned set of marketing efforts may fail because the sales force is ineffective. This front line role of the salesperson means that for many customers the salesperson *is* the company. Allied with the often substantial costs associated with recruiting, training and maintaining the sales force, there are powerful reasons for stressing the importance of the selling task and for justifying attempts to improve effectiveness in this area. Part Two of this text is addressed to this important area of sales techniques.

It should be remembered that the term selling encompasses a whole variety of sales situations and activities. For example, there are those sales positions where the sales representative is required primarily to deliver the product to the customer on a regular or periodic basis. The emphasis in this type of sales activity is very different to the sales position where the sales representative is dealing with sales of capital equipment to industrial purchasers. In addition, some sales representatives deal only in export markets whilst others sell direct to the customers in their homes. One of the most striking aspects of the term selling is thus the wide diversity of selling roles.

Irrespective of this diversity of roles, one trend common to all selling tasks is the increasing emphasis on professionalism in selling. This trend, together with its implications for the nature and role of selling, can be best explained if we examine some of the myths and realities which surround the image of selling.

1.3 IMAGE OF SELLING

Ask any group of people not involved in selling what springs to mind on the mention of the word 'selling' and it will prompt a variety of responses. It will evoke a high proportion of negative, even hostile, responses, including 'immoral', 'dishonest', 'unsavoury', 'degrading', 'wasteful', etc. Is such an unfavourable view justified? We suggest not. In fact the underlying attitudes to selling derive from widely held misconceptions about selling, some of which are outlined below.

(*i*) Selling is not a worthwhile career. This notion is held by many, the common attitude being that if one has talent then it will be wasted in sales. Unfortunately this attitude is often held by those who are in a position to advise and influence young people in their choice of careers. In some academic circles it is fashionable to denigrate careers in selling, and the consequence is that many of our brighter graduates are not attracted to a career in selling.

(*ii*) Good products will sell themselves and thus the selling process adds unnecessarily to costs. This view of selling assumes that if you produce a superior product then there will always be buyers. This may be all right if a firm can produce a technologically superior product, but then it is likely that the additional costs will accrue in terms of research and development, and there will be continued research and development costs involved in keeping ahead. In addition, as is developed later in the text, the role of selling is not solely to sell; it can be used to feed back information from customers to the firm – particularly product performance information – and this is of direct use to research and development!

(*iii*) There is something immoral about selling, and one should be suspicious about those who earn their living from this activity. The origins and reasons for this, the most pervasive and damaging of the misconceptions about selling, are unclear. Nevertheless, such attitudes can make life difficult for the salesperson who has first to overcome the barriers which such mistrust erects in the customer/salesperson relationship.

It has been suggested that some of the more critical responses towards selling derive from a number of misconceptions, but the question still remains as to how and why these misconceptions have arisen and why they still persist. Perhaps, more importantly, those who are concerned to improve the image of selling must be more vociferous, yet objective, in presenting the case for selling. In presenting this case, the first thing to recognise is that misconceptions invariably have some basis of fact. There are always unscrupulous individuals and companies ready to trade on the ignorance and gullibility of the unsuspecting customer. These individuals are not salespeople: at best they are misguided traders and at worst they are crooks. At some times in our lives we inevitably feel that we have purcahsed something that we did not really want or on terms that we could not really afford, because we were subjected to high pressure sales techniques.

Selling then is not entirely blameless, but salespeople are becoming more professional in their approach to customers. Some of the worst excesses in selling have been curbed, some legally, but increasingly voluntarily. To overcome some of the misconceptions, selling needs to sell itself, and the following facts about selling should be more universally aired.

(*i*) There is nothing inherently immoral or unscrupulous about selling or about those involved in this activity. Selling provides a mechanism for exchange and through this process, customers' needs and wants are satisfied. Furthermore, most people, at some stage in their lives, are involved in selling – even if it is only selling their skills and personality in an attempt to obtain a job.

(*ii*) Selling is now a worthwhile career. Many of those who have spent a lifetime in selling have found it to be a challenging, responsible and rewarding occupation. Inevitably a career in selling means meeting people and working with them, and a selling job often offers substantial discretion in being able to plan one's own work schedule.

(*iii*) Good products do not sell themselves. An excellent product may pass unnoticed unless its benefits and features are explained to the customer. What may appear to be a superior product may be totally unsuited to a particular customer. Selling is unique in that it deals with the special needs of each individual customer, and the salesperson, with specialist product knowledge, is in a position to assess these circumstances and advise each customer accordingly.

1.4   THE NATURE AND ROLE OF SALES MANAGEMENT

In the same way as selling has become more professional, so too has the nature and role of sales management. The emphasis is now on the word 'management'. Increasingly, those involved in management are being called upon to exercise in a professional way the key duties of all managers, namely planning, organising and controlling. The emphasis has changed from the idea that to be a good sales manager you had to have the right personality and that the main feature of the job was ensuring that the sales force were out selling sufficient volume. Although such qualities may be admirable, the duties of the sales manager in the modern company have both broadened and changed in emphasis.

Nowadays the sales manager is expected to play a much more strategic role in the company. The sales manager is required to make a key input into the formulation of company plans, this theme being developed in Chapters 3 and 11. There is thus a need to be familiar with the techniques associated with planning, including sales forecasting and budgeting, and these are dealt with in Chapters 12 and 13. The sales manager also needs to be familiar with the concept of marketing to ensure that sales and marketing activities are integrated – a theme expanded in this chapter. In many companies the emphasis is now less on sales volume and more on profits. The sales manager needs to be able to analyse and direct the activities of the sales force towards more profitable business. In dealing with a sales force, the sales manager must be aware of modern developments in human resource management.

Looked at in the manner just outlined, the role of the sales manager may seem to be formidable. He or she must be an accountant, a planner, a personnel manager and a marketer at the same time. However, the prime responsibility is to ensure that the sales function makes the most effective contribution to the achievement of company objectives and goals. In order to fulfil this role, sales managers will undertake the following specific duties and responsibilities.

(*i*) The determination of sales force objectives and goals.
(*ii*) Stemming from the above, forecasting and budgeting.
(*iii*) Sales force organisation, sales force size, territory design and planning.
(*iv*) Sales force selection, recruitment and training.
(*v*) Motivating the sales force.
(*vi*) Sales force evaluation and control.

Because these areas encompass the key duties of the sales manager, they are discussed in detail in Parts Four and Five of the text.

Perhaps one of the most significant developments affecting selling and sales management in recent years has been the evolution of the marketing concept. Because of its importance to selling, we will now turn our attention to the nature of this evolution and its effect upon sales activities..

1.5 THE MARKETING CONCEPT

In tracing the development of the marketing concept it is customary to chart three successive stages in the evolution of modern business practice.

(*i*)   Production orientation.
(*ii*) Sales orientation.
(*iii*) Marketing orientation.

1.5.1 PRODUCTION ORIENTATION

This era was characterised by the focus of company efforts on producing a good or service. More specifically, management efforts were devoted to achieving high production efficiency, often through the large scale production of standardised items. In such a business other functions such as sales, finance and personnel were secondary to the main function of the business, which was to produce. More importantly, the underlying philosophy towards customers was that they would purchase the products, provided that they were available in sufficiently large quantities at a suitably low price.

One of the best known examples of such a philosophy was the Model T factory of Henry Ford. His idea was that if he could produce a standard model vehicle in large quantities using mass production techniques, then he could supply a potential demand for relatively cheap private transport. At the time (in the 1920s in the USA) Ford was correct; there was such a demand and his products proved successful. A production orientation to business was thus suited to an economic climate where potential demand outstripped supply, as was the case in the 1920s prior to the wide-scale introduction of mass production techniques.

However times change, and such a philosophy is not conducive to doing business in today's economic climate, where potential supply usually outstrips demand.

1.5.2 SALES ORIENTATION

With the large-scale introduction of mass production techniques in the 1920s and 1930s, particularly in the USA and Western Europe, and the rapid worldwide increase in competition which accompanied this, many firms adopted a sales orientation.

The sales orientated company is one where the focus of company effort switches to the sales function. The main issue here is not how to produce but, having products, how to ensure that this production is sold. The underlying philosophy towards customers in a sales orientated business is that, if left to their own devices, customers will be slow or reluctant to buy. In any case, even those customers who are seeking to purchase the type of product or service which the company produces will have a wide range of potential suppliers. This situation is exacerbated when, in addition to sufficient capacity on the supply side, demand is depressed. Such was the case in many of the developed economies in the 1930s, and it was in this period that many of the so called 'hard sell' techniques were developed. There is no doubt that many of the techniques developed were dubious, not to say dishonest, and much of the tainted image accompanying selling discussed earlier derives from their use.

Even today, many companies adopt a sales orientated approach to doing business, even though customers are better protected against its worst excesses, as will be discussed in Chapter 8.

1.5.3   MARKETING ORIENTATION

It is unclear exactly when the idea of marketing or customer orientation began to emerge; indeed in some ways the central importance of the customer has perhaps always been recognised in the long history of trading. Not until the 1950s, however, did the ideas associated with the so-called marketing concept begin to emerge and take shape. The marketing concept – initially an American phenomenon – arose partly as a result of a dissatisfaction with the previously described production and sales orientations, partly as a result of a changing environment, and partly as a result of fundamental business sense.

The marketing concept holds that the key to successful and profitable business rests with identifying the needs and wants of customers and providing products and services to satisfy these needs and wants. On the surface such a concept does not appear to be a far reaching and fundamentally different philosophy of business, but in fact the marketing concept requires a revolution in how a company thinks about, and practises, its business activities as compared to production or sales orientation. Central to this revolution in business thinking is the emphasis given to needs and wants of the customer. The contrast between this approach and, for example, that of a sales orientated company is shown in Fig. 1.

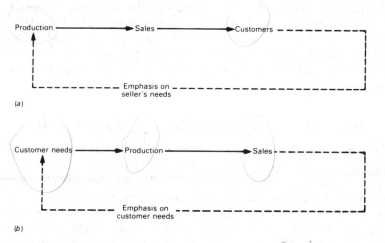

Fig 1   Sales versus market orientation.
(a) Sales orientation. (b) Market orientation.

Praise worthy

Increasingly, companies have come to recognise that this different approach to doing business is essential in today's environment. Consumers are now better educated and more sophisticated than they were. Real incomes have increased steadily over the years and today's consumers now have considerable discretionary spending power to allocate between an increasingly diverse range of products and services. Too many companies have learned the hard way that having what they feel to be a superior product, efficient production, and extensive promotion – laudable though these may be – is not sufficient to confer automatic success. In order to stand any chance of success, the customer and his needs must be placed at the very centre of business planning. In part, this stress on understanding the consumer explains the development of those concepts and techniques aimed at understanding buyer behaviour. In Chapter 2 we develop a framework within which consumer and organisational buying behaviour may be analysed.

1.6   IMPLEMENTING THE MARKETING CONCEPT

Subscribing to a philosophy of marketing, even though an important first step, is not the same as putting that philosophy into practice. Implementing the marketing concept requires more than paying lip service to the ideas inherent in the concept. For a company to be marketing orientated requires that a number of changes take place, in organisation, in practices and in attitudes. Furthermore, to become operational and of real value to a company requires that the discipline of marketing contributes what might be termed a technology of marketing. By this we mean that management requires the development of a set of tools (techniques and concepts) in order to implement the marketing concept. We have already mentioned that the behavioural sciences can lead to an understanding of buyer behaviour; another example is the development of quantitative and qualitative techniques of marketing research for analysing and appraising markets. Some of the more important and useful concepts in marketing are now discussed.

1.6.1 MARKET SEGMENTATION AND TARGETING

Because marketing focuses on customer needs and wants, this requires that companies identify these needs and wants and then develop marketing programmes to satisfy them as a route to achieving company objectives. The diversity of customer needs and wants, and the multiplicity of ways in which these may be satisfied, means that few, if any, companies are in a position to serve effectively all the customers in a market. Market segmentation is the process of identifying those clusters, or segments, of customers in a market which share similar needs and wants and will respond in a similar and unique way to a given marketing effort. Having identified the various segments in a market, a company can then decide which of these segments are most attractive and to which it can market most effectively. Company marketing efforts can then be tailored specifically to the needs of these segments on which the company has decided to target its marketing.

Market segmentation and targeting is one of the most useful concepts in marketing, and a whole set of techniques have been developed to aid companies in its application. Among some of the more important benefits of effective segmentation and targeting are the following.

(i) A clearer identification of market opportunities and particularly the analysis of gaps in a market.
(ii) The design of product and market appeals, which are more finely tuned to the needs of the market.
(iii) The focusing of marketing and sales efforts on those segments with the greatest potential.

There are a number of bases for segmenting markets, which may be used singly or in combination. For example, a manufacturer of toothpaste may decide that the market segments best on the basis of age, i.e. the seller discovers that the different age groups in the market for the product have different wants and needs and vary in what they require from the product. The seller will find that the various segments will respond more favourably, in terms of sales, if he tailors his product and marketing programme more to the needs of each segment. Alternatively, the seller may find that the market for toothpaste segments on the basis of income – the different income groups in the market vary in their product requirements. Finally, the seller may find that the market segments on the basis of a combination of both income and age characteristics. Among some of the more frequently used bases for segmentation are the following.

(*i*) CONSUMER PRODUCTS/MARKETS
- Age.
- Sex.
- Income.
- Social class.
- Geographical location.
- Type of residence [A Classification of Residential Neighbourhoods – ACORN].
- Personality.
- Benefits sought.
- Usage rate, e.g. heavy users v. light users.

(*ii*) INDUSTRIAL PRODUCTS/MARKETS
- End use market/type of industry/product application.
- Benefits sought.
- Company size.
- Geographical location.
- Usage rates.

Whatever the base(s) chosen to segment a market, there is no doubt that the application of the concept of segmentation and targeting is a major step towards becoming marketing orientated.

1.6.2 THE MARKETING MIX

In discussing the notion of market segmentation, we have frequently alluded to the company marketing programme. By far the most important decisions within this marketing programme, and indeed the essence of the marketing manager's task within a company, are decisions on the controllable marketing variables: decisions on prices, products, promotion and distribution. Taken together, these four variables comprise what is termed the *marketing mix* – a concept which, like segmentation and targeting, is central to modern marketing practice.

Generally speaking, company management has a number of variables, or ingredients, which it can control. For example, the management of a company have discretion over the range of products to be produced, their features, quality levels, etc. The task of marketing management is to blend these ingredients together into a successful recipe. The term marketing mix is appropriate, for there are many marketing mix ingredients and even more ways of combining them. In order to simplify the classification problem which this causes, the major ingredients of the mix are often referred to as 'the four Ps' – product, price and promotion, with distribution being referred to as place. (The term 'four Ps' used to describe the marketing mix was probably first used by E. Jerome McCarthy (1960).) In turn, each of the mix elements requires that a number of decisions be made, for example, about the following.

(*i*) PRICE. Price levels; credit terms; price changes; discounts.
(*ii*) PRODUCT. Features; packaging; quality; range.
(*iii*) PROMOTION. Advertising; publicity; sales promotion; personal selling.
(*iv*) PLACE. Inventory; channels of distribution; number of intermediaries.

It will be seen that personal selling is considered to be one component of the promotional decision area of the marketing mix. We shall return to the place of selling in the mix later in this chapter, whilst the notion of a promotional mix is considered in more detail in Chapter 3. At this stage we will consider in greater detail the other elements of the mix.

Product

Many believe that product decisions represent the most important ingredient of the marketing mix. Decisions in this area, they argue, have the most direct and long lasting influence on the degree of success which a company enjoys. At first glance this may seem to constitute evidence of a production as opposed to marketing orientated stance. However it does not. There is no doubt that product decisions are the most important of the marketing decisions which a company makes. It is true that unless there is a potential demand – a true market need – for a product then no matter how good it is, it will not succeed. This is not to say that decisions about products should be made in isolation. It is also true that there are many examples of products which had considerable market potential, but failed because of poor promotional, pricing and distribution decisions. Nevertheless, most salespeople know to their cost the difficulties of selling a poor or inappropriate product, even if that product is heavily advertised and competitively priced. In effect, product decisions determine the upper limit to a company's sales potential. The effectivenss of decisions on the other elements of the mix determine the extent to which this potential is realised.

It should be stressed that the term product covers anything that a company offers to its customers for the purpose of satisfying their needs. In addition to the physical, tangible products offered for sale, there are also services and skills. Non-profit organisations also market their services to potential customers. Increasingly, charities, educational establishments, libraries, museums and even political candidates make use of the techniques of marketing. There are a number of schemes for classifying products, depending upon the basis chosen for classification. For example, a broad distinction can be made between consumer and industrial products, the basis for classification here being the end-use/buyer.

Regardless of how and on what basis a product or service is classified, one of the most important factors to bear in mind about the product is that the customer is purchasing a package of benefits, not product features. This concept of a product is yet another example of a market orientated approach to doing business. It looks at the product from the point of view of what the customer is actually purchasing, i.e. needs and wants. For example, the woman purchasing cosmetics is purchasing beauty, hope, etc. Theodore Levitt (1962) provides us with perhaps one of the most graphic examples of this concept of a product when he states: 'Purchasing agents do not buy quarter inch drills; they buy quarter inch holes.' Viewing the product in this way can provide useful insights which can be used in the marketing of a product. In the sales area it can be used to develop the sales presentation by stressing the ways in which the product or service provides a solution to the customer's problems.

The product life cycle

One of the most useful concepts in marketing derives from the idea that most products tend to follow a particular pattern over time in terms of sales and profits. This pattern is shown in Fig. 2 and is known as the product life-cycle curve.

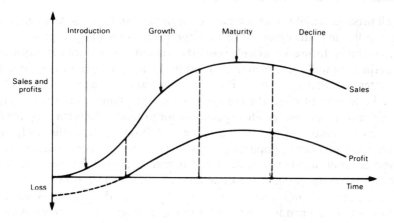

Fig 2   The product life-cycle curve.

The product life cycle is analogous to the life cycle pattern of humans, and has four distinct stages – introduction (birth), growth, maturity and eventually decline. Its shape can be best explained by outlining briefly the nature of each of the stages.

(*i*) INTRODUCTION. In this stage of the product life cycle, sales growth is relatively slow. Dealers must be persuaded to stock and promote the product; consumers must be made aware of its existence, persuaded to be interested, and convinced that it is a worthwhile purchase. They may even have to be educated in how to use the product and their existing purchasing and life-style habits changed. There are no profits at this stage, and heavy launch costs can often mean a large financial deficit.

(*ii*) GROWTH. After the initial slow acceptance, sales begin to escalate at a relatively rapid pace. There is a snowball effect as word-of-mouth communication and advertising begin to take effect. Dealers may request to stock the product. Small profits begin to be made.

(*iii*) MATURITY. The growth of sales begins to slow as the market begins to become saturated. Few new buyers are attracted to the product and there is a high proportion of repeat sales. Attracted by the high profit and sales figures, competitors have now entered the market. Partly because of this increased competition, profits having peaked, then begin to decline during this stage.

(*iv*) DECLINE. Sales begin to fall and already slim profits margins are depressed even further. Customers have begun to become bored with the product and are attracted by newer, improved products. Dealers begin to de-stock the product in anticipation of reduced sales.

Implications of the product life cycle

Not all products exhibit such a typical cycle of sales and profits. Some products have hardly any life cycle at all (a large proportion of new products are unsuccessful in the market place). Similarly, sales may be reduced abruptly even in a period of rapid sales growth as a result of, say, the introduction of a new and better competitive product. Products vary too in the length of time which they take to pass through the life cycle. Unlike the human life span, there is no such thing as an average life expectation for products. Nevertheless, the fact that a great number of products do tend to follow the generalised life cycle pattern has a number of implications for marketing and sales strategies. Some of these are considered in more detail in Chapter 3. Two of the more important implications of the product life-cycle concept are considered now.

The first, and perhaps most obvious, implication of the concept is that even the most successful products have a finite life. Further, there is some evidence that suggests that intensifying competition and rapid technological change are leading to a shortening of product life cycles. This explains the importance and emphasis now attached to the continued development of new products. The sales force have an important role to play in this process. Because of their often daily contact with customers, they are usually the first to detect signs that products are about to embark upon the period of decline. Their often detailed knowledge of customers, competitors and market requirements makes them a potentially very valuable source of new product ideas.

A second implication of the life-cycle concept is that different marketing and sales strategies may be appropriate to each stage. Again this is covered in greater detail in Chapter 3, but clearly sales tactics – indeed the very nature of the selling task – is likely to vary according to the stage of the life cycle. For example, in the introductory stage the emphasis may be on locating potential prospects. In the growth stage, the sales force may find themselves having to deal with the delicate issue of rationing their customers as demand increases more rapidly than capacity. In the maturity and decline stages, the sales force will increasingly have to rely on competitive pricing and special offers in order to combat increasing competition and falling sales.

Pricing

As with the product element of the mix, pricing decisions encompass a whole variety of decision areas. Pricing objectives must be determined, price levels set, decisions must be made as to credit and discount policies, and a procedure established for making price changes. Here we will consider some of the more important inputs to pricing decisions, in particular from the point of view of how they affect selling and sales management.

Inputs to pricing decisions

In the determination of price levels, a number of factors must be considered. The main factors include the following.

(*i*) COMPANY OBJECTIVES. In making pricing decisions, a company must first determine what objectives it wishes its pricing to achieve within the context of overall company financial and marketing objectives. For example, company objectives may specify a target rate of return on capital employed. Pricing levels for individual products should reflect this objective. Alternatively, or additionally, a company may couch its financial objectives in terms of early cash recovery or a specified payback period for the investment.

(*ii*) MARKETING OBJECTIVES. These may shape the pricing decision. For example, a company may determine that the most appropriate marketing strategy for a new product which it has developed is to aim for a substantial market share as quickly as possible. Such a strategy is termed a *penetration strategy*. It is based on stimulating and capturing demand backed by low prices and heavy promotion. At the other extreme, the company might determine that a *market skimming strategy* is appropriate. Here, high initial prices are set – again often backed by high levels of promotional spending – and the cream of the profits is taken before eventually lowering the price. Whatever the financial and marketing objectives set, these determine the framework within which pricing decisions are made. Such objectives should be communicated to sales management and to individual members of the sales team.

(*iii*) DEMAND CONSIDERATIONS. In most markets the upper limit to the prices which a company is able to charge for its products and services is determined by demand. Put simply, one is able to charge only what the market will bear. This tends to over-simplify the complexities of demand analysis and its relationship to pricing decisions. These complexities should not, however, deter the pricing decision-maker from considering demand in his or her deliberations. One of the most straightforward notions about the relationship between demand and price is the concept of a demand curve for a product, as shown in Fig. 3. Although it is a simple concept, the demand curve contains much useful information for the decision-maker. It shows that at lower prices, higher quantities are normally demanded. It is also possible to read off the curve the quantity demanded at any given price. Finally, it is possible to assess how sensitive demand is to changes in price. In other words, we can calculate the percentage change in quantity demanded for any given percentage price increase or decrease. Such information is extremely useful for making pricing decisions, but obtaining information about the relationship between the price and demand is not easy. Factors other than price have an important effect on demand. Despite this, pricing decisions must reflect demand considerations and some estimate should be made of the likely relationship between demand levels and price. Here again, the sales force can play a key role in the provision of such information and many companies make full use of this resource when pricing their products. A final point to be considered is the slope of the demand curve. The one shown in Fig. 3 is a 'conventional' one, in that it slopes downwards to the right; it means that at lower prices, higher quantities are demanded. It is, however, dangerous to assume that this is always the case. In some circumstances it is possible to charge too low a price for a product or service; far from increasing demand, such low prices actually reduce it. This can be the case for products that are bought because they *are* highly priced, i.e. where there is some prestige attached to having purchased what everyone knows is an expensive product. Similarly, low prices may cause the customer to suspect the quality of a product.

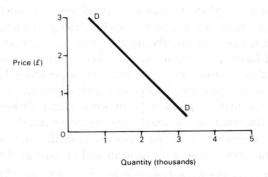

Fig 3   The demand curve.

(*iv*) COST CONSIDERATIONS. If demand determines the upper threshold for price, then costs determine the lower one. In the profit making organisation, in the long run, prices charged need to cover the total costs of production and marketing, with some satisfactory residue for profit. In fact companies often begin the process of making decisions on price by considering their costs. Some techniques of pricing go further, prices being determined solely on the basis of costs; for example, total costs per unit are calculated, a percentage added for profit, and a final price is computed. Such cost plus approaches to pricing, although straightforward, have a tendency to neglect some of the more subtle and important aspects of the cost input. As with demand, cost considerations can be quite complex. One of the important distinctions which a cost plus approach often neglects is the distinction between the fixed and variable costs of producing a product. Fixed costs are those which do not vary – up to the limit of plant capacity – regardless of the level of output, e.g. rent and rates. Variable costs do differ with the level of output – as it increases, so too do total variable costs, and vice versa as production is decreased, e.g. direct labour costs, raw materials, etc. This apparently simple distinction is very useful for making pricing decisions and gives rise to the technique of *break-even analysis*. Figure 4 illustrates this concept. Fixed, variable and total costs are plotted on the chart, together with a sales revenue curve. Where the revenue curve cuts the total cost curve is the break-even point. At this point the company is making neither profit nor loss. From the break-even chart it is possible to calculate the effect on the break-even point of charging different prices and, when this is combined with information on demand, break-even analysis is quite a powerful aid to decision making. Sales managers should

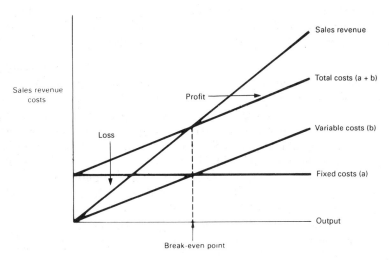

Fig 4   A simple break-even chart.

know something of the different costing concepts and procedures and, whilst they do not need detailed accounting knowledge, they should be familiar with the procedures that go into the costing of the products they are responsible for selling.

(*v*) COMPETITOR CONSIDERATIONS. Few companies are in a position of being able to make pricing decisions without considering the possible actions of competitors. Pricing decisions, particularly short-term tactical price changes, are often made as a direct response to the actions of competitors. Care should be taken in using this tactic, particularly when the movement of price is downwards. Once lowered, price can be very difficult to raise, and where possible a company should consider responses other than price reduction to combat competition.

Distribution

The distribution (or place) element of the marketing mix, particularly the management of physical distribution, has long been felt to be one of the areas in business where substantial improvements and cost savings can be made. Representing, as it often does, a substantial portion of total costs in a company, the distribution area has in recent years attracted considerable attention in terms of new concepts and techniques designed to manage better this important function. The management of distribution has now been recognised as being a key part of the strategic management of a company, and in larger organisations it is often the responsibility of a specialist. Because of this we can do no more here than to give a non-specialist overview of some of the more important aspects of this element of the mix.

   In its broadest sense distribution is concerned with all those activities required to move goods and materials into the factory, through the factory and to the final consumer. Examples of the type of decision areas encompassed in the distribution element of the marketing mix are as follows.

(*i*) THE SELECTION OF DISTRIBUTION CHANNELS. This involves determining in what manner, and through which distribution outlets, goods and services are to be made available to the final consumer. Marketing channels may be very short, e.g. where goods and services are sold direct to the customer such as via mail order. Alternatively, the channel may include a whole set of intermediaries, including brokers, wholesalers and retailers. In addition to selecting the route through which products will reach consumers, decisions must also be made as to the extent of distribution coverage. For example, some companies have a policy of exclusive distribution where only a small number of selected intermediaries are used to distribute company products. In other cases, a company may decide that it requires as wide a distribution cover as possible, and will seek a large number of distribution outlets.

(*ii*) DETERMINING THE LEVEL OF CUSTOMER SERVICE. In addition to selecting channels of distribution, decisions must also be made as to factors such as delivery periods and methods of transportation. Reduced delivery times can, of course, be a significant advantage to a company in marketing its products. On the other hand, such reductions are often accompanied by a necessity to increase inventory levels, thereby increasing costs. A policy decision must therefore be made as to the appropriate level of customer service, after consideration of the relative benefits and costs involved.

(*iii*) TERMS AND CONDITIONS OF DISTRIBUTION. Included under this heading would be conditions of sale on the part of distributors, minimum order/stocking quantities and the determination of credit, payment and discount terms for distributors.

There are other areas to be considered in the distribution element of the marketing mix, and in Chapter 6 we explore channel management in greater detail.

At this point we should note that distribution decisions have a significant impact on sales activities, e.g. the extent of distribution directly influences territory design and route planning (dealt with in detail in Chapter 11). Terms and conditions of distribution influence the framework within which sales are negotiated. The management of physical distribution influences the all-important delivery terms which the sales force are able to offer their customers. Probably no other area of the marketing mix has such a far ranging influence on the sales process.

Promotion

This final element of the marketing mix has the most direct influence on sales because personal selling itself is considered as one element of the total promotional mix of a company. Other elements of this promotional sub-mix include advertising, sales promotion and publicity.

All of these sub-elements are covered throughout the text in a variety of contexts and their relationships with selling are fully examined.

1.7 THE RELATIONSHIP BETWEEN SALES AND MARKETING

Throughout this chapter we have examined the nature and roles of selling and sales management and have discussed a general move towards marketing orientation. In addition, we have seen that sales efforts influence, and are influenced by, decisions taken on the ingredients of a company's marketing mix, which in turn affect its overall marketing efforts. It is essential, therefore, that sales and marketing be fully integrated. The adoption of the marketing concept has, in many companies, been accompanied by changes in organisational structure, together with changes in the view of what constitutes the nature of selling.

An example of the possible organisational implications of adopting the marketing concept is shown in Fig. 5 below which shows the organisation charts of a sales orientated and marketing orientated company.

Perhaps the most notable difference between the pre- and post-marketing orientated company is the fact that sales are later seen to be a part of the activity

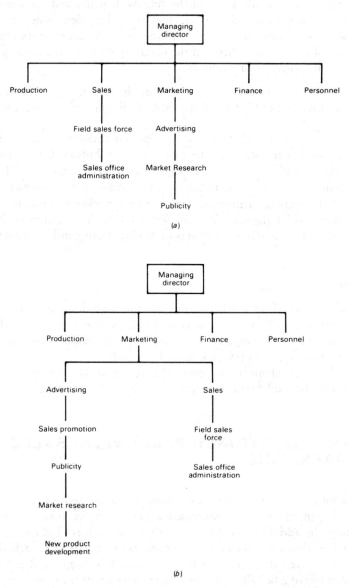

Fig 5   Organisational implications of adopting the marketing concept. (a) Company organisation chart, sales orientated company. (b) Company organisation chart, marketing orientated company.

of the marketing function. In fact, in the marketing orientated company the marketing function takes on a much wider controlling and coordinating role across the range of company activities. This facet of marketing orientation is often misunderstood by those in sales, and a great deal of resentment is often

Marketing strategy and management of personal selling

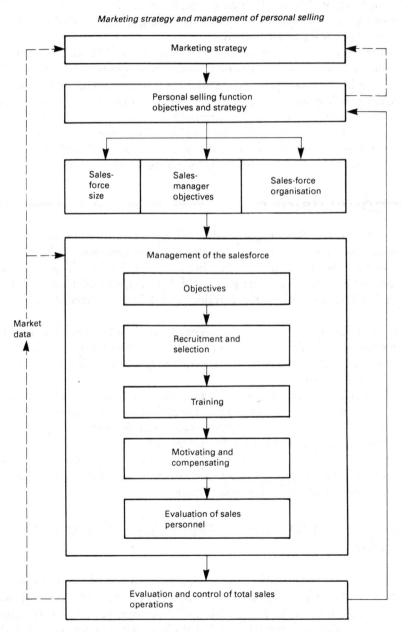

Fig 6   Marketing strategy and management of personal selling.

engendered between sales and marketing. Such resentment is often due to insensitive and undiplomatic management when making the changes often necessary to reorientate a company. Selling is only a part of the total marketing programme of a company, and this total effort should be coordinated by the marketing function. The marketing concept, however, does not imply that sales activities are any less important, nor that marketing executives should hold the most senior positions in a company.

In addition to changes in organisational structure, the influence of the marketing function and the increased professional approach taken to sales, described earlier in this chapter, has meant that the nature and role of this activity has changed. Selling and sales management are now concerned with the analysis of customers' needs and wants and, through the company's total marketing efforts, with the provision of benefits to satisfy these needs and wants.

Figure 6 gives an overview of the relationship between marketing and personal selling and outlines the key areas of sales management.

1.8 CONCLUSIONS

The nature and role of selling and sales management have been outlined and discussed, and some of the more widley held misconceptions about these activities have been explored. It has been suggested that selling and sales management are becoming more professional, and those individuals involved in these activities must now be highly trained and skilled in a range of managerial techniques.

One of the most significant developments in modern business thinking and practice has been the development of the marketing concept. Companies have moved from being production orientated, through being sales orientated to marketing orientation.

Some of the key concepts in marketing were outlined, including market segmentation and targeting, the product life cycle and the marketing mix. The implications of marketing orientation for sales activities and the role of selling in the marketing programme have been demonstrated.

Because of the emphasis given in marketing to the needs and wants of the customer, the next chapter is concerned with exploring further the nature of consumer and organisational buying behaviour.

PRACTICAL EXERCISE – MEPHISTO PRODUCTS LIMITED

'Yet another poor year!' reflected the senior executive of Mephisto Products. 'Profits down by 15 per cent, sales and turnover static in a market which was reckoned to be growing at a rate of some 20 per cent per annum. It cannot go on.' These were the thoughts of Jim Bullins, and he contended that the company would be out of business if the next year turned out to be so bad.

Jim Bullins had been senior executive at Mephisto for the past three years. In each of these years he had witnessed a decline in sales and profits. The company produced a range of technically sophisticated electromechanical control devices for industry. The major customers of Mephisto were in the chemical processing industry. The products were fitted to the customer's processing plant in order to provide safety and cut-out mechanisms, should anything untoward happen in the manufacturing process.

The products were sold through a UK sales force of some twelve people. Each represented a different area of the country and all were technically qualified mechanical or electrical engineers. Although some 95 per cent of Mephisto's sales was to the chemical industry, there were many more applications for electromechanical control devices in a wide variety of industries.

The reason that sales were concentrated in just the one industry was historical, in that the firm's founder, James Watkinson, had some 30 years earlier married the daughter of the owner of a major detergent manufacturer. As an engineer, Watkinson had seen the potential for such devices in this type of manufacture and, with the aid of a small loan from his father-in-law, had commenced manufacture of such devices, initially for his father-in-law's company and later for wider application in the chemical industry. Watkinson had long since resigned from active participation in Mephisto Products, although he still held a financial interest. However the philosophy which Watkinson had brought to the business was one which still pervaded business thinking at Mephisto.

The essence of this philosophy was centred on product and production excellence, backed by strong technical sales support. Watkinson had believed that if the product was right, i.e. well designed and manufactured to the highest level of quality, there would be a market. Needless to say, such a product then needed selling (because customers were not necessarily aware that they had a need for such safety mechanisms) and salespeople were encouraged to use what may be described as high pressure salesmanship, pointing out the consequences of not having such mechanisms in a manufacturing plant. They therefore tended to emphasise the negative aspects (of not having such devices) rather than the positive aspects (of how good they were, time saving in the case of plant breakdown, etc.). Needless to say, in Watkinson's day, such products then needed selling and, even though sales were to industrial purchasers, it was felt that such selling techniques were justified. This philosophy still pertained, and new salespeople were urged to remember that, unless they were pressed, most customers would not consider updating their control equipment.

Little advertising and sales promotion was carried out in the company, although from time to time, when there was a little spare cash, the company did purchase advertising space in *The Chemical Processors' Quarterly*. Pricing was done on a cost-plus basis, with total costs being calculated and a fixed percentage added to account for profits. Prices were thus fixed by the accounts department, and sales had no say in how they were established. This led to much dissent among the salespeople, who constantly argued that prices were not competitive and that if they were cut, sales could be increased substantially.

Delivery times were slow compared to the average in the industry, and there were few discounts for large order quantities, with the salesperson first having to clear such discounts with accounts before agreeing to such an arrangement. Again, Watkinson's old philosophy still prevailed: 'If they want the product badly enough, they will wait for it', and 'Why offer discounts for large quantities – if they did not want that many they would not order them.'

During the previous five years, from being a relatively successful company, market share for Mephisto Products dropped substantially. The market became much more competitive with many new entrants, particularly from EC countries coming into the UK market, which had traditionally been supplied by UK manufacturers. Many of these new entrants had introduced new and updated products to the market, with such products drawing upon recent advances in electronics. These new products were seen by the market as being technically innovative, but the view taken by Mephisto management was that they were faddish and once the electronics novelty had worn off, customers would come back to their superior products.

Unlike many of his colleagues, Jim Bullins was worried by developments over the past five years, and felt that there was a need for many changes. He was aware that the more successful new entrants to the industry had introduced a marketing philosophy into their operations. Compared to ten years ago, it was now common practice for companies to appoint marketing managers. Furthermore, he knew from talking to other people in the industry, that such companies considered sales to be an integral part of marketing. At a recent meeting with his senior staff, he mentioned to the sales manager the possibility of appointing a marketing director. The sales manager, who was shortly expecting to be made sales director, was scathing about the idea. His view was that marketing was suitable for a baked beans manufacturer but not for a company engaged in the manufacture and sale of sophisticated control devices for the chemicals industry. He argued that Mephisto's customers would not be swayed by superficial advertising and marketing ploys.

Although Jim Bullins always took heed of advice from his senior managers, recent sales figures had convinced him that the time had now come to make some changes. He would start, he decided, by appointing a marketing manager in the first instance. This person would have marketing experience and would come, most probably, from the chemical industry. The person appointed would have equal status to the sales manager, and ultimately either the new appointee or the existing sales manager would be promoted to the board of directors.

Discussion questions

1   What do you think is wrong with Mephisto Products' approach to sales and marketing?
2   Comment upon the following as they exist now at Mephisto Products.
    (*i*) Marketing orientation.
    (*ii*) The marketing mix.

(*iii*) The product life cycle.
3   What problems can you anticipate if Jim Bullins goes ahead and appoints a marketing manager?
4   If appointed, what problems can you foresee for the new marketing manager?
5   What general advice can you give to the company to make it more marketing orientated?

EXAMINATION QUESTIONS

1   Discuss the place of selling in the marketing mix.
2   How does the role of selling tend to differ between:
    (*i*)   industrial products; and
    (*ii*) consumer products?

2 Consumer and Organisational Buyer Behaviour

2.1 DIFFERENCES BETWEEN CONSUMER AND ORGANISATIONAL BUYING

There are a number of important differences between consumer and organisational buying which have important implications for the marketing of goods and services in general and the personal selling function in particular.

2.1.1 FEWER ORGANISATIONAL BUYERS

Generally, a company marketing industrial products will have fewer potential buyers than one marketing in consumer markets. Often 80 per cent of output, in the former case, will be sold to perhaps 10–15 organisations. This means that the importance of one customer to the industrial marketer is far in excess of that to the consumer marketing company. However this situation is complicated in some consumer markets where the importance of trade intermediaries e.g. supermarkets, is so great that, although the products have an ultimate market of many millions of people, the companies' immediate customers rank alongside those of important industrial buyers.

2.1.2 ORGANISATIONAL BUYERS ARE MORE RATIONAL

Although organisational buyers, being people, are affected by emotional factors, e.g. like or dislike of a salesperson, the colour of office equipment, etc., it is probably true that, on the whole, organisational buying is more rational. Often decisions will be made on economic criteria. This is because industrial buyers have to justify their decisions to other members of their organisation. Caterpillar tractor salespeople based their sales presentation on the fact that, although the initial purchase price of their tractors was higher than competition, over the life of the tractor costs were significantly lower. This rational, economic appeal proved very successful.

2.1.3 ORGANISATIONAL BUYING MAY BE TO SPECIFIC REQUIREMENTS

It is not uncommon in idustrial marketing for buyers to determine product specifications and for sellers to tailor their product offerings to meet them. This is feasible because of the large potential revenue of such products, e.g. railway engines. This is much less a feature of consumer marketing, where a product offering may be developed to meet a need of a market segment but, beyond that, meeting individual needs would prove uneconomic.

2.1.4 RECIPROCAL BUYING MAY BE IMPORTANT IN ORGANISATIONAL BUYING

Because an industrial buyer may be in a powerful negotiating position with a seller, it may be possible for him to demand concessions in return for placing his order with him. In some situations the buyer may demand that the seller buys some of his products in return for securing the order. A buyer of tyres for a company may demand that, in return for the contract, the tyre producer buys its company cars from them.

2.1.5 ORGANISATIONAL SELLING/BUYING MAY BE MORE RISKY

Industrial markets are sometimes characterised by a contract being agreed before the product is made. Further, the product itself may be highly technical and the seller may be faced with unforeseen problems once work has started. Thus, when Rolls-Royce won the contract to build an engine for Lockheed, technical problems associated with its development made the deal unprofitable for Rolls-Royce. More recently, Scott-Lithgow won an order to build an oil rig for British Petroleum, but the price proved uneconomic given the nature of the problems associated with its construction.

2.1.6 ORGANISATIONAL BUYING IS MORE COMPLEX

Many industrial purchases, notably those which involve large sums of money and which are new to the company, involve many people at different levels of the organisation. The managing director, product engineers, production managers, purchasing manager and operatives may influence the decision of which expensive machine to purchase. The sales task may be to influence as many of these people as possible and may involve multi-level selling by means of a sales team, rather than an individual salesperson (Corey, 1983).

2.2 THE CONSUMER DECISION-MAKING PROCESS

Behavioural scientists regard consumer purchasing as a problem-solving or need satisfaction process. Thus, an electronic calculator may be bought in order to solve a problem – inaccuracy or slowness in arithmetic – which itself defines the need – fast and accurate calculations. In order to define which calculator to buy a consumer may pass through a series of steps (Engel and Blackwell, 1982).

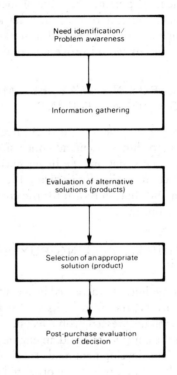

Fig 7   The consumer decison-making process.

2.2.1 NEEDS

In the case of the calculator, the needs (stimulated by problem identification) are essentially *functional*. In this situation the salesperson would be advised, after identifying the buyer's needs, to demonstrate the speed and accuracy of the calculators he is selling. Successful selling may involve identifying needs in more detail – for example, are special features required or does the buyer only have to perform a standard, basic set of calculations, implying a less elaborate and cheaper calculator. However, for other products need-satisfaction may be in terms of more *emotional* or *psychological* needs. For example, a Sheaffer pen is bought largely for its status rather than any marginal functional superiority over other pens. An accurate assessment of the kinds of needs which a product is satisfying will enable a salesperson to plan the sales presentation correctly, presenting the product as a means of satisfying the buyer's needs or solving the buyer's problems.

How do needs arise? They may occur as a natural process of life; for example, the birth of children in a family may mean that a larger car is required. They may, also, arise because of stimulation. An advertisement for video-recorders or a salesperson's talk may create the need for extra in-house entertainment and, at the same time, provide a means of satisfying that need.

2.2.2 INFORMATION GATHERING

Many needs can only be satisfied after a period of information search. Thus a prospective car purchaser who requires a small, economical car may carry out a considerable search before deciding on the model which best satisfies these needs. This search may involve visiting car showrooms, watching car programmes on television, reading car magazines and *Which* reports and talking to friends. Clearly, many sources of information are sought besides that provided by the salesperson in the showroom. Indeed, in some situations the search may omit the salesperson until the end of this process. The buyer may reduce the number of alternatives to a manageable few and contact the salesperson only to determine the kind of deal offered on the competing models.

2.2.3 EVALUATION OF ALTERNATIVES AND SELECTION OF THE BEST SOLUTION

Evaluation may be thought of as a system as depicted in Fig. 8.

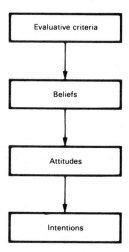

Fig 8   The evaluation system.

(*i*) EVALUATIVE CRITERIA. These are the dimensions used by consumers to compare or evaluate products or brands. In the car example the relevant evaluative criteria may be fuel economy, purchase price and reliability.

(*ii*) BELIEFS. These are the degrees to which, in the consumer's mind, a product possesses various characteristics, e.g. roominess.

(*iii*) ATTITUDES. These are the degrees of liking or disliking a product, and are in turn dependent on the evaluative criteria used to judge the products and the beliefs about the product measured by those criteria. Thus beliefs imply knowledge, e.g. model X does 36 miles per gallon at a steady 56 miles per hour, whereas attitudes imply liking or disliking, e.g. model X is poor with regard to fuel economy.

(*iv*) INTENTIONS. These measure the probability that attitudes will be acted upon. The assumption is that favourable attitudes will increase purchase intentions, i.e. the probability that the consumer will buy.

Given this system, it makes sense for a salesperson to find out from a prospect the evaluative criteria he is using to judge alternative products. For example, a stereo system salesperson will attempt to find out whether a potential buyer is evaluating alternative stereo units primarily in terms of external design or sound quality. Further, it can be effective to try to change evaluative criteria. For example, if the stereo system salesperson believes that the competitive advantage of his product range lies in its sound quality but the buyer's criterion is primarily external design, he can attempt to emphasise the quality of the sound of the product and minimise the importance of external design. Alternatively, if the primary consideration of the buyer is sound quality but a competitor's system is preferred, the sales task is to change attitudes in favour of his system. Tools at his disposal include the use of performance comparisons from hi-fi magazines, and in-shop demonstrations.

2.2.4 POST-PURCHASE EVALUATION OF DECISION

The art of effective marketing is to create customer satisfaction. Most business rely on repeat purchasing, which implies that customers must gain satisfaction from their purchases (otherwise this will not occur). Festinger (1957) introduced the notion of 'cognitive dissonance' partly to explain the anxiety felt by many buyers of expensive items shortly after purchase. The classic case of this is the car buyer who assiduously reads car advertisements after he has bought his car, in an effort to dispel the anxiety caused by him not being sure that he has made the correct purchase.

Salespeople often try to reassure a buyer, after the order has been placed, that he has made the right decision, but the outcome of the post-purchase evaluation is dependent on many factors besides the salesperson's reassuring words. The quality of the product and the level of after-sales service play an obvious part in creating customer goodwill, and it is the salesperson who can help the buyer in ensuring that the product he buys best matches his needs in the first place. This implies that it may not be in the salesperson's long-term interest to pressure buyers into buying higher-priced items which possess features not really wanted – although this may increase short-term profit margins (and commission) it may lead to a long-term fall in sales as consumers go elsewhere to replace the item.

2.3 FACTORS AFFECTING THE CONSUMER DECISION-MAKING PROCESS

There are a number of factors which affect the consumer decision-making process and the outcome of that process. These can be classified under three headings:

(*i*)   the buying situation;
(*ii*) psychological influences;
(*iii*) social influences.

2.3.1 THE BUYING SITUATION

Howard and Sheth (1969) identified three types of buying situation.

(*i*)   Extensive problem solving.
(*ii*) Limited problem solving.
(*iii*) Automatic response.

When a problem or need is new, the means of solving that problem are expensive and uncertainty is high, a consumer is likely to conduct extensive problem solving. This will involve a high degree of information search and close examination of alternative solutions. Faced with this kind of buyer the salesperson can create immense goodwill by providing information and assessing alternatives from his product range in terms of how well their benefits conform to the buyer's needs. The goodwill generated with this type of buyer in such a buying situation may be rewarded by a repeat purchase when the buying situation changes to one of limited problem solving. Thus successful car sales-people often find themselves with a group of highly loyal buyers who purchase from them, even if the dealership changes, because of the trust built up during this stage.

Limited problem solving occurs when the consumer has some experience with the product in question and may be inclined to stay loyal to the brand previously purchased. However, a certain amount of information search and evaluation of a few alternatives occurs as a rudimentary check that the right decision is being made. This process provides a limited opportunity for salespeople of competing products to persuade consumers that they should switch model or brand by providing relevant comparative information and, perhaps, by providing risk-reducing guarantees, e.g. free replacement of any defective parts.

Companies who have built up a large brand franchise will wish to move their customers to the state of automatic response. Advertising may be effective in keeping the brand in the forefront of the consumer's mind and in reinforcing already favourable attitudes towards the brand. In this situation, personal selling to the ultimate consumer may be superfluous. Companies selling consumer durables may offer generous trade-in terms for their old models: Black and Decker employ this technique whereby old, unusable lawnmowever can be traded-in as part payment on a new model.

2.3.2 PSYCHOLOGICAL INFLUENCES

A second group of factors which influences the consumer decision-making process concerns the psychology of the individuals concerned. Relevant concepts include personality, motivation, perception and learning.

Although personality may explain differences in consumer purchasing, it is extremely difficult for a salesperson to judge accurately how extrovert or introvert, conventional or unconventional, a customer is, for example. Indeed, reliable personality measurement has proved difficult, even for qualified psychologists.

Similarly, the true reason or motive for purchase may be obscure. However, by careful probing a salesperson is likely to find out some of the real motives for purchase some of the time. Motivation is clearly linked to needs; the stronger a need is perceived by a consumer the more likely he is to be moved towards the satisfaction of that need. Thus, a salesperson can increase buyer motivation by stimulating need recognition, by showing the ways in which needs can be fulfilled and by attempting to understand the various motives which may be at work in the decision-making process. These may be functional, e.g. time saved by a convenience food, or psychological, e.g. the status imparted by the ownership of a Jaguar or BMW car.

Not everyone with the same motivations will buy the same products, however. One of the reasons for this is that how someone decides to act depends upon his *perception* of the situation. One buyer may perceive a salesperson as being honest and truthful while another may not. Three selective processes may be at work on consumers.

(*i*) SELECTIVE EXPOSURE. Only certain information sources may be sought and read.

(*ii*) SELECTIVE PERCEPTION. Only certain ideas, messages and information from those sources may be perceived.

(*iii*) SELECTIVE RETENTION. Only some of them may be remembered.

In general, people tend to forget more quickly and to distort or avoid messages that are substantially at variance with existing attitudes.

Learning is also important in consumer decision-making. Learning refers to the changes in a person's behaviour as a result of his experiences. A consumer will learn which brand names imply quality and which salesperson to trust.

2.3.3 SOCIAL INFLUENCES

Major social influences on consumer decision-making include social class, reference groups, culture and the family.

The first of these factors, social class, has been regarded as an important determinant of consumer behaviour for many years. Social class in marketing is based upon the occupation of the head of the household. The practical importance of social class is reflected in the fact that respondents in market research surveys are usually classified by their social class, and most advertising media give readership figures broken down by social class groupings. Recently, however, the use of this variable to explain differences in purchasing has been criticised. It is often the case that people within the same social class may have different consumption patterns. Within the C2 group, i.e. skilled manual workers, it has been found that some people spend a high proportion of their income on buying their own house, furniture, carpets and in-home entertainment, while others prefer to spend their money on more transitory pleasures such as drinking, smoking and playing bingo.

Such findings have led to a new classificatory system called ACORN (A Classification of Residential Neighbourhoods) which classified people according to the type of area they live in. This has proved to be a powerful discriminator between different lifestyles, purchasing patterns and media exposure (Baker *et al.*, 1979).

The term 'reference group' is used to indicate a group of people that influence a person's attitude or behaviour. Where a product is conspicuous, for example clothing or cars, the brand or model chosen may have been strongly influenced by what the buyer perceives as acceptable to his reference group, e.g. a group of friends, the family, or work colleagues. Reference group acceptability should not be confused with popularity. The salesperson who attempts to sell a car using the theme 'that it's very popular' may conflict with the buyer's desire to aspire to an 'exclusive' reference group, for which a less popular, more individual, model may be appropriate.

Culture refers to the traditions, taboos, values and basic attitudes of the whole society within which an individual lives. It is of particular relevance to international marketing, since different countries have different cultures, affecting the conduct of business and how products are used. In Arabian countries, for example, a salesperson may find himself conducting a sales presentation in the company of a competitor's salesperson. In France chocolate is sometimes eaten between slices of bread!

The family is sometimes called a primary reference group and may play a significant part in consumer buyer behaviour; the decision as to which product or brand to purchase may be a group decision, with each family member playing a distinct part. Thus, in the purchase of motor cars, it has been found that the husband usually decides upon the model, while his wife chooses the colour (Doyle and Hutchinson, 1973). The purchase of cereals may be strongly influenced by children. The cleaning properties of a carpet fibre may be relatively unimportant to a man but of crucial importance to his wife. When a purchase is a group decision, a salesperson will be wise to view the benefits of his products in terms of each of the decision-makers or influencers.

2.4 ORGANISATIONAL BUYER BEHAVIOUR

Organisational buyer behaviour has usefully been broken down into three elements by Fisher (1976).

(*i*) STRUCTURE. The 'who' factor – who participates in the decision-making process, and their particular roles.

(*ii*) PROCESS. The 'how' factor – the pattern of information getting, analysis, evaluation and decision-making which takes place as the purchasing organisation moves towards a decision.

(*iii*) CONTENT. The 'why' factor – the evaluative criteria used at different stages of the process and by different members of the decision-making unit.

2.4.1 STRUCTURE

An essential point to understand in organisational buying is that the buyer or purchasing officer is often not the only person who influences the decision, or who actually has the authority to make the ultimate decision. Rather, the decision is in the hands of a decision-making unit (DMU), or buying centre as it is sometimes called. This is not necessarily a fixed entity. The people in the DMU may change as the decision-making process continues. Thus a managing director may be involved in the decision that new equipment should be purchased, but not in the decision as to which manufacturer to buy it from.

Webster (1979) has identified five roles in the structure of the DMU.

(*i*) USERS. Those who actually use the product.

(*ii*) DECIDERS. Those who have the authority to select the supplier/model.

(*iii*) INFLUENCERS. Those who provide information and add decision criteria throughout the process.

(*iv*) BUYERS. Those who have authority to execute the contractual arrangements.

(*v*) GATEKEEPERS. Those who control the flow of information, e.g. secretaries who may allow or prevent access to a DMU member, or a buyer whose agreement must be sought before a supplier can contact other members of the DMU.

The factors which influence the nature of the DMU will be examined later. Obviously, for different types of purchase the exact formation will vary. For very important decisions the structure of the DMU will be complex, involving numerous people within the buying organisation. The salesperson's task is to identify and reach the key members in order to convince them of his products' worth. Often, talking only to the purchasing officer will be insufficient, since he may be only a minor influence on which supplier is chosen.

When the problem to be solved is highly technical, suppliers may work with engineers in the buying organisation in order to solve problems and secure the order. An example where this approach was highly successful involved a small US company who secured a large order from a major car company owing to its ability to work with them in solving the technical problems associated with the development of an exhaust gas recirculation valve (Cline and Shapiro). In this case, their policy was to work with company engineers and to keep the purchasing department out of the decision until the last possible moment, by which time only they were qualified to supply the part.

Where DMU members are inaccessible to salespeople, advertising may be used as an alternative. Also, where users are an important influence and the product is relatively inexpensive and consumable, free samples given by the salespeople may be effective in generating preference.

2.4.2 PROCESS

Figure 9 describes the decision-making process for an industrial product (Robinson *et al.*, 1967). The exact nature of the process will depend on the buying situation. In some situations some stages will be omitted; for example, in a routine re-buy situation the purchasing officer is unlikely to pass through stages (*iii*) (*iv*) and (*v*) (search for suppliers and an analysis and evolution of their proposals). These stages will be bypassed, as the buyer, recognising a need – perhaps shortage of stationery – routinely reorders from his existing supplier.

In general, the more complex the decision and the more expensive the item, the more likely it is that each stage will be passed through and that the process will take more time.

(*i*) NEED OR PROBLEM RECOGNITION. Needs and problems may be recognised through either internal or external factors. An example of an internal factor would be the realisation of undercapacity leading to the decision to purchase plant or equipment. Thus, internal recognition leads to active behaviour (*internal/active*). Some problems which are recognised internally may not be acted upon. This condition may be termed *internal/passive*. A production manager may realise that there is a problem with a machine but, given more pressing problems, decide to live with it. Other potential problems may not be recognised internally, and only become problems because of *external cues*. A production manager may

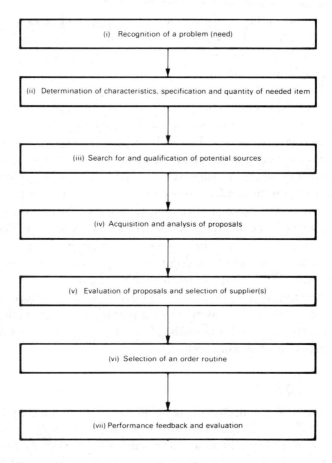

Fig 9   The organisational decision-making process (buy phases).

be quite satisfied with the production process until he is made aware of another more efficient method. Clearly these different problems have important implications for the salesperson. The internal/passive condition implies that there is an opportunity for the salesperson, having identified the condition, to highlight the problem by careful analysis of cost inefficiencies and other symptoms, so that the problem is perceived to be more pressing and in need of solution (internal/active). The internal/active situation requires the salesperson to demonstrate a differential advantage of one of his products over the competition. In this situation problem stimulation is unnecessary, but where internal recognition is absent, the salesperson can provide the necessary external cues. A fork-lift truck sales representative might stimulate problem recognition by showing how his trucks can save his customer money, due to lower maintenance costs, and lead to more efficient use of warehouse space through higher lifting capabilities.

(*ii*) DETERMINATION OF CHARACTERISTICS, SPECIFICATION AND QUANTITY OF NEEDED ITEM. At this stage of the decision-making process the DMU will draw up a description of what is required. For example, it might decide that five lathes are required to meet certain specifications. The ability of a salesperson to influence the specifications can give his company an advantage at later stages of the process.

(*iii*) SEARCH FOR AND QUALIFICATION OF POTENTIAL SERVICES. A great deal of variation in the degree of search takes place in organisational buying. Generally speaking, the cheaper, less important the item, and the more information the buyer possesses, the less search takes place.

(*iv*) ACQUISITION AND ANALYSIS OF PROPOSALS. Having found a number of companies who, perhaps through their technical expertise and general reputation, are considered to be qualified to supply the product, proposals will be called and analysis of them undertaken.

(*v*) EVALUATION OF PROPOSALS AND SELECTION OF SUPPLIER(S). Each proposal will be evaluated in the light of the criteria deemed to be important to each DMU member. It is important to realise that various members may use different criteria when judging proposals. Although this may cause problems, the outcome of this procedure is the selection of a supplier or suppliers.

(*vi*) SELECTION OF AN ORDER ROUTINE. Next the details of payment and delivery are drawn up. Usually this is conducted by the purchasing officer. In some buying decisions this stage is merged into stages (*iv*) and (*v*) when delivery is an important consideration in selecting a supplier.

(*vii*) PERFORMANCE FEEDBACK AND EVALUATION. This may be formal, where a purchasing department draws up an evaluation form for user departments to complete, or informal through everyday conversation.

The implications of all this are that a salesperson can affect a sale through influencing need recognition, through the design of product specifications and by clearly presenting the advantages of his product over competition in terms which are relevant to DMU members. By early involvement, a salesperson can benefit through the process of *creeping commitment*, whereby the buying organisation becomes increasingly committed to one supplier through its involvement in the process and the technical assistance it provides.

2.4.3 CONTENT

This aspect of organisational buyer behaviour refers to the criteria used by members of the DMU to evaluate supplier proposals. These criteria are likely to be determined by the performance criteria used to evaluate the members themselves. Thus a purchasing manager who is judged by the extent to which he reduces purchase expenditure is likely to be more cost conscious than a production engineer who is evaluated in terms of the technical efficiency of the production processes he designs.

As with consumers, organisational buying is characterised by both functional (economic) and psychological (emotive) criteria. Key functional considerations may be, for plant and equipment, return on investment, while for materials and component parts they might be cost savings, together with delivery reliability, quality and technical assistance. Because of the high costs associated with production down-time, a key concern of many purchasing departments is the long-run development of the organisation's supply system. Psychological factors may also be important, particularly when suppliers' product offerings are essentially similar. In this situation the final decision may rest upon the relative liking for the supplier's salesperson.

The implications of understanding the content of the decision are that, first, a salesperson may need to change his sales presentation when talking to different DMU members. Discussion with a production engineer may centre on the technical superiority of the product offering, while much more emphasis on cost factors may prove beneficial when talking to the purchasing officer. Second, the criteria used by buying organisations change over time as circumstances change. Price may be relatively unimportant to a company when trying to solve a highly visible technical problem, and the order will be placed with the supplier who provides the necessary technical assistance. Later, after the problem has been solved and other suppliers become qualified, price may be of crucial significance.

2.5 FACTORS AFFECTING ORGANISATIONAL BUYER BEHAVIOUR

Cardozo (1980) identified three factors which influence the composition of the DMU, the nature of the decision-making process and the criteria used to evaluate product offerings. These factors are:

(*i*)   the buy class;
(*ii*)   the product type;
(*iii*)   the importance of purchase to buying organisation.

2.5.1 THE BUY CLASS

Industrial purchasing decisions were studied by Robinson *et al.* (1967), who concluded that buyer behaviour was influenced by the nature of the buy class. They distinguished between a new task, a modified re-buy and a straight re-buy.

A *new task* occurs when the need for the product has not arisen previously so that there is little or no relevant experience in the company, and a great deal of information is required. A *straight re-buy*, on the other hand, occurs where an organisation buys previously purchased items from suppliers already judged acceptable. Routine purchasing procedures are set up to facilitate straight re-buys. The *modified re-buy* lies between the two extremes. A regular requirement for the type of product exists, and the buying alternatives are known, but sufficient change has occurred to require some alteration of the normal supply procedure.

The buy classes affect organisational buying in the following ways. First, the structure of the DMU changes. For a stright re-buy possibly only the purchasing officer is involved, whereas for a new buy senior management, engineers, production managers and purchasing officers are likely to be involved. Modified re-buys often involve engineers, production managers and purchasing officers, but senior management, except when the purchase is critical to the company, is unlikely to be involved. Second, the decision-making process is likely to be much longer as the buy class changes from a straight re-buy to a modified re-buy and, then, a new task. Third, in terms of influencing DMU members, they are likely to be much more receptive for new task and modified re-buy situations than straight re-buys. In the latter case the purchasing manager has already solved the purchasing problems and he has other problems to deal with. So why make it a problem again?

The first implication of this buy class analysis is that there are big gains to be made if the salesperson can enter the new task at the start of the decision-making process. By providing information and helping with any technical problems which can arise, the salesperson may be able to create goodwill and creeping commitment which secures the order when the final decision is made. The second implication is that since the decision process is likely to be long, and many people are involved in the new task, supplier companies need to invest heavily in sales manpower for a considerable period of time. Some firms employ missionary sales teams, comprising their best salespeople, to help secure big new-task orders.

Salespeople in straight re-buy situations must ensure that no change occurs when they are in the position of the supplier. Regular contact to ensure that the customer has no complaints may be necessary, and the buyer may be encouraged to use automatic recording systems. For the non-supplier the salesperson has a difficult task unless poor service or some other factor has caused the buyer to become dissatisfied with his present supplier. The obvious objective of the salesperson in this situation is to change the buy class from a straight re-buy to a modified re-buy. Price alone may not be enough since changing supplier represents a large personal risk to the purchasing officer. The new supplier's products might be less reliable, and delivery might be unpredictable. In order to reduce this risk, the salesperson may offer delivery guarantees with penalty clauses and be very willing to accept a small (perhaps uneconomic) order at first in order to gain a foothold. Many straight re-buys are organised on a contract basis, and buyers may be more receptive to listening to non-supplier salespeople prior to contract renewal.

2.5.2 THE PRODUCT TYPE

Products can be classified according to four types – materials, components, plant and equipment, and MROs.

(*i*) Materials to be used in the production process, e.g. steel.

(*ii*) Components to be incorporated in the finished product, e.g. alternator.

} Product constituents

(*iii*) Plant and equipment.   Production facilities

(*iv*) Products and services for maintenance, repair and operation (MROs), e.g. spanners, welding equipment and lubricants.

This classification is based upon a customer's perspective – how the product is used – and may be used to identify differences in organisational buyer behaviour. First, the people who take part in the decision-making process tend to change according to product type. For example, it has been found that senior management tend to get involved in the purchase of plant and equipment or, occasionally, when new materials are purchased if the change is of fundamental importance to company operations, e.g. if a move from aluminium to plastic is being contemplated. Rarely do they involve themsleves in component or MRO supply. Similarly, design engineers tend to be involved in buying components and materials but not normally MRO and plant and equipment. Second, the decision-making process tends to be slower and more complex as product type moves from:

MRO → Components → Materials → Plant and equipment

For MRO items, 'blanket contracts' rather than periodic purchase orders are increasingly being used. The supplier agrees to resupply the buyer on agreed price terms over a period of time. Stock is held by the seller and orders are automatically printed out by the buyer's computer when stock falls below a minimum level. This has the advantage to the supplying company of effectively blocking the efforts of the competitors' sales forces for long periods of time.

Classification of suppliers' offerings by product type gives the sales force clues as to who is likely to be influential in the purchase decision. The sales task is then to confirm this in particular situations and attempt to reach those people involved. A salesperson selling MROs is likely to be wasting effort attempting to talk to design engineers, whereas attempts to reach operating management are likely to prove fruitful.

2.5.3 IMPORTANCE OF PURCHASE TO BUYING ORGANISATION

A purchase is likely to be perceived as being important to the buying organisation when it involves large sums of money, when the cost of making the wrong decision, e.g. in lost production, is high and when there is considerable uncertainty about the outcome of alternative offerings. In such situations, many people at different organisational levels are likely to be involved in the decision and the process is likely to be long, with extensive search and analysis of information. Thus extensive marketing effort is likely to be required, but great opportunities present themselves to sales teams who work with buying organisations to convince them that their offering has the best pay off; this may involve acceptance trials, e.g. private diesel manufacturers supplying British Rail with prototypes for testing, engineering support and testimonials from other users. Additionally, guarantees of delivery dates and after-sales service may be necessary when buyer uncertainty regarding these factors is high.

2.6 CONCLUSIONS

Understanding buyer behaviour has important implications for salespeople and sales management. Recognition that buyers purchase products in order to overcome problems and satisfy needs implies that an effective sales approach will involve the discovery of these needs on the part of the salesperson. Only then can he sell the offering from the range of products marketing by his company which best meets these needs.

When the decision-making unit is complex, as in many organisational buying situations, the salesperson must attempt to identify and reach key members of the DMU in order to persuade them of his product's benefits. He must also realise that different members may use different criteria to evaluate his product and, thus, may need to modify his sales presentation accordingly.

The next chapter concerns the development of sales strategies which reflect the buyer behaviour patterns of the market place.

PRACTICAL EXERCISE – THE CASE OF THE LOST COMPUTER SALE

Jim Appleton, managing director of Industrial Cleaning Services, had decided that a personal computer could help solve his cash flow problems. What he wanted was a machine which would store his receipts and outgoings so that at a touch of a button he could see the cash flow at any point in time. A year ago he got into serious cash flow difficulties simply because he didn't realise that, for various reasons, his short-term outflow greatly exceeded his receipts.

He decided to visit a newly opened personal computer outlet in town on Saturday afternoon. His wife, Mary, was with him. They approached a salesman seated behind a desk.

JIM: Good afternoon. I'm interested in buying a personal computer for my business. Can you help me?

SALESPERSON: Yes, indeed, sir. This is the fastest growing network of personal computer centres in the country. I have to see a colleague for a moment but I shall be back in a few minutes. Would you like to have a look at this brochure and at the models we have in the showroom?

Salesperson gives them the brochures, and leaves them in the showroom.

> MARY: I don't understand computers. Why have some got screens and others not?
>
> JIM: I don't know. Perhaps they haven't had delivery of screens on some models yet. What baffles me are all these buttons you have to press. I wonder if you have to do a typing course to use one?

Jim and Mary look round the showroom asking each other questions and getting a little confused. The salesman arrives after five minutes.

> SALESPERSON: Sorry to take so long but at least it's given you a chance to see what we have in stock. You tell me you want a computer for work. I think I have just the one for you.

Salesperson takes Jim and Mary to a model.

> SALESPERSON: This could be just up your street. Not only will this model act as a word processor, it will do your accounts, financial plans and stock control as well. It has full graphic facilities so that you can see trend lines on the screen at the touch of the button.
>
> MARY: It looks very expensive. How much will it cost?
>
> SALESPERSON: A lot less than you think. This one costs £3,000, which is quite cheap.
>
> MARY: I've seen advertisements in newspapers for computers which are a lot less expensive.
>
> SALESPERSON: Yes, but do they have computer graphic facilities and do they have a storage capacity of 300,000 bytes?
>
> MARY: I don't know, but they looked quite good to me.
>
> JIM: It looks very complicated to use.
>
> SALESPERSON: No more complicated than any of the other models. The computer comes with a full set of instructions. My twelve year old son could operate it.
>
> JIM: What's this button for?
>
> SALESPERSON: That moves the cursor. It allows you to delete or amend any character you wish.
>
> JIM: I see.
>
> SALESPERSON: I've left the best till last. Included in the price are three software programmes which allow the machine to be used for spreadsheet analysis, stock control and word processing. I'm sure your business will benefit from this computer.
>
> JIM: My business is very small. I only employ five people. I'm not sure it's ready for a computer yet. Still, thank you for your time.

Discussion questions

1   What evaluative criteria did Jim and Mary use when deciding whether to buy a computer and which model to buy?

2 Did the salesperson understand the motives behind the purchase? If not, why not? Did he make any other mistakes?

3 Imagine that you were the salesperson. How would you have conducted the sales interview?

EXAMINATION QUESTIONS

1 Compare and contrast the ways in which consumers and organisations buy products and services.

2 Of what practical importance is the study of organisational buyer behaviour to the personal selling function?

3 Sales Strategies

3.1 SALES AND MARKETING PLANNING

It is important to recognise the fact that, to be effective, sales activities need to take place within the context of an overall strategic marketing plan. Only in this way are we likely to ensure that our sales efforts complement, rather than compete with, the rest of our marketing activities. Sales strategies and tactics may only be arrived at, implemented and assessed against a framework of company-wide objectives and strategic planning processes. As a prelude to discussing sales strategies and tactics later in this chapter, the nature and purpose of strategic market plans and the place of selling in these plans is outlined and discussed.

3.2 THE PLANNING PROCESS

The nature of the planning process is outlined in Fig. 10 opposite. This deceptively simple process can be likened to that of operating a domestic central heating system. One first determines the temperature required, timing, etc. (setting objectives), and the procedures which must be followed in order to make sure that this is achieved (determining operations). Next one has to organise oneself to implement appropriate procedures, including making sure that all the necessary resources are available (organisation). At this stage one can go ahead and commence operation of the system (implementation). Finally, one needs to check how the system is operating, in particular the temperature level which is being achieved (measuring results). Any deviations in required temperature are then reported and corrected through the thermostatic system (re-evaluation and control).

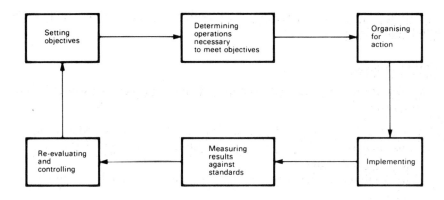

Fig 10   The planning process.

3.3 ESTABLISHING MARKETING PLANS

In fact there is no universal way of establishing a marketing plan; neither is the process simple in actual practice. Conceptually, however, the process is comparatively simple, comprising a series of logical steps.

3.3.1 BUSINESS DEFINITION

As a prerequisite to the determination of marketing plans, careful consideration should be given to defining (or re-defining) the overall role or mission of the business. This issue is perhaps best addressed by senior management asking and answering the question 'What business are we in?' Always, the definition of the role of a business should be couched in terms of what customer needs are being served by a business rather than in terms of what products or services are being produced. For example, the manufacturer of microcomputers might define the business as being in the business of rapid problem-solving. In the automobile industry, companies might define their business as being the provision of transport, status, etc., rather than the manufacture of cars.

This process of business definition is extremely important. Not only does it ensure that a company thinks in terms of its customers' wants and needs but, in terms of the planning process, it forms a focusing mechanism for much of what follows.

3.3.2 ANALYSIS OF CURRENT MARKETING SITUATION

Business definition is followed by analysis of the current marketing situation. The precise content of this step in the preparation of the marketing plan will vary from company to company, but normally the analysis will encompass the following factors.

Market analysis

Examples of the data and analysis required under this heading would include the following.

(*i*)   Current and recent size and growth of market. In the multi-product company this analysis needs to be made in total, by product/market and by geographical segment.

(*ii*) The analysis of customer needs, attitudes and trends in purchasing behaviour.

(*iii*) Current marketing mix.

(*iv*) Competitor analysis, including an appraisal of the following:
  - current strategy;
  - current performance, including market share analysis;
  - their strengths and weaknesses;
  - expectations as to their future actions.

In addition to analysing existing competition, the much more difficult task of appraising potential new entrants should be carried out at this stage.

(*v*)   The analysis of broad macro-environment trends – economic, demographic, technological, political and cultural, which might influence the future of the company's products.

Analysis of strengths/weaknesses, opportunities and threats (SWOT analysis)

Here management must make a realistic and objective appraisal of company strengths and weaknesses in the context of potential opportunities and threats. Opportunities and threats to the future of a business stem primarily from factors outside the direct control of a company and in particular from trends and changes in those factors which were referred to earlier as the macro-environment – namely economic, political, technological, and cultural factors. It is important to recognise that the determination of what constitutes an opportunity/threat, and indeed the appraisal of strengths and weaknesses, must be carried out concurrently. An 'apparent' strength, for example a reputation for quality, becomes a real strength only when it can be capitalised on in the market place.

3.3.3 STATEMENT OF OBJECTIVES

On the basis of the preceding steps the company must now determine specific objectives and goals which it wishes to achieve. These objectives, in turn, form the basis for the selection of marketing strategies and tactics.

Companies often have objectives in a number of areas – financial objectives, technological objectives and so on. Needless to say, here we are concerned primarily with marketing objectives, although these must be supportive of and consistent with objectives in other areas. In addition to this element of consistency, objectives should be expressed unambiguously, preferably quantitatively, and with an indication of the time span with which the objectives are planned to be achieved. This time span of planned activities often gives rise to some confusion in the planning literature. Marketing plans are often categorised as being short range, intermediate range and long range; the confusion arises from the fact that there is no accepted definition of what constitutes the appropriate time horizon for each of these categories. What is felt to comprise long-term planning in one company – say 5–10 years – may be considered intermediate in another. It is suggested that the different planning categories are identical in concept although clearly they differ in detail. Furthermore the different planning categories are ultimately related to each other – achieving long-term objectives requires first that intermediate and short-term objectives be met.

One of the most important documents in a company, however, and one which the sales manager will play a key part in the preparation of, is the annual marketing plan. The remainder of this chapter discusses planning in the context of the preparation of this annual document.

3.3.4 DETERMINING MARKET AND SALES POTENTIAL – FORECASTING SALES

A crucial step in the development of marketing plans is the assessment of market and sales potential followed by the preparation of a detailed sales forecast. Market potential is the maximum possible sales that are available for an entire industry during a stated period of time. Sales potential is the maximum possible portion of that market which a company could reasonably hope to achieve under the most favourable conditions. Finally the sales forecast is the portion of the sales potential that the company estimates that it will achieve. The sales forecast is in fact a very important step in the preparation of company plans. Not only are the marketing and sales functions directly affected in their planning considerations by this forecast, but other departments, including production, purchasing and personnel, will use the sales forecast in their planning activities. Sales forecasting, therefore, is a prerequisite to successful planning and is considered in detail in Chapter 12.

3.3.5 GENERATING AND SELECTING STRATEGIES

Once marketing objectives have been defined and market potential assessed, consideration may be given to the generation and selection of strategies. Broadly, strategies encompass the set of approaches which the company will use to achieve its objectives.

This step in the process is complicated by the fact that there are often many alternative ways in which each objective can be achieved. For example, an increase in sales revenue of 10 per cent can be achieved by increasing prices, increasing sales volume at the company level (increasing market share) or increasing industry sales. At this stage it is advisable, if time consuming, to generate as many alternative strategies as possible. In turn, each of these strategies can be further evaluated in terms of their detailed implications for resources and in the light of the market opportunities identified earlier. Finally, each strategy should be examined against the possibility of counter-strategies on the part of competitors.

From this list of alternative strategies a choice must be made with regard to the broad marketing approach which the company considers will be the most effective in achieving objectives. This must then be translated into a strategy statement which must be communicated to and agreed with all those managers who will influence its likely degree of success or failure. Once again, the specific contents of such a strategy statement will vary between companies, but as an example a strategy statement might encompass the following areas.

(*i*) A clear statement of marketing objectives.
(*ii*) A description of the choice of strategies for achieving these objectives.
(*iii*) An outline of the broad implications of the selected strategies with respect
      to following key areas in marketing.
      – Target market.
      – Positioning.
      – Marketing mix.
      – Marketing research.

At this stage the strategy statement should give a clear and concise indication of where the major marketing efforts of the company will be focused. Once this has been discussed and agreed we can progress to the next step of preparing a detailed plan of action.

3.3.6 PREPARING THE MARKETING PROGRAMME

The strategy statement prepared in the previous step provides the input for the deterination of the detailed programme required to implement these strategies. The first step in the preparation of this programme is the determination of the marketing mix. Detailed decisions must be made with respect to product policy, pricing, promotion and distribution. Further, care needs to be taken to ensure that the various elements of the marketing mix are integrated, i.e. that they work together to achieve company objectives in the most effective manner.

At this stage what has previously been an outline plan for guiding decision making becomes a detailed operating plan. It is on the basis of this part of the plan that the day-to-day marketing activities and tactics of the company will be organised, implemented and assessed.

3.3.7 ALLOCATING NECESSARY RESOURCES – BUDGETING

Having made detailed decisions with respect to the elements of the marketing mix, the next step is to assemble a budget for each of these elements. In most companies limited resources ensure that managers from the different functional areas have to compete for these scarce resources. At this stage it is likely that much discussion will take place between those responsible for each element of the marketing mix. In addition it may be found that initial marketing objectives, strategies and detailed plans for the marketing programme to achieve the forecast level of sales may, in the light of financial and other resource constraints, be unrealistic. In this event modifications to the original plan may have to be made.

It should be noted that at this stage an estimate can be made of both costs and revenues and a forecast profit and loss statement prepared.

3.3.8 IMPLEMENTATION AND CONTROL

The procedure so far should have resulted in the preparation of a detailed document setting out what is to be done, when it will be done, who is responsible and estimated costs and revenues. Once approved, details of the marketing plan should be communicated to everyone involved. This communication is an essential, and often neglected, aspect of marketing planning. It is surprising how many companies have elaborate marketing plans which are not implemented because key people have not been informed or have not agreed the proposed plan.

Finally, the plan should include an outline of the control mechanisms that will be applied to the plan. This should include details of major objectives and key parameters in the measurement of the degree of success in achieving the objectives. This part of the marketing plan should specify what is to be measured, how it is to be measured and what data is required for measurement. It may also include details of what action is to be taken in the light of deviations from the plan. This so-called contingency planning is a key feature of any planning process, recognising as it does that plans need to be flexible in order to accommodate possible unforeseen or unpredictable changes in the market.

The overall marketing planning process is summarised in Fig. 11.

3.4 THE PLACE OF SELLING IN THE MARKETING PLAN

So far we have examined the procedure by which marketing plans are prepared. Needless to say, the sales function has an important role to play in this process. Here we examine the nature of this role and, in particular, look at the contribution which the sales function makes to the preparation of the marketing plan and how the sales function is, in turn, influenced by the marketing plan itself.

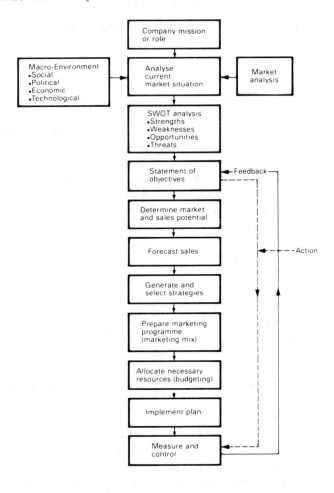

Fig 11   An overview of the marketing planning process.

3.4.1 THE CONTRIBUTION OF THE SALES FUNCTION

We have already seen that throughout the planning process alternative courses of action need to be identified and decisions taken as to which of these alternatives is the most appropriate. Both of these – identifying alternatives and choosing between them – require accurate and timely information. One of the key roles of the sales function in the planning process is the provision of such information. This will become clearer if we examine just some of the stages in the planning process where the sales function can make a valuable contribution. These stages include:

(*i*)   analysis of current market situation;
(*ii*) determining sales potential/sales forecasting;

(*iii*) generating and selecting strategies;
(*iv*) budgeting, implementation and control.

Analysis of current market situation

Its proximity to the market place places the sales function and its personnel in a unique position to contribute to the analysis of the current market situation facing the company. In particular, the sales function is often well placed to contribute to the analysis of customer needs and trends in purchasing behaviour. The sales manager can also make a valuable contribution with respect to knowledge about competitors and their standing in the market place. This informational role of the sales manager should not be ignored; through his sales force he is ideally equipped to provide up-to-date accurate information based on feedback from customers.

Determining sales potential/sales forecasting

As we shall see in Chapter 12, an important responsibility of the sales manager is the preparation of sales forecasts for use in planning, Short-, medium- and long-term forecasts by the sales manager form the basis for allocating company resources in order to achieve anticipated sales.

Generating and selecting strategies

Although the final decision about the appropriate marketing strategies to adopt in the market place rests with marketing management, the sales manager must be prepared, and encouraged, to make an input to this decision. Once again, the sales function is ideally placed to comment on the appropriateness of any suggested strategies.

A point worth mentioning here is that the sales manager should actively encourage his sales staff to comment upon the appropriateness of company marketing strategies. Often the field sales force can assess accurately how existing target markets will respond to company marketing initiatives.

Budgeting, implementation and control

The preparation of the sales forecast is a necessary prerequisite to the preparation of detailed plans. The sales forecast is also used in the preparation of the sales budget.

On the basis of the sales forecast, the sales manager must determine what level of expenditure will be required to achieve the forecasted level of sales. The important thing to remember about this budget is that it is the cornerstone of the whole budgeting procedure in a company. Not only the activities of the sales department, but also production, personnel, finance, and research and development will be affected by this budget. Because of this importance, sales budgets are considered in more detail in Chapter 13. At this stage it is sufficient to note that in preparing the sales budget the sales manager must prepare an outline of the essential sales activities required to meet the sales forecast, together with an estimate of their costs. The precise contents of the annual sales budget will vary between companies, but will normally include details of salaries, direct selling expenses, administrative costs and commissions and bonuses.

Having agreed the sales budget for the department, the sales manager must assume responsibility for its implementation and control. In preparing future plans, an important input is information on past performance against budget and, in particular, any differences between actual and budgeted results. Such 'budget variances', both favourable and unfavourable, should be analysed and interpreted by the sales manager as an input to the planning process. The reasons for budget variances should be reported, together with details of any remedial actions which were taken and their effects.

3.4.2 THE INFLUENCE OF THE MARKETING PLAN ON SALES ACTIVITIES: SALES STRATEGIES AND TACTICS

Any planning process is effective only to the extent that it influences action. An effective marketing planning system therefore influences activities, both strategic and tactical, throughout the company. Perhaps this influence is most clearly seen through decisions relating to the marketing programme or marketing mix.

Sales strategies are most directly influenced by planning decisions on the promotional element of the marketing mix. Here we will consider briefly the notion of a 'mix' of promotional tools, outlining the considerations in the choice of an appropriate mix and the implications for sales strategies. In particular, the important and often misunderstood relationship between advertising and selling is explained and discussed. We will conclude this section by examining briefly the nature of sales tactics.

The promotional mix

Earlier in this chapter we suggested that an important facet of marketing planning is the preparation of a marketing programme, the most important step in this preparation being the determination of the marketing mix – product, price, distribution and promotion. As selling is in fact only one element in the promotion part of this mix, it is therefore customary to refer to the promotion mix of a company.

This promotion mix (also called the communications mix) is made up of four major elements:

(*i*) advertising;
(*ii*) sales promotion;

(*iii*) publicity; and
(*iv*) personal selling.

In most companies all four can contribute to company sàles, but a decision has to be made as to where to place the emphasis. This decision is made at the planning stage. In addition, it is important that the elements of the promotion mix work together to achieve company objectives, and an important planning task of management is the coordination of promotional activities.

Several factors influence the planning decision as to where to place the emphasis within the promotion mix. In some firms the emphasis is placed on the sales force with most, if not all, of the promotional budget being devoted to this element of the mix. In others, advertising or sales promotion are seen as being much more efficient and productive than personal selling. Perhaps the most striking aspect of the various promotional tools is the extent to which they can be substituted, one for another. Companies within the same industry differ markedly in where they place the promotional emphasis. This makes it dangerous to be specific about developing the promotional mix within a particular company. As a guide, however, some of the more important factors influencing this decision are outlined below.

(*i*) TYPE OF MARKET. In general, advertising and sales promotion play a more important role in the marketing of consumer products, whereas personal selling plays the major role in idustrial marketing. The reasons for this stem from the differences between industrial and consumer marketing, which were outlined in Chapter 2, and are most obvious where we contrast the marketing of fast moving comsumer goods (fmcg) with the marketing of often highly technical, expensive capital goods to industry. Despite this, it is a mistake to conclude – as is often done – that advertising does not have a role to play in the marketing of industrial products. Indeed, the potential contribution of advertising is often mistakenly undervalued by the sales personnel and discounted as a waste of valuable company resources. The relationship between advertising and sales is considered later in this chapter.

(*ii*) STAGE IN THE BUYING PROCESS. In Chapter 2 it was suggested that for both industrial and consumer products it is useful to consider the stages which the prospective purchaser passes through en route to making a purchase decision. Although there are a number of ways in which this process may be conceptualised, essentially it consists of the potential purchaser moving from a position of being unaware of a company and/or its products, through to being convinced that the products or services of this company are the most appropriate to the buyer's needs. The sequential nature of this process is shown in Fig. 12. Evidence suggests that, for a given outlay, advertising and publicity are more effective in the earlier stages of moving potential purchasers through from unawareness to comprehension. Personal selling, on the other hand, is more cost effective than other forms of promotional activity at the conviction and purchase stages. This is not to suggest that 'cold calling' is not an important area of sales activity; however, as we shall see later, such cold calling is rendered much more effective if the customer is already aware of your company and its products.

(*iii*) PUSH VERSUS PULL STRATEGIES. One of the most important determinants in the choice of promotional mix is the extent to which a company decides to concentrate its efforts in terms of its channels of distribution. This can perhaps be best illustrated if we contrast a push strategy with that of a pull strategy.

   – A *push strategy* is where the focus of marketing effort is aimed at pushing the product through the channel of distribution. The emphasis is on ensuring that wholesalers and retailers stock the product in question. The notion is that if channel members can be induced to stock a product they, in turn, will be active in ensuring that your product is brought to the attention of the final customer. In general a push strategy entails a much greater emphasis on personal selling and trade promotion in the promotional mix.

   – A *pull strategy* relies much more heavily on advertising to promote the product to the final consumer. The essence of this approach is based on the notion that if sufficient consumer demand can be generated for a product this will result in final consumers asking retailers for the product. Retailers will then ask their wholesalers for the product, who

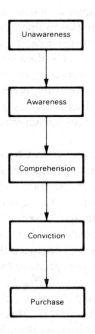

Fig 12   Stages in the buying process.

will in turn contact the producer. In this way the product is 'pulled' through the channel by creating consumer demand via aggressive advertising. (Channel management is considered in detail in Chapter 6.)

(*iv*) STAGE IN THE PRODUCT LIFE CYCLE. Chapter 1 introduced the notion of the product life cycle. Again there is some evidence to suggest that the different promotional tools vary in their relative effectiveness over the various stages of this cycle. In general, advertising and sales promotion are most effective in the introduction and growth stages of the life cycle, whereas it is suggested that the emphasis in personal selling needs to increase as the market matures and eventually declines. Needless to say, although there is no doubt that the stage of the product life cycle does influence the choice of marketing strategy, great care should be taken in evaluating the consequences of this influence for sales strategies.

Coordinating promotional efforts: the relationship between advertising and selling

In discussing the factors affecting the choice of promotional tools, it may have appeared that to some extent these tools are mutually exclusive – for example, one chooses to concentrate either on advertising or personal selling. This is not the case; the relationship between the various promotional tools, including personal selling, should be complementary and coordinated. Perhaps this rather obvious point would not need to be stressed were it not for the fact that often this complementary relationship is misunderstood. Nowhere is this misunderstanding more evident than in the relationship between advertising and selling.

It is a sad fact that many sales managers and their sales forces believe that expenditure on advertising is a waste of company resources. Very rarely, they argue, does a customer ever purchase simply because a product is advertised, particularly where that customer is an industrial purchaser. Because of this, the argument continues, the money 'wasted' on advertising would be better spent where it will have a direct and immediate effect – on the sales force. Increasingly, the evidence suggests that this notion that advertising money is wasted in industrial markets is misplaced. Among the functions that advertising can perform in such markets are the following.

(*i*) Corporate advertising can help to build the reputation of a company and its products.
(*ii*) Advertising is particularly effective in creating awareness among prospective clients. The sales representative facing a prospect who is unaware of the company or product faces a much more difficult selling task than the representative who can build on an initial awareness.
(*iii*) Advertising can aid the sales representative in the marketing of new products by shouldering some of the burden of explaining new product features and building comprehension.

(*iv*) Advertising using return coupons may be used to open up new leads for the sales force.

Overall, by far the greatest benefit of advertising in industrial markets is seen, not through a direct effect on sales revenue, but in the reduction of overall selling costs. Evidence suggests that, given adequate frequency, this reduction in selling costs to customers exposed to advertising may be as high as 30 per cent. Conversely, the non-advertiser may find himself at a serious disadvantage. His cost of selling to customers exposed to competitors' advertising may be increased by as much as 40 per cent.

On the other hand, in consumer goods marketing, whereas advertising is generally thought to be the most effective promotion tool, personal selling and a well-trained sales force can contribute significantly to increased market penetration by influencing stockists to allocate more shelf space to company products, persuading new dealers to stock them, etc.

At all times, sales and advertising should be coordinated together to achieve company objectives. It is important for sales personnel to be informed about company advertising campaigns. This advertising should be utilised in selling, the advertising theme being reinforced in the sales presentation.

From sales strategies to tactics

We have seen that a number of factors influence the setting for sales strategies. It was suggested that this influence is most direct in determining the relative emphasis to be given to sales activities in overall company and promotional strategy. Sales strategies are of course also influenced by the marketing and sales objectives specified in the marketing planning document. As an illustration, a marketing objective of increased market share may mean that the sales manager has to ensure that sales in the forthcoming year increase by 10 per cent. Further, the planning document should specify the route or strategy by which this objective will be accomplished, e.g. 'Additional sales effort is to be targeted on the opening of new accounts.' Sales objectives and strategies, therefore, also stem directly from the planning process, after consulation and agreement with relevant personnel.

Having agreed these strategic guidelines, a more detailed set of activities must be built into the planning process. The sales manager must determine the specific actions required to achieve sales goals, i.e. tactics.

Tactics encompass the day-to-day activities of the sales function in the achievement of marketing and sales objectives. Tactics also include actions which require to be taken in response to unexpected short-term events in the market place, for example a special promotional effort by a competitor. The relationship between objectives, strategies and tactics is shown in Fig. 13.

Tactical decisions represent what might be termed a 'fine tuning' of sales activities and encompass many of the decision areas covered in greater detail

Fig 13   The relationship between objectives, strategies and tactics.

elsewhere in this text; for example, the deployment of sales personnel – territory design and planning (Chapter 11) – can be considered a tactical aspect of sales. Similarly, the design of incentive systems (Chapter 10) should form part of a tactical plan, designed to accomplish sales goals within the framework of sales strategies.

The importance of sound tactics should not be underestimated; even the best-formed strategies often fail for want of proper tactics. As an example of the use and importance of tactics in selling, we will consider briefly an aspect of purchasing which is of vital interest to many companies, namely brand/supplier loyalty.

Brand/supplier loyalty

If we examine the purchase of products and services over time, we find that often the purchasing sequence of individuals indicates that they repeatedly buy the same brand of a product, or, if the product is an industrial one, that they consistently buy from a particular supplier. For such individuals, if we imagine that the brand or supplier in question is called X, the purchasing sequence would be as shown below:

Purchase occasion	1	2	3	4	5	6
Brand purchased/supplier	X	X	X	X	X	X

There is no doubt that brand/supplier loyalty does exist. Moreover, the cultivation of such loyalty among customers often accounts for a significant part of tactical marketing and sales effort, representing, as it does, a substantial market asset to a company.

Before considering the part that sales tactics can play in this process of cultivating brand loyalty, it is important to explain precisely what is meant by brand loyalty. This apparently simple notion in fact gives rise to some misunderstanding.

Let us return to our purchasing sequence shown above. Although we have suggested that such a sequence is associated with a brand-loyal customer, the existence of such an array of purchases for a customer does not, of itself, constitute evidence that this customer *is* brand loyal. There are in fact a number of possible explanations for this purchasing behaviour. One such explanation might be the fact this customer concentrates much of his purchasing in one particular retail outlet and it so happens that this particular retail outlet only stocks brand X of this product, i.e. the customer exhibits loyalty, but to the store, rather than the brand. Another possible explanation is that this customer in fact pays little regard to the particular brand or supplier; he is not consciously brand loyal at all, rather he has simply slipped into the habit of purchasing this brand and cannot be bothered to switch. In this second example it is of course true to say that at least the customer must be reasonably satisfied with the brand he is purchasing consistently; presumably if he were not, or became dissatisfied for any reason, he would then make the decision to switch. Nevertheless, this is not true brand loyalty.

True brand or supplier loyalty exists when a customer makes a conscious decision to concentrate his purchases on a particular brand, because he considers that supplier or brand superior to others. There may be a number of reasons/bases for such perceived superiority, e.g. superior quality, better delivery and after-sales services, the availability of credit, or some combination of these or other factors. In fact, in discussing the possible reasons for brand/supplier loyalty, we enter the realms of motives, perceptions, attitudes, etc. – complex behavioural areas discussed in the previous chapter.

The concept of brand/supplier loyalty therefore is a difficult one and care should be taken in interpreting the often conflicting evidence for its causes. Nevertheless, there are some indications that the salesperson can play a key role in helping to establish brand/supplier loyalty amongst a firm's customers. One of the reasons for this is that learning theory suggests that we have a tendency to repeat experiences that give us pleasure and to avoid those that do not. One of the most powerful and lasting impressions that serve as a source of pleasure or displeasure in purchasing activities are experiences in the face-to-face encounters with sales staff. Favourable attitudes and behaviour of sales personnel in dealing with their customers can contribute significantly to the creation of brand/supplier loyalty.

3.5 CONCLUSIONS

The framework for sales strategies and tactics has been established. We have seen that these are developed and operated within the framework of marketing planning. The sales function makes a valuable contribution to the establishment of marketing plans, providing, as it does, key data on customers, markets, competitors, sales forecasts and budgets. In turn, selling activities are directly influenced by decisions taken at the marketing planning stage.

We have looked at planning decisions for the marketing programme or marketing mix and, specifically, at the promotional mix in a company. Factors such as type of product market, steps in the buying process, push versus pull strategies and stage in the product life-cycle have all been shown to influence promotional and therefore sales strategies.

Finally, we looked at sales tactics, the relationship between advertising and selling, and the important area of brand/supplier loyalty. It was shown that advertising plays a key role in aiding the sales effort, reducing selling costs and easing the sales task. Brand/supplier loyal customers are a valuable asset to any company and the sales force is central to the establishment and maintenance of such customer loyalty.

PRACTICAL EXERCISE – AUCKLAND ENGINEERING PLC

Jim Withey, sales manager for Auckland Engineering PLC, a well-established engineering company based in the Midlands, had been contemplating the memo he had received two days earlier from his newly appointed marketing director.

Memo
To: J. Withey, sales manager
From: D. C. Duncan, marketing director
Subject: Preparation of annual marketing plan Jan.–Dec. 1991
Date: 16 Jan. 1990.
You will recall that at our series of preliminary meetings to discuss future marketing plans for the company, I suggested that I was unhappy with the seemingly haphazard approach to planning. Accordingly, you will recall it was agreed between departmental heads that each would undertake to prepare a formal input to next month's planning meeting.

At this stage I am not seeking detailed plans for each product market, rather I am concerned that you give some thought to how your department can contribute to the planning process. Being new to the company and its product/markets, I am not entirely up to date on what has been happening to the market for our products, although as we all know our market share at 3·5 per cent is down on last year. I would particularly like to know what information your department could contribute to the analysis of the situation.

To help you in your own analysis I have summarised below what I feel came out of our first planning meetings.
• Business definition. It was agreed that the business needs re-defining in customer terms. An appropriate definition for our company would be as follows:
'Solutions to engine component design and manufacturing problems.'

- Strengths, weaknesses, opportunities and threats, i.e. SWOT analysis.

The main *strengths* of our company are as follows.
- We have excellent customer awareness and an image of reliability and quality.
- Our sales force is technically well qualified.
- Our manufacturing flexibility is second to none. We can respond quickly and effectively to individual customer needs.

Our main *weaknesses* are as follows.
- Our prices are approximately 10 per cent above the industry average.
- We are spending a far higher proportion of our turnover on advertising than some of our main competitors.
- Our sales force is not skilled in generating new leads.

Major *opportunities* are as follows.
- Some of our major competitors are having difficulty keeping their customers because of quality and delivery problems. Buyers in the industry seem particularly prone to switching their suppliers.
- Recent legislation in the industry means that our research and development programme on the new TDIX component, with its emphasis on lower exhaust emission levels, should prove advantageous.
- Recent and forecast trends in the exchange rate should help our export marketing efforts.

Major *threats* are shown below.
- Our largest customer is threatening to switch to another supplier because of our higher average prices.
- Apart from the TDIX programme, we have not been keeping pace with the rapid technological change in the industry.
- Some of our major export markets are threatened by the possiblity of important restrictions.

- *Objectives.*
  Financial.
  - To increase our return on capital employed by 5 per cent after taxes.
  - Our net profit in the forthcoming year to be £2·0 million.
  Marketing.
  - Sales revenue to be increased to £18 million in the forthcoming year.
- *Marketing strategy.*
  Target markets.
  - Major manufacturers of diesel engines worldwide.
  Positioning.
  - Highest engineering quality and after-sales service in the supply of specialist low volume diesel engine components.

I would of course welcome your comments on my analysis of the situation, together with your views on the appropriateness of the objectives I have set.

In addition, for the next meeting I suggest that as sales manager you give some thought as to where the relative emphasis should be placed in our promotional effort. As I have already mentioned in my summary of our preliminary meetings, we seem to be spending an excessive amount on advertising compared to our competitors. Perhaps you could appraise me of your thoughts on this, as I understand that you were instrumental in raising our advertising budget from 3 per cent to 5 per cent of our turnover last year. As you are well aware, from a limited budget we must decide where to place the relative emphasis in our promotional mix. Perhaps you would indicate what you feel are the major considerations in this decision.

Discussion questions

1 Give a brief outline of the ways in which you as sales manager can contribute to the marketing planning process at Auckland Engineering.
2 Looking at Mr Duncan's analysis of your previous meetings, what issues/problems do you see which are of particular relevance to the activities of the sales force?
3 How would you respond to Mr Duncan's comments on the promotional mix and, in particular, to his comments about the level of advertising expenditure?
4 What is the point in conducting a SWOT analysis?

EXAMINATION QUESTIONS

1 Explain the differences between marketing strategies and sales strategies.
2 What is the relationship between objectives, strategies and tactics.

PART TWO
Sales Technique

4 Sales Responsibilities and Preparation

4.1 SALES RESPONSIBILITIES

The *primary* responsibility of a salesperson is to conclude a sale successfully. This task will involve the identification of customer needs, presentation and demonstration, negotiation, handling objections and closing the sale. These skills are discussed in detail in Chapter 5. In order to generate sales successfully a number of *secondary* functions are also carried out by most salespeople. Although termed secondary, they are vital to long-term sales success. These are:

(*i*)   prospecting;
(*ii*) maintaining customer records and information feedback;
(*iii*) self-management;
(*iv*) handling complaints;
(*v*)   providing service.

4.1.1 PROSPECTING

Prospecting is the searching for and calling upon customers who, hitherto, have not purchased from the company. This activity is not of uniform importance across all branches of selling. It is obviously far more important in industrial selling than retail selling; for example, a salesperson of office equipment may call upon many new potential customers, whereas a furniture salesperson is unlikely to search out new prospects – they come to him as a result of advertising and, perhaps, high street location.

  A problem sometimes associated with salespeople who have worked for the same company for many years is that they rely on established customers to provide repeat orders rather than actively seeking new business. Certainly, it is usually more comfortable for the salesperson to call upon old contacts, but the nature of much industrial selling is that, because product life is long, sustained sales growth depends upon searching out and selling to new customers.

Sources of prospects

(*i*) EXISTING CUSTOMERS. This is a highly effective method of generating prospects and, yet, tends to be under-used by many. A wealth of new prospects can be obtained simply by asking satisfied customers if they know of anyone who may have a need for the kinds of products or services being sold. This technique has been used successfully in life insurance and industrial selling but has application in many other areas also.

Having obtained the names of potential customers, the salesperson, if appropriate, can ask his customer if he may use his name as a reference. The use of reference selling in industrial marketing can be highly successful since it reduces the perceived risk for a potential buyer.

(*ii*) TRADE DIRECTORIES. A reliable trade directory such as *Kompass* or *Dunn and Bradstreet* can prove useful in identifying potential industrial buyers. The *Kompass* directory, for example, is organised by industry and location and provides such potentially useful information as:
- name, address and telephone number of companies;
- names of board members;
- size of firm, by turnover and number of employees;
- type of products manufactured or distributed.

For trade selling, the *Retail Directory* provides information regarding potential customers, organized by various types of retail outlet. Thus a salesperson selling a product suitable for confectioners and newsagents could use the listing of such retailers under the CTN heading (confectioners, tobacconists and newsagents) to obtain relevant names, addresses, telephone numbers and, also, an indication of size through the information given regarding number of branches.

(*iii*) INQUIRIES. Inquiries may arise as a natural consequence of conducting business. Satisfied customers may by word-of-mouth create inquiries from 'warm' prospects. Many companies stimulate inquiries, however, by advertising (many industrial advertisements use coupon return to stimulate leads), direct mail and exhibitions. This source of prospects is an important one and the salesperson should respond promptly. The inquirer may have an urgent need seeking a solution and may turn to the competition if faced with a delay. Even if the customer's problem is not so urgent, slow response may foster unfavourable attitudes towards the salesman and his company's products.

The next priority is to screen out those inquiries which are unlikely to result in a sale. A telephone call has the advantage of giving a personalised response, and yet is relatively inexpensive and not time consuming. It can be used to check how serious the inquiry is and to arrange a personal visit should the inquiry prove to have potential. This process of checking leads to establish their potential is known as *qualifying*.

(*iv*) THE PRESS. Perhaps underused as a source of prospects, the press is nevertheless important. Advertisements and articles can give clues to potential new sources of business. Articles may reveal diversification plans which may mean a company suddenly becomes a potential customer; advertisements for personnel may reveal plans for expansion, again suggesting potential new business.

(*v*) COLD CANVASSING. This method involves calling in every prospect who might have a need for the salesperson's product. A brush salesperson, for example, may attempt to call upon every house in a village. A variant of this method is the 'cool canvass', where only certain groups of people are canvassed, i.e. those who are more likely to buy since they possess some qualifying feature; for example, only companies over a certain size may be judged viable prospects. Calling cold on big company buyers is unlikely to be successful, however. A more effective approach is to send a letter in advance explaining the business the company is in, followed by a call to make an appointment (Lee, 1984).

4.1.2 CUSTOMER RECORDS AND INFORMATION FEEDBACK

A systematic approach to customer record-keeping is to be recommended to all repeat-call salespeople. An industrial salesperson should record the following information.

(*i*)   Name and address of company.
(*ii*)   Name and position of contact(s).
(*iii*) Nature of business.
(*iv*)   Date and time of interview.
(*v*)   Assessment of potential.
(*vi*)   Buyer needs, problems and buying habits.
(*vii*) Past sales with dates.
(*viii*) Problems/opportunities encountered.
(*ix*)   Future actions on the part of salesman (and buyer).

Record cards should be provided by management and salespeople encouraged to use them as part of the sales plan before each visit.

Salespeople should also be encouraged to send back to head office information which is relevant to the marketing of company products. Test market activity by competition, news of imminent product launches, rumours of policy changes on the part of trade and industrial customers, competitors, and feedback on company achievement regarding product performance, delivery and after-sales service are just some of the kinds of information which may be useful to management.

4.1.3 SELF-MANAGEMENT

This aspect of the sales job is of particular importance since he is often working alone with the minimum of personal supervision. A salesperson may have to organise his or her own call plan. This involves dividing territory into sections to be covered day by day and deciding the best route to follow between calls. Often it makes sense to divide a territory into segments radiating outwards, with the salesperson's home being at the centre. Each segment is designed to be small enough to be covered by the salesperson during one day's work.

Many salespeople believe that the most efficient routing plan involves driving out to the furthest customer and, then zig-zagging back to home base. However it can be shown that adopting a round-trip approach will usually result in lower mileage. Such considerations are important with respect to efficiency, as an alarming amount of time can be spent on the road as opposed to face to face with buyers. A survey conducted on behalf of the Institute of Marketing into selling practice in the UK (PA Consultants, 1979) found that, on average, only 20 – 30 per cent of a salesperson's normal working day is spent face to face with customers. Although this study was conducted over 10 years ago, matters have not improved since then. In fact, this figure is now nearer 20 per cent rather than 30 because salespeople are increasingly called upon to carry out ancillary work such as customer surveys, service work and merchandising. Some companies take this responsibility out of the salesperson's hands and produce daily worksheets showing who is to be called on and in what order.

Another factor which may be the responsibility of the salesperson is deciding on call frequency. It is sensible to grade customers according to potential. For example, consumer durable salesmen may categorise the retain outlets they are selling into A, B and C grades. A grade outlets may be visited every fortnight, B grade every month and C grade once every three months. The principle applies to all kinds of selling, however, and may be left to the salesperson's discretion or organised centrally as part of the sales management function. The danger of delegating responsibility to salespeople is that the criteria used to decide frequency of visit are 'friendliness with the buyer' or 'ease of sale' rather than sales potential. On the other hand, it can be argued that a reponsible salesperson is in the best position to decide how much time needs to be spent with each customer.

4.1.4 HANDLING COMPLAINTS

Dealing with complaints may seem, at first, to be a time-consuming activity which diverts a salesperson from his primary task of generating sales. A marketing orientation for a sales force, however, dictates that the goal of an organisation is to create customer satisfaction in order to generate profit. When dissatisfaction identifies itself in the form of a complaint, this necessary condition for long-term survival is clearly not being met.

Complaints vary in their degree of seriousness and in the authority which the salesperson holds in order to deal with them. No matter how trivial the complaint may seem, the complainant should be treated with respect and the matter dealt with seriously. In a sense, dealing with complaints is one of the after-the-sale services provided by suppliers. It is therefore part of the mix of benefits a company offers its customers, although it differs in essence since the initial objective is to minimise its necessity. Nevertheless, the ability of the salesperson to empathise with the customer and his problem and to react sympathetically can create considerable goodwill and help foster long-term relationships.

With this in mind, many companies give the customer the benefit of the doubt when this does not involve high cost, even though they suspect that the fault may be caused by inappropriate use of the product on the part of the customer; for example, garden fork manufacturers may replace prematurely broken forks, even though the break may have been caused by work for which the fork was not designed.

When the salesperson does not have the authority to deal with the complaint immediately, his job is to submit the relevant information in written form to head office so that the matter can be taken further.

4.1.5 PROVIDING SERVICE

Salespeople are in an excellent position to provide a 'consultancy' service to their customers. Since they meet many customers each year, they become familiar with solutions to common problems. Thus an industrial salesperson may be able to advise his customers on improving productivity or cutting costs. Indeed the service element of industrial selling is often incorporated into the selling process itself, e.g. computer salespeople may offer to conduct an analysis of customer requirements and produce a written report in order to complete a sale. The salesperson who learns solutions to common problems and provides useful advice to his customers builds an effective barrier to competitive attacks and strengthens buyer-seller relationships.

Another area where salespeople provide service is in trade selling. They may be called upon to set up in-store displays and other promotions for wholesalers and retailers. Some companies employ people to do this on a full-time basis. These people are called merchandisers and their activities provide support to traditional salespeople, who can thus spend more time selling.

Salespeople may also be called upon to provide after-sales service to customers. A sales engineer may be required to give advice on the operation of a newly acquired machine or provide assistance in the event of a breakdown. Sometimes he may be able to solve the problem himself, while in other cases he will call in technical specialists to deal with the problem.

4.2 PREPARATION

The ability to think on one's feet is of great benefit to a salesperson, since he will be required to modify his sales presentation to suit the particular needs and problems of his various customers and to respond quickly to unusual objections and awkward questions. However, there will be much to be gained by careful preparation of the selling task. Some customers will have similar problems; some questions and objections will be raised repeatedly. A salesperson can therefore usefully spend time considering how best to respond to these recurring situations.

Within this section attention will be given to preparation not only for the selling task, in which there is little or no scope for the salesperson to bargain with the buyer, but also for where selling may involve a degree of negotiation between buyer and seller. In many selling situations, buyers and sellers may negotiate price, timing of delivery, product extras, payment and credit terms, and trade-in values. These will be termed *sales negotiations*. In others, the salesperson may have no scope for such discussions; in essence the product is offered on a take-it-or-leave-it basis. Thus, the salesperson of bicycles to dealers may have a set price list and delivery schedule with no authority to deviate from them. This will be termed *pure selling*.

4.2.1 PREPARATION FOR PURE SELLING AND SALES NEGOTIATIONS

A number of factors can be examined in order to improve the chances of sales success in both sales negotiations and pure selling.

Product knowledge and benefits

Knowledge of product features is insufficient for sales success. Because people buy products for the benefits they confer, successful salespeople relate product features to consumer benefits; product features are the means by which benefits are derived. The way to do this is to look at products from the customer's point of view. Table 1 shows a few examples.

By analysing the products he is selling in this way, a salesman will communicate in terms which are meaningful to buyers and therefore be more convincing. In industrial selling, the salesperson may be called upon to be an adviser or consultant who is required to provide solutions to problems. In some cases this may involve a fairly deep understanding of the nature of the customer's business, in order to be able to appreciate his problems fully and to suggest the most appropriate solution. Thus the salesperson must not only know his products' benefits but the types of situation in which each would be appropriate. In computer selling, for example, successful selling requires an appreciation of which system is most appropriate given customer needs and resources. This may necessitate a careful examination of customer needs through a survey conducted

Table 1. *Product features and customer benefits*

Product feature	Customer benefit
Retractable nib on ballpoint pen	Reduces chances of damage
High rev. speed on spin dryer	Clothes are dried more thoroughly
High reach on forklift truck	Greater use of warehouse space
Stream-feeding (photocopiers)	Faster copying
Automatic washing machine	More time to spend on doing other less mundane activities

by the seller. Sometimes the costs of the survey will be paid for by the prospective customer, later to be subtracted from the cost of the equipment should an order result.

Preparation of sales benefits should not result in an inflexible sales approach. Different customers have different needs which implies they seek different benefits from products they buy. One high-earning salesperson of office equipment attributed his success to the preparation he conducted before every sales visit; this involved knowing his product's capabilities, understanding his client's needs, and matching these together by getting his wife to test him every evening and at the weekend (Kennedy *et al.*, 1980).

Knowledge of competitors' products and their benefits

Knowledge of competitive products offers several advantages.

(*i*) It allows a salesperson to offset the strengths of competitors' products, which may be mentioned by potential buyers, against their weaknesses. For example, a buyer might say 'Competitor X's product offers cheaper maintenance costs', to which a salesperson might reply 'Yes, but these cost savings are small compared to the fuel savings you get with our machine.'

(*ii*) In industrial selling sales engineers may work with a buying organisation in order to solve a technical problem. This may result in a product specification being drawn up in which the sales engineers may have an influence. It is obviously to their benefit that the specification reflects the strengths and capabilities of their products rather than competition. Thus knowledge of competitive strengths and weaknesses will be an advantage in this situation.

Competitive information can be gleaned from magazines, e.g. *Which?* sales catalogues and price lists, from talking to buyers and from direct observation, e.g. of prices in supermarkets. It makes sense to keep such information on file for quick reference.

Sales presentation planning

Although versatility, flexibility and the ability to 'think on one's feet' are desirable attributes, there are considerable advantages to presentational planning.

(*i*)　The salesperson is less likely to forget important consumer benefits associated with each product within the range he is selling.

(*ii*)　The use of visual aids and demonstrations can be planned into the presentation at the most appropriate time to reinforce the benefit the salesperson is communicating.

(*iii*)　It builds confidence in the salesperson, particularly the newer less experienced type, that he is well-equipped to do the job efficiently and professionally.

(*iv*)　Possible objections and questions can be anticipated and persuasive counterarguments prepared. Many salespeople who, to an outsider, seem naturally quick-witted have developed this skill through careful preparation beforehand, imagining themselves as buyers and thinking of objections that they might raise if they were in such a position. For example, many price objections can be countered by reference to higher product quality, greater durability, high productivity and lower offsetting life-cycle costs, e.g. lower maintenance, fuel or manpower costs.

Setting sales objectives

The essential skill in setting call objectives is to phrase them in terms of what the salesperson wants the customer to do rather than what the salesperson will do. The type of objective set may depend upon the *sales cycle* of the product and the stage reached in that cycle with a prospective customer.

The sales cycle refers to the time which can reasonably be expected to pass before an order is concluded. With many retail sales this is short; often, unless a sale is concluded during the first visit, the customer will buy elsewhere. In this situation it is reasonable to set a sales close objective. With capital goods, like aeroplanes, gas turbines and oil rigs, the sales cycle is very long, perhaps running into years. Clearly, to set a sales objective in terms of closing the sale is inappropriate. For producers with longer sales cycles, sensible objectives may be:

(*i*)　for the customer to define clearly what his requirements are;

(*ii*)　to have the customer visit the production site;

(*iii*)　to have the customer try the product, e.g. fly on an aircraft;

(*iv*)　to have the customer compare the product versus competitive products in terms of measurable performance criteria, e.g. for pile driving equipment this might be the number of metres driven per hour.

The temptation, when setting objectives, is to determine them in terms of what the salesperson will do. An adhesive salesperson may decide that the objective of his visit to a buyer is to demonstrate the ease of application and adhesive properties of a new product. While this demonstration may be a valuable and necessary part of the sales presentation, it is not the ultimate goal of the visit. This may be to have the customer test the product over a four-week period, or for him to order a quantity for immediate use.

Understanding buyer behaviour

The point was made in Chapter 2 that many organisational buying decisions are complex, involving many people whose evaluative criteria may differ, and that the purchasing officer may play a minor role in deciding which supplier to choose, particularly with very expensive items.

The practical implication of these facts is that careful preparation may be necessary for industrial salespeople, either when selling to new companies or when selling to existing customers where the nature of the product is different. In both situations, time taken trying to establish who the key influencers and decision-makers are will be well rewarded. In different companies there may be different key people, e.g. secretaries, (office stationery), production engineers (lathes), design engineers (components), managing directors (computers), so the salesperson needs to be aware of the real need to treat each organisation individually.

Other practical information which a salesperson can usefully collect includes the name and position of each key influencer and decision-maker, the times most suitable for interview, the types of competitive products previously purchased by the buying organisation, and any threats to a successful sale or special opportunities afforded by the situation. Examples in the last category would include personal prejudices held by key people against the salesperson, his company, or its products, while positive factors might include common interests which could form the basis of a rapport with the buyer, or favourable experiences with other types of products sold by the salesperson's company.

4.2.2 PREPARATION FOR SALES NEGOTIATIONS

In addition to the factors outlined in the previous section, a sales negotiator will benefit by paying attention to the following additional factors during preparation.

Assessment of the balance of power

In the sales negotiation, seller and buyer will each be expecting to conclude a deal which is favourable to themselves. The extent to which each is successful will depend upon their negotiating skills and the balance of power between the parties. This balance will be determined by four key factors.

(*i*) THE NUMBER OF OPTIONS AVAILABLE TO EACH PARTY. If a buyer has only one option – to buy from the seller in question – then that seller is in a powerful position. If the seller, in turn, is not dependent on the buyer, but has many attractive potential customers for his products, then again he is in a strong position. Conversely, when a buyer has many potential sources of supply, and a seller has few potential customers, the buyer should be able to extract a good deal. Many buyers will deliberately contact a number of potential suppliers to strengthen their bargaining position.

(*ii*) THE QUANTITY AND THE QUALITY OF INFORMATION HELD BY EACH PARTY. ('Knowledge is power' – Machieavelli.) If a buyer has access to a seller's cost structure then he is in a powerful position to negotiate a cheaper price, or at least avoid paying too high a price. If a seller knows how much a buyer is willing to pay, then his power position is improved.

(*iii*) NEED RECOGNITION AND SATISFACTION. The greater the salesperson's understanding of the needs of the buyer and the more capable he is of satisfying those needs, the stronger will be his bargaining position. In some industrial marketing situations, suppliers work with buying organisations to solve technical problems in the knowledge that to do so will place them in a very strong negotiating position. The more the buyer believes that his needs can be satisfied by only one company, the weaker his negotiating stance. In effect, the seller has reduced the buyer's number of options by uniquely satisfying his needs.

(*iv*) THE PRESSURES ON THE PARTIES. Where a technical problem is of great importance to a buying organisation, its visibility high and its solution difficult, any supplier who can solve it will gain immense bargaining power. If, on the other hand, there are pressures on the salesperson, perhaps because of low sales returns, then a buyer should be able to extract extremely favourable terms during negotiations in return for purchasing from him.

The implications of these determinants of the balance of power are that before negotiations (and, indeed, during them) a salesperson will benefit by assessing the relative strength of his power base. This implies that he needs information. If the seller knows the number of companies who are competing for the order, their likely stances, the criteria used by the buying organisation when deciding between them, the degree of pressure on key members of the decision making unit, and any formula they might use for assessing price acceptability, an accurate assessment of the power balance should be possible.

This process should lessen the chances of pricing too low or of needlessly giving away other concessions like favourable payment terms. Judicious negotiators will at this stage look to the future to assess likely changes in the balance of power. Perhaps power lies with the supplier now, but overpowering or 'negotiating too sweet a deal' might provoke retribution later when the buyer has more suppliers from which to choose.

Determination of negotiating objectives

It is prudent for negotiators to set objectives during the preparation stage. This reduces the likelihood of being swayed by the heat of the negotiating battle and of accepting a deal which, with hindsight, should have been rejected. This process is analogous to a buyer at an auction paying more than he can afford because he allows himself to be swept along by the bidding. Additionally, when negotiation is conducted by a team, discussion of objectives helps coordination and unity.

It is useful to consider two types of objectives (Kennedy *et al.*, 1980).

(*i*) 'MUST HAVE' OBJECTIVES. The 'must have' objectives define a bargainer's minimum requirements; for example, the minimum price at which a seller is willing to trade. This determines the negotiating breakpoint.

(*ii*) 'WOULD LIKE' OBJECTIVES. These are the maximum a negotiator can reasonably expect to get; for example, the highest price a seller feels he can realistically obtain. This determines the opening positions of buyers and sellers.

Figure 14 describes a negotiating scenario where a deal is possible since there is overlap between the highest price the buyer is willing to pay (buyer's 'must have' objective) and the lowers price the seller is willing to accept (seller's 'must have' objective). The price actually agreed will depend upon the balance of power between the two parties and their respective negotiating skills.

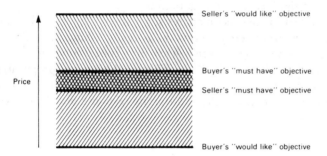

Fig 14   A negotiating scenario (adapted from Winkler, 1981).

Concession analysis

Since negotiation implies movement in order to achieve agreement, it is likely that concessions will be made by at least one party during the bargaining process. Preparation can aid negotiators by analysing the kinds of concessions which might be offered to the other side. The key to this concession analysis is to value concessions the seller might be prepared to make through the eyes of the buyer. By doing this it may be possible to identify concessions which cost the seller very little and yet be highly valued by the buyer. For example, to offer much quicker delivery than is usual may cost a seller very little because of spare capacity, but if this is highly valued bythe buyer the seller may be able to trade it in return for a prompt payment agreement.

Below are listed the kinds of issues which may be examined during concession analysis.

(*i*) Price.
(*ii*) Timing of delivery.
(*iii*) The product – its specification, optional extras.
(*iv*) The price – ex works price, price at the buyer's factory gate, installation price, in-service price?
(*v*) Payment – on despatch, on receipt, in working order, credit terms?
(*vi* Trade-in terms, e.g. cars.

The aim of concession analysis is to ensure that nothing which has value to the buyer is given away freely during negotiations. A skilful negotiator will attempt to trade concession for concession so that ultimately an agreement which satisfies both parties is reached.

Proposal analysis

A further sensible activity during the preparation stage is to estimate the proposals and demands the buyer is likely to make during the course of negotiation, and the seller's reaction to them. This is analogous to the anticipation of objections in pure selling – it helps when quick decisions have to be made in the heat of the negotiation.

It is also linked to concession analysis, for when a buyer makes a proposal, for example favourable credit terms, he is really asking the seller to grant a concession. The skilful salesperson will ask for a concession in return – perhaps a less onerous delivery schedule. By anticipating the kinds of proposals the buyer is likely to make, the seller can plan the kinds of counter-proposals he wishes to make. In some situations, the appropriate response may be the 'concession close' (see Chapter 5).

4.3 CONCLUSIONS

This chapter has examined the responsibilities of salespeople, i.e. to gain sales, to prospect for new customers, to maintain customer records and provide information feedback, to manage their work, to handle complaints, and to provide service.

An important element in managing their work is preparation, this being examined in detail. A distinction is made between sales negotiations, where a certain amount of bargaining may take place, and pure selling, where the salesman is given no freedom to bargain. Important in preparation is:

(*i*) product knowledge and customer benefits;
(*ii*) knowledge of competitors' products and their benefits;
(*iii*) sales presentation planning;

(*iv*) setting sales and negotiation objectives;
(*v*) understanding buyer behaviour;
(*vi*) assessing the power balance;
(*vii*) concession analysis;
(*viii*) proposal analysis.

The next chapter on personal selling skills considers how to use this preparation in the actual selling situation.

PRACTICAL EXERCISE – THE O'BRIEN COMPANY

The O'Brien Company manufactures and markets a wide range of luggage including suitcases, handbags and briefcases. The company is organised into two divisions – consumer and industrial. The consumer division sells mainly through retail outlets whereas the industrial division markets direct to companies, who buy luggage (especially briefcases) for use by their executives.

You have recently been appointed as a salesperson for the industrial division and have been asked to visit a new potential client with a view to selling him briefcases.

The potential customer is Brian Forbes, the managing director (and owner) of a medium-sized engineering company in the Midlands with subsidiaries in Manchester, Leeds and Bristol. They employ a sales force of twenty men selling copper piping. In addition, it is estimated that the company employs around forty marketing, personnel, production and accountancy executives.

The O'Brien Company markets two ranges of executive briefcase. One is made from good quality plastic, with imitiation hide lining. It is available in black only and is priced at £25 for the lockable version and £22 for the non-lockable type. The other de-luxe range is manufactured from leather and real hide and is priced at £95. Colours available are black, brown, dark blue and claret. Additional features are a number-coded locking device, a variable depth feature which allows the briefcase to be expanded from its usual 3½ inches to 5½ inches, individual gilt initialling on each briefcase, an ink-resistant interior compartment for pens, and three pockets inside the lid to take different sized papers/documents. The plastic version has only the last of these features and is 3 inches in depth.

Quantity discounts for both ranges are as follows:

Quantity	Reduction
10–19	2%
20–39	3%
40–79	4%
80 or more	6%

Very little is known about Brian Forbes or his company apart from the information already given. However, by chance, an acquaintance of yours who works as a salesman for a machine tool company has visited Mr Forbes earlier in the year.

Discussion questions

1   What are your sales objectives? What exta information would be useful?
2   Prepare a sales presentation for the briefcases.
3   Prepare a list of possible objections and your responses to them.

EXAMINATION QUESTIONS

1   What considerations should be taken into account when deciding on the amount of prospecting a salesperson should do?
2   Discuss the contribution of preparation to the selling process.

5 Personal Selling Skills

The basic philosophy underlying the approach to personal selling adopted in this book is that selling should be an extension of the marketing concept. This implies that, for long-term survival, it is in the best interests of the salesperson and his or her company to identify customer needs and aid customer decision-making by selecting from the product range those products which best fit the customer's requirements. This is not to deny the importance of personal persuasion. In the real world, it is unlikely that a product has clear advantages over its competition on all points, and it is clearly part of the selling function for the salesperson to emphasise those superior features and benefits which his product possesses. However the model for personal selling advocated here is that of a salesperson acting as a need identifier and problem solver. The view of the salesperson as being a slick fast-talking confidence trickster is unrealistic in a world where most sellers depend upon repeat business and where a high proportion of selling is conducted with professional buyers.

As with the development of all skills, the theoretical approach described in this chapter needs to be supplemented by practical experience. Many companies use role playing as a method of providing new salespeople with the opportunity to develop their skills in a situation where sales trainees can observe and correct behaviour. An example of such an exercise, where students and salespeople can apply some of the techniques outlined in this chapter is given at the end of Chapter 10.

In order to develop personal selling skills it is useful to distinguish six phases of the selling process.

(*i*)   The opening.
(*ii*) Need and problem identification.
(*iii*) Presentation and demonstration.
(*iv*) Dealing with objections.
(*v*)   Negotiation.
(*vi*) Closing the sale.

These phases need not occur in this order; objections may be raised during presentation, or during negotiation or a trial close may be attempted at any point during the presentation if buyer interest is high.

5.1 THE OPENING

Initial impressions can cloud later perceptions, and so it is important to consider the ways in which a favourable initial response can be achieved.

Buyers expect salespeople to be business-like in their personal appearance and behaviour. Untidy hair and a sloppy manner of dress can create a lack of confidence. Further, the salesperson who does not respect the fact that the buyer is likely to be a busy person, with many demands on his time, may cause irritation on the part of the buyer.

The salesperson should open with a smile, a handshake and, in situations where he or she is not well known to the buyer, introduce himself and the company he represents. Common courtesies should be followed. For example, he should wait for the buyer to indicate that he can sit down or, at least, ask the buyer if he may sit down. Attention to detail, like holding one's briefcase in the left hand so that the right can be used for the handshake, removes the possibility of an awkward moment when a briefcase is clumsily transferred from right to left as the buyer extends his hand in greeting.

Opening remarks are important since they set the tone for the rest of the sales interview. Normally they should be business-related since this is the purpose of the visit; they should show the buyer that the salesperson is not about to waste his time. Where the buyer is well known and where, by his own remarks, the buyer indicates a willingness to talk about a more social matter, the salesperson will obviously follow. This can generated close rapport with the buyer, but the salesperson must be aware of the reason for him being there, and not be excessively diverted from talking business. Opening remarks might be:

TRADE SALESPERSON: Your window display looks attractive. Has it attracted more custom?

INDUSTRIAL SALESPERSON: We have helped a number of companies in the same kind of business as you are in to achieve considerable savings by the use of our stock control procedures. What methods do you use at present to control stock.

RETAIL SALESPERSON: I can see that you appear to be interested in our stereo equipment. What kind of system had you in mind?

The cardinal sin which many retail salespeople make is to open with 'Can I help you?' which invites the response 'No, thank you, I'm just looking.'

5.2 NEED AND PROBLEM IDENTIFICATION

Most salespeople have a range of products to sell. A car salesperson has many models ranging from small economy cars to super luxury top-of-the-range models. The computer salesperson will have a number of systems to suit the needs and resources of different customers. A bicycle retailer will have models from many different manufacturers to offer customers. A pharmaceutical salesperson will be able to offer doctors a range of drugs to combat varous illnesses. In each case, the seller's first objective will be to discover the problems and needs of his customers. Before a car salesperson can sell a car, he needs to understand the circumstances of his customer. What size of car is required? Is the customer looking for high fuel economy or performance? Is a boot or a hatchback preferred? What kind of price range is being considered? Having obtained this information the salesperson is in a position to sell the model which best suits the needs of the buyer. A computer salesperson may carry out a survey of customer requirements prior to suggesting an appropriate computer system. A bicycle retailer should ask who is the bicycle for, what type is preferred, e.g. BMX or racing bicycle, and the colour preference, before he can make sensible suggestions as to which model is most suitable. A pharmaceutical salesperson will discuss with doctors the problems which have arisen with patient treatment; perhaps an ointment has been ineffective or a harmful side-effect has been discovered. This gives the salesperson the opportunity to offer a solution to such problems by means of one of his company's products.

This 'needs analysis' approach suggests that early in the sales process the salesperson should adopt a question-and-listen posture. In order to encourage the buyer to discuss his problems and needs, salespeople tend to use 'open' rather than 'closed' questions. An open question is one which requires more than a one word or one phrase answer.

(*i*) 'Why do you believe that a computer system is inappropriate for your business?'
(*ii*) 'What were the main reasons for buying the XYZ photocopier?'
(*iii*) 'In what ways did the ABC ointment fail to meet your expectations?'

A closed question, on the other hand, invites a one word or one phrase answer. These can be used to obtain purely factual information, but excessive use can hinder rapport and lead to an abrupt type of conversation which lacks flow. Examples of closed questions are:

(*i*) 'Would you tell me the name of the equipment you currently use?'
(*ii*) 'Does your company manufacture 1000 cc marine engines?'
(*iii*) 'What is the name of your chief mechanical engineer?'

In practice, a wide variety of questions may be used during a sales interview (DeCormier and Jobber, 1989). Thirteen types of question and their objectives, together with examples are given in Table 2.

Table 2. *Types of question used in personal selling*

Type of question	Objective	Example
Tie down question	Used for confirmation or to commit a prospect to a position	You want the program to work, don't you?
Leading question	Direct or guide a prospect's thinking	How does that coat feel on you?
Alternative question	Used to elicit an answer by forcing selection from two or more alternatives	Would you prefer the red or blue model?
Statement/Question	A statement is followed by a question which forces the prospect to reflect upon the statement	This machine can spin at 5000 rpm and process 3 units per minute. What do you think of that productivity?
Sharp angle question	Used to commit a prospect to a position	If we can get it in blue, is that the way you would want it?
Information gathering questions	Used to gather facts	How many people are you currently employing?
Opinion gathering questions	Used to gather opinions or feelings	What are your feelings concerning the high price of energy?
Confirmation questions	Used to elicit either agreement or disagreement about a particular topic	Do my recommendations make sense?
Clarification questions	Reduce ambiguities, generalities and non-committal words to specifics	When you say . . . exactly what do you mean?
Inclusion questions	Present an issue for the prospect's consideration in a low risk way	I don't suppose you'd be interested in a convertible hard-top, would you?
Counterbiasing	To attain sensitive information by making potentially embarrassing situation appear acceptable	Research shows that most drivers exceed the speed limit. Do you ever do so?
Transitioning	Used to link the end of one phase to the next phase of the sales process	In addition to that is there anything else that you want to know? (No) What I'd like to do now is talk about . . .
Reversing	Used to pass the responsibility of continuing the conversation back to the prospect by answering a question with a question	(When can I expect delivery?) When do you want delivery?

(*Source*: DeCormier and Jobber, 1989)

Salespeople should avoid the temptation of making a sales presentation without finding out the needs of their customers. It is all too easy to start a sales presentation in the same rigid way, perhaps by highlighting the current bargan of the week, without first questioning the customer as to his needs.

At the end of this process, the salesperson may find it useful to summarise the points that have been raised to confirm an understanding with the buyer. For example:

> Fine, Mr and Mrs Jones. I think I have a good idea of the kind of property you are looking for. You would like a four-bedroom house within fifteen minutes drive of Mr Jones' company. You are not bothered whether the house is detached or semidetached, but you do not want to live on an estate. The price range you are considering is between £120,000 and £150,000. Does this sum up the kind of house you want, or have I missed something?

5.3 THE PRESENTATION AND DEMONSTRATION

Once the problems and needs of the buyer have been identified, the presentation follows as a natural consequence.

The first question to be addressed is presentation of what? The preceding section has enabled the salesperson to choose the most appropriate product(s) from his range to meet customer requirements. Second, having fully discussed what the customer wants, the salesperson knows which product benefits to stress. A given product may have a range of potential features which confer benefits to customers, but different customers place different priorities on them. In short, having identified the needs and problems of the buyer, the presentation provides the opportunity for the salesperson to convince the buyer that he can supply the solution.

The key to this task is to recognise that buyers purchase benefits and are only interested in product features in as much as they provide the benefits that the customer is looking for. Examples of the relationship between certain product features and benefits are given in Chapter 4. Training programmes and personal preparation of salespeople should pay particular attention to deriving the customer benefits their products bestow.

Benefits should be analysed at two levels: those benefits which can be obtained by purchase of a particular type of product; and those that can be obtained by purchasing that product from a particular supplier. For example, automatic washing machine salespeople need to consider the benefits of an automatic washing machine compared with a twin-tub, as well as the benefits that his company's automatic washing machines have over competitors' models. This proffers maximum flexibility for the salesperson in meeting various sales situations.

The danger of selling features rather than benefits is particularly acute in industrial selling because of the highly technical nature of many industrial products, and the tendency to employ sales engineers rather than salespeople. Perkins Diesels found this to be a problem with their sales team after commissioning market research to identify strengths and weaknesses of their sales and marketing operation (Reed, 1983), but it is by no means confined to this sector. Hi-fi salespeople who confuse and infuriate customers with tedious descriptions of the electronic wizardry behind the products they sell are no less guilty of this sin.

A simple method of relating features and benefits in a sales presentation is to link them by using the following phrases:

(*i*)   'which means that';
(*ii*)   'which results in';
(*iii*) 'which enables you to'.

For example, an estate agent might say, 'The house is situated four miles from the company where you work (product feature) which means that you can easily be at work within fifteen minutes of leaving home' (customer benefit). Or an office salesperson might say 'The XYZ photocopier allows streamfeeding (product feature) which results in quicker photocopying' (customer benefit). Finally, a car salesperson may claim that 'This model is equipped with overdrive (product feature) which enables you to reduce petrol consumption on motorways' (customer benefit).

The term 'presentation' should not mislead the salesperson into believing that he alone should do all the talking. The importance of asking questions is not confined to the needs and problem identification stage. Asking questions as part of the presentation serves two functions. First, it checks that the salesperson has understood the kinds of benefits the buyer is looking for. After explaining a benefit it is sound practice to ask the buyer 'Is this the kind of thing you are looking for?' Second, asking questions establishes whether the buyer has understood what the salesperson has said. A major obstacle to understanding is the use of technical jargon which is unintelligible to the buyer. Where a presentation is necessarily complicated and lengthy, the salesperson would be well advised to pause at varous points and simply ask if there are any questions. This gives the buyer the opportunity to query anything that is not entirely clear. This questioning procedure allows the salesperson to tailor the speed and content of his presentation to the circumstances which face him. Buyers have different backgrounds, technical expertise and intelligence levels. Questioning allows the salesperson to communicate more effectively because it provides the information necessary for the seller to know how to vary his presentation to different buyers.

Many sales situations involve risk to the buyer. No matter what benefits the salesperson discusses, the buyer may be reluctant to change from his present supplier or change his present model because to do so may give rise to unforeseen problems – delivery may be unpredictable or the new model may be unreliable. Assurances from the salesperson are, of themselves, unlikely to be totally convincing – after all, he would say that wouldn't he! Risk is the hidden reason behind many failures to sell. The salesperson accurately identifies customer needs and relates product benefits to those needs; the buyer does not offer much resistance, but somehow he does not buy. A likely reason is that he plays safe, sticking to his present supplier or model in order to lessen the risk of aggravation should problems occur.

How, then, can a salesperson reduce risk? There are four major ways:

(*i*)   reference selling;
(*ii*) demonstrations;
(*iii*) guarantees;
(*iv*) trial orders.

5.3.1 REFERENCE SELLING

Reference selling involves the use of satisfied customers in order to convince the buyer of the effectiveness of the salesman's product. During the preparation stage a list of satisfied customers, arranged by product type, should be drawn up. Letters from satisfied customers should also be kept and used in the sales presentation in order to build confidence. This technique can be highly effective in selling, moving a buyer from being merely interested in the product to being convinced that it is the solution to his problem.

5.3.2 DEMONSTRATIONS

Demonstrations also reduce risk because they prove the benefits of the product. A major producer of sales training films organises regional demonstrations of a selection of them in order to prove their quality to training managers. Industrial goods manufacturers will arrange demonstrations to show their products' capabilities in use. Car salespeople will allow customers to test drive cars.

For all but the most simple of products it is advisable to divide the demonstration into two stages. The first stage involves a brief description of the features and benefits of the product and an explanation of how it works. The second stage entails the actual demonstration itself. This should be conducted by the salesperson. The reason behind this two-stage approach is that it is often very difficult for the viewers of the demonstration to understand the principles of how a product works while at the same time watching it work. This is because the viewers are receiving competing stimuli. The salesperson's voice may be competing for the buyers' attention with the flashing lights and noise of the equipment.

Once the equipment works, the buyers can be encouraged to use it themselves under the salesperson's supervision. If the correct equipment, to suit the buyers' needs, has been chosen for demonstration, and it performs reliably, the demonstration can move the buyers very much closer to purchase.

There now follows more practical advice upon what must be regarded as an extremely important part of the personal selling process, for without a demonstration the salesperson is devoid of one of his or her principal selling tools.

Pre-demonstration

(*i*)   Make the process as brief as possible, but not so brief as not to be able to fulfil the sales objective of obtaining an order, or of opening the way for further negotiations. It is basically a question of 'balance', in that the salesperson must judge the individual circumstances and 'tailor' the demonstration accordingly. Some potential buyers will require lengthier or more technical demonstrations than others.

(*ii*)   Make the process as simple as possible, bearing in mind that some potential purchasers will be more technically minded than others. Never 'over-pitch' such technicality, because potential buyers will generally pretend that they understand, and will not want to admit that they do not because of 'loss of face'. They will see the demonstration through, and probably make some excuse at the end to delay the purchase decision. The likelihood is that they will not purchase (or at least not purchase from you). This point is deliberately emphasised, because it is a fact that many potential sales are lost through demonstrations that are too technical.

(*iii*) Rehearse the approach to likely objections with colleagues (e.g. with one acting as an 'awkward' buyer). Work out how such objections can be addressed and overcome through the demonstration. The use of interactive video is useful here, as you can witness your mistakes and rehearse a better demonstration and presentation.

(*iv*) Know the product's selling points and be prepared to advance these during the course of the demonstration. Such selling points must, however, be presented in terms of benefits to the customer. Buyer behaviour must, therefore, be ascertained beforehand. By so doing, it will be possible to maximise what is euphemistically called the 'you' or 'u' benefits.

(*v*)   The demonstration should not go wrong if it has been adequately rehearsed beforehand. However, machines do break down and power supplies sometimes fail. Be prepared for such eventualities (e.g. rehearse an appropriate verbal 'routine', and have a back-up successful demonstration available on video). The main point is not to be caught out unexpectedly and be prepared to launch into a contingency routine as smoothly as possible.

Conducting the demonstration

(*i*)   Commence with a concise statement of what is to be done or proved.

(*ii*)   Show how potential purchasers can participate in the demonstration process.

(*iii*) Make the demonstration as interesting and as satisfying as possible.

(*iv*) Show the potential purchaser how the product's features can fulfil his or her needs or solve his or her problems.

(*v*) Attempt to translate such needs into a desire to purchase.

(*vi*) Do not leave the purchaser until he or she is completely satisfied with the demonstration. Such satisfaction will help to justify ultimate expenditure and will also reduce the severity and incidence of any complaints that might arise after purchasing.

(*vii*) Summarise the main points by re-emphasising the purchasing benefits that have been put forward during the demonstration. Note that we state purchasing benefits and *not* sales benefits because purchasing benefits relate to individual buying behaviour.

(*viii*) The objective of a demonstration should be:
(a) to enable the salesperson to obtain a sale immediately (e.g. a car demonstration drive given to a member of the public); or
(b) to pave the way for future negotiations (e.g. a car demonstration drive given to a car fleet buyer).

(*ix*) Depending upon the objective above, in the case of (a) ask for the order now, or in the case of (b) arrange for further communiation in the form of a meeting, a telephone call, a letter, an additional demonstration to other members of the decision making unit, etc.

Advantages of demonstrations

(*i*) Demonstrations are a useful ancillary in the selling process. They add realism to the sales routine in that they utilise more human senses than mere verbal descriptions or visual presentation.

(*ii*) When a potential customer is partaking in a demonstration it is easier for the salesperson to ask questions in order to ascertain buying behaviour. This means that the salesperson will not need to emphasise inappropriate purchasing motives later in the selling process.

(*iii*) Such demonstrations enable the salesperson to maximise the 'u' benefits to potential purchasers. In other words, the salesperson can relate product benefits to match the potential buyer's buying behaviour and adopt a more creative approach, rather than concentrating upon a pre-prepared sales routine.

(*iv*) Customer objections can be more easily overcome if they can be persuaded to take part in the demonstration process. In fact, many potential objections may never even be aired, because the demonstration process will make them invalid. It is a fact that a sale is more likely to ensue if fewer objections can be advanced initially, even if such objections can be satisfactorily overcome.

(*v*) There are advantages to customers in that it is easier for them to ask questions in a more realistic way in order to ascertain the product's utility more clearly and quickly.

(*vi*) Purchasing inhibitions are more quickly overcome and buyers declare their purchasing interest sooner than in face to face selling/buyiing situations. This makes the demonstration a very efficient sales tool.

(*vii*)   Once a customer has participated in a demonstration there is less likelihood of 'customer remorse' (i.e. the doubt that value for money is not good value after all). By partaking in the demonstration and tacitly accepting its results, the purchaser has *bought* the product and not been *sold* it.

5.3.3 GUARANTEES

Guarantees of product reliability, after-sales service, and delivery supported by penalty clauses can build confidence towards the salesperson's claims and lessen the costs to the buyer should something go wrong. Their establishment is a matter for company policy rather than the salesperson's discretion but, where offered, the salesperson should not under-estimate their importance in the sales presentation.

5.3.4 TRIAL ORDERS

The final strategy for risk reduction is for salespeople to encourage trial orders, even though they may be uneconomic in company terms and in terms of salespeople's time in the short term, when faced with a straight re-buy (see Chapter 2). Buyers who habitually purchase supplies from one supplier may recognise that change involves unwarranted risk. It may be that the only way for a new supplier to break through this impasse is to secure a small order which, in effect, permits the demonstration of his company's capability to provide consistently high-quality products promptly. The confidence, thus built, may lead to a higher percentage of the customer's business in the longer term.

5.4 DEALING WITH OBJECTIONS

Objections should not always be viewed with dismay by salespeople. Many objections are simply expressions of interest by the buyer. What the buyer is asking for is further information because he is interested in what the salesperson is saying. The problem is that he is not, as yet, convinced. Objections highlight the issues which are important to the buyer.

An example will illustrate these points. Suppose an industrial salesperson working for an adhesives manufacturer is faced with the following objection: 'Why should I buy your new adhesive gun when my present method of applying adhesive – direct from the tube – is perfectly satisfactory?' This type of objection is clearly an expression of a desire for additional information. The salesperson's task is to provide it in a manner which does not antagonise the buyer and, yet, is convincing. It is a fact of human personality that the argument which is supported by the greater weight of evidence does not always win the day; people do not like to be proved wrong. The very act of changing a supplier may be resisted because it may imply criticism of a past decision on the part of the buyer. For a salesperson to disregard the emotional aspects of dealing with objections is to court disaster. The situation to be avoided is where the buyer digs his heels in on principle, because of the attitude of the salesperson.

So, the effective approach for dealing with objections involves two areas: the preparation of convincing answers; and the development of a range of techniques for answering objections in a manner which permits the acceptance of these answers without loss of face on the part of the buyer. The first area has been covered in the previous chapter. A number of techniques will now be reviewed to illustrate how the second objective may be accomplished.

5.4.1 LISTEN AND DO NOT INTERRUPT

Experienced salespeople know that the impression given to buyers by the salesperson who interrupts the buyer in midstream is that the salesperson believes that:

(*i*)   the objection is obviously wrong;
(*ii*) it is trivial;
(*iii*) it is not worth the salesperson's time to let the buyer finish.

Interruption denies the buyer the kind of respect he is entitled to receive and may lead to a misunderstanding of the real substance behind the objection.

The correct approach is to listen carefully, attentively and respectfully. The buyer will appreciate the fact that the salesperson is taking the problem seriously and the salesperson will gain through having a clear and full understanding of what the problem really is.

5.4.2 AGREE AND COUNTER

This approach maintains the respect the salesperson shows to the buyer. The salesperson first agrees that what the buyer is saying is sensible and reasonable, before then putting forward an alternative point of view. It therefore takes the edge off the objection and creates a climate of agreement rather than conflict. For example:

BUYER: The problem with your tractor is that it costs more than your competition.

SALESPERSON: Yes, the initial cost of the tractor is a little higher than competitors' models, but I should like to show you how, over the life-time of the machine, ours works out to be far more economical.

This example shows why the method is sometimes called the 'yes . . . but' technique. The 'yes' precedes the agree statement, while the 'but' prefaces the counter-argument. There is no necessity to use these words, however. In fact, in some sales situations the buyer may be so used to having salespeople use them that the technique loses some of its effectiveness. Fortunately there are other approaches which are less blatant. For example:

(*i*) 'I can appreciate your concern that the machine is more expensive than the competition. However, I should like to show you . . .'

(*ii*) 'Customer XYZ made the same comment a year ago. I can assure you that he is highly delighted with his decision to purchase because the cost savings over the life-time of the machine more than offset the initial cost difference.'

(*iii*) 'That's absolutely right! The initial cost is a little higher. That's why I want to show you . . .'

The use of the reference selling technique can be combined with the agree and counter method to provide a powerful counter to an objection. For example, salespeople of media space in newspapers which are given away free to the public often encounter the following objection.

BUYER: (e.g. car dealer): Your newspaper is given away free. Most of the people who receive it throw it away without even reading it.

SALESPERSON: I can understand your concern that a newspaper which is free may not be read. However a great many people do read it to find out what second hand cars are on the market. Mr Giles of Grimethorpe Motors has been advertising with us for two years and he is delighted with the results.

5.4.3 THE STRAIGHT DENIAL

This method has to be handled with a great deal of care since the danger is that it will result in exactly the kind of antagonism which the salesperson is wishing to avoid. However it can be used when the buyer is clearly seeking factual information. For example:

BUYER: I expect that this upholstery will be difficult to clean.

SALESPERSON: No, Mr Buyer, absolutely not. This materials is made from a newly developed synthetic fibre which resists stains and allows marks to be removed simply by using soap, water and a clean cloth.

5.4.4 QUESTION THE OBJECTION

Sometimes an objection is raised which is so general as to be difficult to counter. In this situation the salesperson should question the nature of the objection in order to clarify the specific problem at hand. Sometimes this results in a major objection being reduced to one which can easily be dealt with.

BUYER: I'm sorry but I don't like the look of that car.

SALESPERSON: Could you tell me exactly what it is that you don't like the look of?

BUYER: I don't like the pattern on the seats.

SALESPERSON: Well in fact this model can be supplied in a number of different upholstery designs. Shall we have a look at the catalogue to see if there is a pattern to your liking?

Another benefit of questioning objections is that, in trying to explain the exact nature of the objection, the buyer may himself realise it is really quite trivial.

5.4.5 FORESTALL THE OBJECTION

With this method, the salesperson not only anticipates an objection and plans his counter, but actually raises the objection himself as part of his sales presentation.

There are two advantages of doing this. First, the timing of the objection is controlled by the salesperson. Consequently, it can be planned so that it is raised at the most appropriate time for it to be dealt with effectively. Second, since it is raised by the salesperson, the buyer is not placed in a position where, having raised a problem, he feels that he must defend it.

The danger with using this method, however, is that the salesperson may highlight a problem the buyer had not thought of. It is most often used where a salesperson is faced with the same objection being raised time after time. Perhaps buyers are continually raising the problem that the salesperson is working for one of the smallest companies in the industry. The salesperson may pre-empt the objection in the following manner: 'My company is smaller than most in the industry which means that we respond quicker to our customers' needs and try that bit harder to make sure our customers are happy.'

5.4.6 TURN THE OBJECTION INTO A TRIAL CLOSE

A *trial close* is where a salesperson attempts to conclude the sale without prejudicing the chances of continuing the selling process with the buyer should he refuse to commit himself.

The ability of a salesperson to turn the objection into a trial close is dependent upon perfect timing and considerable judgment. Usually it will be attempted after the selling process is well under way, and the salesperson judges that only one objection remains. Under these conditions he might say the following: 'If I can satisfy you that the fuel consumption of this car is no greater than that of the Vauxhall Cavalier, would you buy it?'

When dealing with objections, the salesperson should remember that heated arguments are unlikely to win sales – buyers buy from their friends not their enemies.

5.4.7 HIDDEN OBJECTIONS

Not all prospects state their objections. They may prefer to say nothing because to raise an objection may cause offence or may prolong the sales interaction. Such people may believe that staying on friendly terms with the salesperson and at the end of the interview stating that they will think over the proposal is the best tactic in a no-buy situation. The correct salesperson response to hidden objections is to ask questions in an attempt to uncover their nature. If a salesperson believes that a buyer is unwilling to reveal his or her true objections, he or she should ask such questions as

(*i*) 'Is there anything so far you are unsure about?'
(*ii*) 'Is there anything on your mind?'
(*iii*) 'What would it take to convince you?'

Uncovering hidden objections is crucial to successful selling because to convince someone it is necessary to know what he/she needs to be convinced of. However, with uncommunicative buyers this may be difficult. As a last resort the salesperson may need to 'second guess' the reluctant buyer and suggest an issue which they believe is causing the problem and ask a question such as:

'I don't think you're totally convinced about the better performance of our product, are you?'

5.5 NEGOTIATION

In some selling situations, the salesperson or sales team have a degree of discretion with regard to the terms of the sale. Negotiation may therefore enter into the sales process. Sellers may negotiate price, credit terms, delivery times, trade-in values and other aspects of the commercial transaction. The deal which is arrived at will be dependent upon the balance of power (see Chapter 4) and the negotiating skills of the respective parties.

The importance of preparation has already been mentioned in the previous chapter. The buyer's needs, the competition which the supplier faces and knowledge about the buyer's business and the pressures upon him should be estimated. However, there are a number of other guidelines to aid the salespeople actually engaged in the negotiation process.

5.5.1 START HIGH BUT BE REALISTIC

There are several good reasons for making the opening stance high. First, the buyer might agree to it! Second, it provides room for negotiation. A buyer may come to expect concessions from a seller in return for purchasing. This situation is prevalent in the car market. It is unusual for a car salesperson not to reduce the advertised price of a car to a cash purchaser. When considering how high to go, the limiting factor must be to keep within the realistic expectations of the buyer, otherwise he may not be willing to talk to the seller in the first place.

5.5.2 ATTEMPT TO TRADE CONCESSION FOR CONCESSION

Sometimes it may be necessary to give a concession simply to secure the sale. A buyer might say that he is willing to buy if the seller drops his price by £100.

If the seller has left himself negotiating room, then this may be perfectly acceptable. However in other circumstances, especially when the seller has a degree of power through being able to meet buyer requirements better than competition, the seller may be able to trade concessions from the buyer. A simple way of achieving this is by means of the 'if . . . then' technique (Kennedy *et al.*, 1980).

(*i*) 'If you are prepared to arrange collection of these goods at our premises, then I am prepared to knock £10 off the purchase price.'
(*ii*) 'If you are prepared to make payment within twenty-eight days, then I am willing to offer a 2½% discount.'

This is a valuable tool at the disposal of the negotiator since it promotes movement towards agreement and yet ensures that proposals to give the buyer something are matched by proposals for a concession in return.

It is sensible, at the preparation stage, to evaluate possible concessions in the light of their costs and values, not only to the seller but also, to the buyer. In (*i*) above, the costs of delivery to the seller might be much higher than the costs of collection to the buyer. The net effect of the proposal, therefore, is that the salesperson is offering a benefit to the buyer at very little cost to himself.

5.5.3 BUYERS' NEGOTIATING TECHNIQUES

Buyers also have a number of techniques which they use in negotiations. Sellers should be aware of their existence, for sometimes their effect can be devastating. Kennedy *et al.* (1980) describe a number of techniques designed to weaken the position of the unsuspecting sales negotiator.

First, the shot-gun approach involves the buyer saying 'Unless you agree immediately to a price reduction of 20% we'll have to look elsewhere for a supplier.' In a sense, this is the 'if . . . then' technique played on the seller, but in this setting the consequences are more serious. The correct response depends upon the outcome of the assessment of the balance of power conducted during preparation. If the buyer does have a number of options, all of which offer the same kind of benefits the seller's product offers, then the seller may have to concede. If the seller's product offers clear advantages over competition, then the salesperson may be able to resist the challenge.

A second ploy used by buyers is the 'sell cheap, the future looks bright' technique: 'We cannot pretend that our offer meets you on price, but the real pay-off for you will come in terms of future sales.' This may be a genuine statement – in fact the seller's own objective may have been to gain a foothold in the buyer's business. At other times it is a gambit to extract the maximum price concession from the seller. If the seller's position is reasonably strong he should ask for specific details and firm commitments.

A final technique is known as 'Noah's Ark' – because it's been around that long! The buyer says, tapping a file with his finger, 'You'll have to do much better in terms of price. I have quotations from your competitors which are much lower.' The salesperson's response depends upon his level of confidence. He can call his bluff and ask to see the quotations; he can take the initiative by stating that he assumes the buyer is wishing for him to justify his price; or, if flushed with the confidence of past success, he can say 'Then I advise you to accept one of them.'

5.6 CLOSING THE SALE

The skills and techniques discussed so far are not, in themselves, sufficient for consistent sales success. A final ingredient is necessary to complete the mix − the ability to close the sale.

Some salespeople believe that an effective presentation should lead the buyer to ask for the product without the salesperson needing to close the sale himself. This sometimes happens, but more usually it will be necessary for the salesperson to take the initiative. This is because no matter how well the salesperson identifies buyer needs, matches product benefits to them and overcomes objections, there is likely to be some doubt still present in the mind of the buyer. This doubt may manifest itself in the wish to delay the decision. Would it not be better to think things over? Would it not be sensible to see what competitor XYZ has to offer? The plain truth, however, is that if the buyer does put off buying until another day it is as likely that he will buy from the competition. While the seller is there he is at an advantage over the competition; thus part of the salesperson's job is to try to close the sale.

Why, then, are some salespeople reluctant to close a sale? The problem lies in the fact that most people fear rejection. Closing the sale asks the buyer to say yes or no. Sometimes is will be no and the salesperson will have been rejected. Avoiding closing the sale does not result in more sales, but rejection is less blatant. The most important point to grasp, then, is not to be afraid to close. Accept the fact that some buyers will inevitably respond negatively, but be confident that more will buy than if no close had been used.

A major consideration is timing. A general rule is to attempt to close the sale when the buyer displays heightened interest or a clear intention to purchase the product. Salespeople should therefore look out for such *buying signals* and respond accordingly. Purchase intentions are unlikely to grow continuously throughout the sales presentation; they are more likely to rise and fall as the presentation progresses (see Fig. 15). The true situation is reflected by a series of peaks and troughs. An example will explain why this should be so. When a salesperson talks about a key benefit which exactly matches the buyer's needs, purchase intentions are likely to rise sharply. However the buyer then perhaps raises a problem, which decreases the level, or perhaps doubts arise in the buyer's mind as to whether the claims made for the product are completely justified. This causes purchase intentions to fall, only to be followed by an increase as the salesperson overcomes the objection or substantiates his claim.

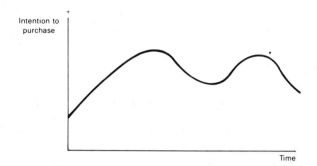

Fig 15 The level of buyer's purchase intentions throughout a sales presentation.

In theory the salesperson should attempt to close at a peak. In practice, judging when to close is difficult. The buyer may be feigning disinterest, and throughout a sales interview several peaks may be expected to occur. Which peak should be chosen for the close? Part of the answer lies in experience. Experienced salespeople know intuitively if intentions are sufficiently favourable for a close to be worthwhile. Also, if need and problem identification has been conducted properly, the salesperson knows that a rough guide to when to close is after he has matched all product benefits to customer needs; theoretically, intentions should be at a peak then.

Not all buyers conform to this theoretical plan, however, and the salesperson should be prepared to close even if his planned sales presentation is incomplete. The method to use is the *trial close*. This technique involves asking for the order in such a way that if the timing is premature the presentation can continue with the minimum of interruption. Perhaps early in the presentation the customer might say 'Yes, that's just what I'm looking for', to which the salesperson replies 'Good, when do you think you would like delivery.' Even if the buyer says he has not made up his mind yet, the salesperson can continue with his presentation or ask the customer a question, depending on which is most appropriate to the given situation.

A time will come during the sales interview when the salesperson has discussed all the product benefits and answered all the customer's questions. It is, clearly, decision time; the buyer is enthusiastic but is hesitating. There are a number of closing techniques which the salesperson can use.

5.6.1 SIMPLY ASK FOR THE ORDER

The simplest technique involves asking directly for the order.

(*i*)   'Shall I reserve you one?'
(*ii*) 'Would you like to buy it?'
(*iii*) 'Do you want it?'

The key to using this technique is to keep silent after you have asked for the order. The salesperson has asked a closed question implying a yes or no answer. To break the silence effectively lets the buyer off the hook. He will forget the first question and reply to the salesperson's later comment.

5.6.2 SUMMARISE AND THEN ASK FOR THE ORDER

This technique allows the salesperson to remind the buyer of the main points in the sales argument in a manner which implies that the moment for decision has come and that buying is the natural extension of the proceedings.

> Well, Mr Smith, we have agreed that the ZDXL4 model meets your requirements of low noise, high productivity and driver comfort at a cost which you can afford. May I go ahead and place an order for this model?

5.6.3 THE CONCESSION CLOSE

This involves keeping one concession in reserve to use as the final push towards agreement: 'If you are willing to place an order now, I'm willing to offer an extra 2½ per cent discount.'

5.6.4 THE ALTERNATIVE CLOSE

This closing technique assumes that the buyer is willing to purchase but moves the decision to whether the colour should be red or blue, the delivery should be Tuesday or Friday, the payment in cash or credit, etc. In such circumstances the salesperson suggests two alternatives, the agreement to either thus closing the sale.

(*i*) 'Would you like the red one or the blue one?'
(*ii*) 'Would you like it delivered on Tuesday or Friday?'

This technique has been used by salespeople for many years and consequently should be used with care, especially with professional buyers who are likely to have experienced its use many times and know exactly what the salesperson is doing.

5.6.5 THE OBJECTION CLOSE

This closing technique has been mentioned briefly earlier in this chapter. It involves the use of an objection as a stimulus to buy. If the salesperson is convinced that the objection is the major stumbling block to the sale, he can gain commitment from the buyer by saying: 'If I can convince you that this model is the most economical in its class, will you buy it?' A positive response from the buyer and reference to an objective statistical comparison by the seller effectively seals the sale.

5.6.6 ACTION AGREEMENT

In some situations it is inappropriate to attempt to close the sale. For many industrial goods the sales cycle is long and a salesperson who attempts to close the sale at early meetings may cause annoyance. In selling pharmaceutical products, for example, salespeople do not try to close a sale but instead attempt to achieve 'action agreement' whereby either the salesperson or the doctor agree to do something before their next meeting. This technique has the effect of helping the doctor–salesperson relationship to develop and continue.

A useful characteristic for salespeople is persistence. Making a decision to spend large quantities of money is not easy. In most sales situations, no one product is better than its competitors on all evaluative criteria. This means that the salespeople for all of these products stand some chance of success. The final decision may go to the one who is the most persistent in his attempts to persuade the customer that the product meets the buyer's needs. Children learn very quickly that if they are initially refused what they want, asking a second or third time may be successful. The key is knowing where to draw the line before persistence leads to annoyance.

Once the sale is agreed, the salesperson should follow two rules. First, he should never display emotions. No matter how important the sale is, and how delighted the salesperson feels, he should remain calm and professional. There will be plenty of opportunity later to be euphoric. Second, he should leave as quickly as is courteously possible. The longer he stays around, the greater the chance the buyer will change his mind, and cancel the order.

5.7 CONCLUSIONS

The skills involved in personal selling are explored in this chapter. The necessary skills are examined under the following headings.

(*i*)   The opening.
(*ii*) Need and problem identification.
(*iii*) Presentation and demonstration.
(*iv*) Dealing with objections.
(*v*)   Negotiation.
(*vi*) Closing the sale.

The emphasis in this chapter is on identifying the needs and problems of the potential buyer and presenting a product or service as a means of fulfilling that need or solving that problem.

Having identified the skills necessary for successful selling, Part Three examines the types of environment in which selling takes place.

PRACTICAL EXERCISE – THE MORDEX PHOTOCOPIER COMPANY

You have an appointment to see George Kirby, sales office manager of Plastic Foods Ltd, with regard to the hire of a Mordex photocopier. You are bristling with anticipation as you know the present contract which Plastic Foods has with Clearprint, your closest competitor, is up for renewal. You have not met Mr Kirby before.

As you enter Mr Kirby's office you notice that Mr Kirby appears a little under pressure.

After introducing yourself, you say 'I'd like to talk with you about how we can improve the efficiency of your photocopying operation. I see that you use the Clearprint ZXR photocopier at the moment. What kinds of documents do you photocopy in the sales office?'

The discussion continues, with you attempting to assess his staff's requirements as regards photocopying facilities and his attitude towards the Clearprint machine.

One need is the ability of the photocopier to collate automatically, since some of the documents which are photocopied are quite lengthy. Another requirement is for the photocopy to be of the highest quality since it is usual for photocopies of standard letters to be sent to clients. The Clearprint photocopier does *not* have a collating facility, and the quality, while passable, is not totally satisfactory. Further, there are sometimes delays in repairing the machine when it breaks down, although generally it is quite reliable.

At the end of the discussion you summarise the points that have been raised: staff time is being wasted collating lengthy documents, the quality of photostat is not totally satisfactory, repairs are not always carried out promptly. Mr Kirby agrees that this is a fair summary.

Discussion questions

During the sales interview the following objections were raised. How would you deal with them?

1 'I'm sorry, I have an urgent meeting in ten minutes time. Can we make it quick?'
2 'We haven't had any major problems with the Clearprint so far.'
3 'Doesn't your firm have a bad reputation?'
4 'Aren't your hiring charges much higher than Clearprint's?'
5 'How do I know your service will be any better than Clearprint's?'
6 'My staff have got used to using the Clearprint. I'll have to spend time showing them how to use your machine.'
7 'Let me think about it. The Clearprint rep. is coming next week. I should like to discuss the points you've raised with him.'

EXAMINATION QUESTIONS

1   If the product is right and the sales presentation is right, there is no need to close the sale. Discuss.
2   Discuss the ways in which a salesperson can attempt to identify buyer needs.

PART THREE
Sales Environment

6 Sales Settings

6.1 SALES CHANNELS

Before industrialisation, distribution was a simple matter, with producers selling to their immediate neighbours, who often collected the goods themselves. Modern day manufacturing, more cosmopolitan consumers, better transportation and communications, and business specialisation has meant that channel decisions are now quite complex. Distribution costs have risen relative to production. In fact, as a result of automation and computerisation, production costs as a percentage of total cost are now considerably lower than they were only a few years ago. Marketing management must continually reappraise its channels of distribution in an attempt to effect cost savings. Company policy decides the marketing channels and this determines how the sales force is organised.

A sales channel is merely the route that goods take through the selling process from a supplier to a customer. Sometimes the channel is direct, and the goods sold are incorporated into a manufacturing process which results in a different end-product. This, in turn, is sold through a different channel. Such a product example is carburettors, which are sold to automobile manufacturers; the automobiles are then sold to car distributors and the car distributors sell to the end consumers. When one considers a product from the raw material stage to the end product, many different sales channels can be involved at different stages in the manufacturing process. A sales channel can also be indirect, whereby a manufacturer sells to a wholesaler or agent, who sells in smaller lots to other customers. This process is known as 'breaking bulk'.

6.1.1 SELECTING/REAPPRAISING SALES CHANNELS

When selecting or reappraising channels, the company must take into consideration a number of factors.

(*i*)   The market.
(*ii*) Channel costs.
(*iii*) The product.
(*iv*) Profit potential.
(*v*)   Channel structure.
(*vi*) Product life-cycle.
(*vii*) Non-marketing factors.

The market

This must be analysed with a view to ensuring that as many potential consumers as possible will have the opportunity to purchase the product or service. Channel compatibility with similar products in the market place is important; consumers are quite conservative and any radical move from the accepted norm can be viewed with suspicion. Unless there are sound reasons for so doing, it does not make sense to go outside the established channel. For instance, a canned food processor would not normally consider selling through mail order unless the company was providing a very specialist type of food or perhaps providing it as part of a hamper pack. Instead, the company would use the traditional distribution outlets like food multiples and cash and carry.

Channel costs

Generally the shortest channels are the costliest. Thus the company selling direct will achieve a large market coverage, but in addition to increased investment in the sales force the firm will also incur heavier transportation and warehousing costs. However, against this must be balanced the fact that there will be a greater profit margin, by virtue of the fact that distributive intermediaries are obviated and their margins will not have to be met. In addition to these financial criteria, short channels have the advantage of being nearer to the end users, which means that the company is in a better position to anticipate and meet their needs.

There has been a trend in recent years for manufacturers to shorten their channels in order to control more effectively the distribution of their products, particularly where expensive advertising has been used to pre-sell the goods to the consumer.

The product

Generally, low-cost low-technology items are more suited to longer channels. More complex items, often requiring much after-sales service, tend to be sold through short channels. This is why most industrial products are sold direct from the producer to the user. The width of the product line is also important, in that a wide product line may make it worthwhile for the manufacturer to market direct because the salesperson has a larger product portfolio with which to interest the customer, and this makes for more profit-earning potential.

A narrow product line is more suited to a longer channel because, along the distribution chain, it can be combined with complementary products of other manufacturers, resulting in a wider range of items with which to interest the customer. In this particular case the distributive intermediaries, not the manufacturers, are performing the final selling function. A good illustration of the above is the manufacturer of bathroom fittings who would normally sell to builders' merchants. Builders' merchants then sell these fittings to builders alongside other merchandise that builders require.

Profit potential

There comes a point when the costs of attempting to obtain more sales through the channel outweigh the revenue and profits to be gained from those increased sales. For instance, a manufacturer of an exclusive and expensive perfume would not distribute through supermarkets or advertise during peak time television viewing. If the company did, then sales would no doubt increase, but the costs of achieving those sales would make it an unprofitable exercise. It is really an accounting problem, and a balance must be struck between channel expense, profit and gross margins.

A manufacturer using short channels is more likely to have high gross margins, but equally higher channel expenses. The manufacturer using longer channels will have relatively lower gross margins, coupled with lower channel expenses.

Channel structure

To a great extent a manufacturer's choice of distributive intermediaries is governed by the members in that channel. If the members of the channel are strong (by virtue of, say, a powerful trade association), then it will be difficult for the manufacturer to go outside the established channel.

In some cases it may be difficult to gain entry to the channel unless the product is somehow differentiated by way of uniqueness or lower price than those products already established in the channel. A good example here would be the potential difficulty that a new detergent manufacturer would have in attempting to sell products through food multiples. The manufacturer would have to convince members of the channel that the detergent was in some way better than those already on the market, or offer advantageous prices and terms. In addition, detergent is mainly marketed using a 'pull' strategy of marketing, relying upon consumer advertising to create brand loyalty and pre-sell the product. The manufacturer would thus have to spend a lot on mass advertising to create brand loyalty for the product, or attempt to 'push' the product through the channel by providing trade incentives, with probably a lower end price than competitive products coupled with a larger profit margin for retailers. It can, therefore, be seen that it would be a very daunting task for a new detergent manufacturer to enter the market in a big way without large cash resources at its disposal.

Product life-cycle

Considerations must be given to how far the product is along the product life-cycle. A new concept or product just entering the life-cycle may require intensive distribution to start with to launch it onto the market. As it becomes established it may be that after-sales service criteria become important, leading to a move to selective distribution, with only those dealers that are able to offer the necessary standard of after-sales service being allowed to sell the product.

In the case of television sets the wheel has turned full circle, from intensive distribution to selective distribution (for the reasons just mentioned) and back to intensive distribution. This is because the servicing of televisions has now become a relatively simple matter, in that televisions are now constructed similarly and standard units are replaced when repairs are needed. A television repairer no longer needs to be a specialist in one particular brand. Television manufacturers now realise that, with comparative parity between models, consumers are less likely to be drawn towards a particular brand because of its supposed technical superiority or standard of after-sales service. The most crucial factor now is price. Thus, maximum exposure at the point of sale has become the manufacturer's objective.

Non-marketing factors

These usually relate to the amount of finance available. It may be, in the case of, say, an innovative product, that the firm is unable to exploit this to its fullest advantage because of financial constraints. In such a case the firm may have to distribute through a middleman because it cannot afford to employ a field sales force. Conversely, the firm may use a non-conventional channel like mail order which requires minimal investment in salespeople, although the physical characteristics of the product may not make it suitable for mail order.

Non-marketing factors often apply when selling internationally, since many companies unfortunately view export orders as a supplement to home trade and are prepared to offer an agency to anybody who is likely to obtain orders, irrespective of their commercial standing. A fuller discussion of international aspects takes place in Chapter 7, but it is worth noting that there are cases of companies who entered into export agency agreements when they were small and exporting was relatively unimportant to them. As the companies grew they came to regard exporting as being essential, but it proved difficult and expensive to unwind hastily entered-into agency agreements. The companies in many cases had to persevere with the original arrangements, often against long-term best interests.

6.1.2 CHARACTERISTICS OF SALES CHANNELS

It should be realised that marketing channels are one of the more stable elements in the marketing mix. A channel is costly and complex to change, unlike, say, price which is relatively easy to manipulate. For instance, a switch from selective to intensive distribution is a top management policy decision which will have a direct effect upon sales force numbers, and even upon the type of selling methods to be used.

The main problem that companies have to face is in choosing the most appropriate channel, and from the viewpoint of sales management this includes the type of sales outlet that must be serviced. Basically, a manufacturer has the choice of one of four types of distribution at its disposal.

(*i*) DIRECT. Here the manufacturer does not use a middleman, and sells and delivers direct to the customer.

(*ii*) SELECTIVE. Here the manufacturer sells through a limited number of middlemen who are chosen because of their special abilities or facilities to enable the product to be marketed more effectively.

(*iii*) INTENSIVE. The intention is to achieve maximum exposure at the point of sale, and the manufacturer will sell through as many outlets as possible. The servicing and after-sales aspects are probably not so important here. Product examples are cigarettes, breakfast cereals and detergents.

(*iv*) EXCLUSIVE. The manufacturer sells to a restricted number of dealers. An obvious example is the car industry, where distributive intermediaries must provide the levels of stockholding, after-sales service, etc., deemed appropriate by manufacturers; their reputations depend ultimately upon the service backup given by their distributors.

A discussion of different sales setting follows later in the chapter, but consideration is first made of segmentation, which has a direct bearing upon the choice of channel.

6.2 SEGMENTATION

When a company decides to sell to a specific target market, it is employing market segmentation. This is basically an attempt to group or to classify customers according to similar needs or purchasing characteristics. These needs can relate to non-product as well as product benefits.

To be effective, market segments must be clearly identifiable and substantial enough to be potentially profitable. The objective of segmentation is to group individuals so that their collective response to marketing inputs is similar.

Broadly speaking, segmentation partitions the market into industrial, retail, wholesale, consumer and international areas. Each of these is dealt with later in this chapter. More specific segmentation includes the following.

(*i*) CULTURAL. This is important in international markets, as well as in domestic markets where large cultural or ethnic groupings occur.

(*ii*) DEMOGRAPHIC. This contains factors such as age, income, sex, occupation, size of family, type of dwelling, religion, social class or grade.

(*iii*) GEOGRAPHIC. Here, segmentation includes nations, regions within a nation, areas within regions, cities and districts.

(*iv*) PSYCHOGRAPHIC. This is concerned with groupings based upon personality types, including life styles. It could also include interests and hobbies.

Once the company has achieved segmentation it can more clearly concentrate and aim its promotional effort at a particular target market. (By promotional effort is meant all the marketing activities that are employed in getting the goods or service from the company into the hands of the customer.) The main marketing elements involved in achieving this goal are selling and advertising. In a 'sellers market', similar to that which pertained in the United Kingdom after World War Two, there was little need for promotional activity because demand exceeded supply and whatever was produced was taken up immediately by the market. This also applies in a state socialist society where the government can control the economy by limitation or expansion of production, which should (in theory) match demand. In a free market economy, supply normally exceeds demand (assuming no artificial shortages) and, as a result, companies use various promotional tactics in an attempt to attract more customers.

Sales promotions can be directed either to the trade or to consumers, and these are considered in the next section.

6.3 SALES PROMOTIONS

Sales promotions embrace a variety of techniques that organisations can use as part of their total marketing effort. Examples of possible objectives that may be achieved through sales promotional activities include:

(*i*)   the encouragement of repeat purchases;
(*ii*)   the building of long-term customer loyalty;
(*iii*) the encouragement of consumers to visit a particular sales outlet;
(*iv*) the building up of retail stock levels;
(*v*)   the widening or increasing of the distribution of a product or brand.

Sales promotions include:

(*i*)   price reductions;
(*ii*)   vouchers or coupons;
(*iii*) gifts;
(*iv*) competitions;
(*v*)   lotteries;
(*vi*) cash bonuses.

In turn the techniques can cover:

(*i*)   consumer promotions;
(*ii*)   trade promotions;

(*iii*) sales force promotions;
(*iv*) sponsorship.

The importance of sales promotions has increased steadily since the 1960s, as has the sophistication of methods used. It is sometimes implied that sales promotion is a second rate or peripheral marketing activity, but companies are increasingly realising the importance of a well-planned and coordinated programme of sales promotion.

Within the United Kingdom, sales promotional activities have matured since the late 1960s. At that time few attempts were made to measure the effectiveness of such activity, and advertising agencies tended to branch out into sales promotions with the aim of offering an all-inclusive package to their clients in an attempt to combat competition from the emerging sales promotion agencies. The mid-1970s brought increased economic pressure to bear on all business activities, and this had the effect of making advertising agencies become more concerned about reductions in company advertising budgets. They began to pay greater attention to the effectiveness of sales promotions, and began to adopt a more integrated approach to advertising and sales promotion. There was also a move towards fee-based sales promotional agencies, which implied a longer-term relationship between agency and client, rather than the ad hoc commission structure that had existed before.

As a result of this increased competition from sales promotional agencies, advertising agencies have tended, since the late 1970s, to concentrate more upon sales promotional activities, and have begun to offer sales promotion alongside advertising as an integrated promotional package. Hence, since the late 1960s there has been a gradual erosion of the line between sales promotion and advertising.

Sales promotions can be divided into three main areas of activity:

(*i*)   consumer promotions;
(*ii*) trade promotions; and
(*iii*) personnel motivation.

Each of these is examined separately.

6.3.1 CONSUMER PROMOTIONS

These are often referred to as 'pull' techniques, in that they are designed to stimulate final demand and move products through the sales channel, with the consumer providing the impetus.

The most widely used consumer promotion is the price reduction or price promotion. There are various techniques which fall into this category.

(*i*) The item is marked '*x* pence off'. This can be manufacturer or retailer organised.

(*ii*) An additional quantity is offered for the normal price, e.g. 'two for the price of one' or '10% bigger – same price as before.'

(*iii*) Price-off coupons, either in or on the pack, may be redeemed against future purchase of the product.

(*iv*) Introductory discount price offers on new products.

A view held by many organisers of such promotions is that the consumer, in economically difficult times, is more likely to be attracted by the opportunity to save money than by incidental free offers or competitions. Price promotions are predominantly used by fast-moving consumer goods producers, especially in the grocery trade.

Premium offers are marketing techniques which give extra value to goods or services in the short term as part of a promotional package. Under this category are the following.

(*i*) SELF-LIQUIDATING PREMIUMS. An offer of merchandise is communicated to the customer in, on or off the pack. The price charged to the customer covers the cost of the item to the promoter. The promoter is able to purchase such merchandise in bulk and thereby pass savings on to the customers who feel that they are getting good value for money. Such promotions are usually linked with the necessity to collect labels or cut out tokens, etc., from a number of purchases of the same, or same range of, products. Thus the premium need not necessarily be connected with the product that carried the premium; the idea is to stimulate purchases of the product – selling the premium is of secondary importance. Recently, there has been a move towards customised self-liquidating premiums, an example being luxury bathrobes bearing the company logo. Such items are offered by drink and tobacco companies who face advertising restrictions, but other producers are beginning to adopt this type of promotion.

(*ii*) ON-PACK GIFTS. Here the premium is usually attached to the product. The premium may be product-related, e.g. a toothbrush attached to toothpaste, or not product-related, e.g. an item of merchandise such as shampoo taped to a magazine for women.

(*iii*) CONTINUITIES. These are sets of merchandise which can be collected through a series of purchases, e.g. picture cards, chinaware, glassware, etc., forming part of a set. The premium is either with the product or the purchaser has to send off for the premium.

(*iv*) COUPON PLANS. Coupons, contained within the pack, may be collected over time and exchanged for a variety of products in a catalogue. Coupon techniques may be used by one producer or supplier as a promotion for its goods or services, or the plan may include a number of different producers' products under one name. These schemes have largely replaced trading stamps, which were used in a similar way although trading stamps are now making a comeback.

(*v*) FREE SAMPLES. These are sample packs of products offered with brand-related products, attached to magazines, given away separately in retail outlets, delivered door-to-door, etc.

Merchandise as a premium does not have the universal appeal
it may have a more pointed appeal than cash or a price reductio
chosen, and the way in which it is offered, may pre-select a spec..
customer, but the offer can at least be targeted at the right market segn..
Providing the additional response generated more than covers the cost of the
premium and the administration/distribution costs, the promotion will be cost
effective.

The choice of premium and sales promotional technique is a crucial decision,
and the problem is to find a premium which is 'different' or unusual, has broad
customer appeal and is available in sufficient quantity to meet demand.

Lotteries and competitions are widely used in North America as are consumer
promotions. They are also popular in the United Kingdom, but since 1980 they
have suffered a decline. The advantage of running a competition is that it should
be cost effective if the cost of the prizes is spread over a large enough number
of entrants.

Competitions for consumer goods are usually promoted on the pack
concurrent with in-store promotion. The entry form is usually located on or
near the product and it is usually required that each entry is accompanied by
proofs of purchase. More recently, free draws have become popular whereby
a purchase is not necessary and one shopper merely fills in his or her name on
an entry form and 'posts' it in an entry box in the retail outlet.

There is much scope for individuality and creativity in this method of
promotion. It does, however, need much pre-planning and administration, which
is probably the reason why competitions tend to be aimed at the national level,
and involve high value prizes such as holidays and cars, so that consumer
response is great enough to cover the costs of the promotion. Lotteries and
sweepstakes are also used as promotional techniques, particularly by the retail
outlets, which use them to attract custom into the store.

Joint promotions are not specific to consumer goods, but are to be seen more
often as companies attempt to find new promotional techniques. They may
involve two or more companies, who tend to be related not by product type
but rather by similar customer profits. There are a number of such arrangements.

(i) Between retailer and producer, where a branded good may carry a voucher
redeemable at a particular store or chain.
(ii) Between two or more producers, where one manufacturer's product carries
a promotion for the other, and vice versa. Here the relation by customer
profile and not product similarities becomes evident.
(iii) Between a service organisation and a producer, e.g. between a travel
company and a breakfast cereal manufacturer, or a dry cleaner and a clothes
manufacturer.

6.3.2 TRADE PROMOTIONS

The aim of trade promotions is usually to 'push' products through the sales
channel towards the customer. Similar to consumer promotions, incentives are

offered in the form of extra rewards such as cash discounts, increased margins on sales, dealer competitions, exhibitions, provision of demonstrators, holidays (often in the guise of a conference or product launch), etc.

The objectives of retailer-distributor promotions are:

(*i*)   to achieve widespread distribution of a new brand;
(*ii*) to move excess stockd on to retailers' shelves;
(*iii*) to achieve the required display levels of a product;
(*iv*) to encourage greater overall stockholding of a product;
(*v*)   particularly in the case of non-cocnsumer products, to encourage salespeople at distributor level to recommend the brand;
(*vi*) to encourage support for overall promotional strategy.

There are a number of problems associated with trade promotions. Too frequent use of promotions can mean that a salesperson directs his or her attention to the one product involved and neglects other products in the product line. The objectives of the promoter may conflict with those of the retailer or distributor; consequently some sales employees are not permitted to accept incentives or participate in trade contests because their management wish to maintain strict control over their selling activities. There is also a danger that a trade promotion may be used to push an uncompetitive brand or inferior product. Therefore, long-term measures to promote sales are not feasible, and the manufacturer would be better advised to look to product improvement as part of long-term strategy. The British Code of Sales Promotion Practice states:

> No promotion directed towards employees should be such as to cause any conflict with their loyalty to their employer. In case of doubt, the prior permission of the employer, or his responsible manager should be obtained.

Although business gifts are not strictly speaking sales promotions, they are relevant to this section. The business gift sector is characterised by seasonal demand, and it is estimated that 80 per cent of this business is conducted in the last two months of every year. Apart from the obvious connotation that it puts the recipient under some moral obligation to purchase, it also serves as an advertising medium if the company logo is incorporated in the gift. From 1981 the Institute of Purchasing and Supply has taken a serious and critical interest in the use of business gifts, especially where the 'giving' was tied to the placing of orders. They argued that such gifts could influence the buyer's objectivity, and that they should be restricted to such nominal items as calendars, diaries, pens, etc. Recently, the giving of business gifts has declined, as employers have placed restrictions upon what their employees may receive, and the Institute of Purchasing and Supply has published a 'blacklist' of companies operating what they consider to be gift schemes over and above items of nominal value.

6.3.3 PERSONNEL MOTIVATION

These are essentially promotions to the sales force, but many apply to distributors and retailers. The most widely used sales force promotion is the sales incentives scheme. Rewards are offered to all participants on an equal basis and these rewards are over and above the normal sales compensation. Such rewards are offered as prizes in a competition to those individuals or groups who perform best against a specific set of objectives. The problem is that average or below average performers may not feel sufficiently motivated to put in any extra effort if they consider that only top performers are likely to win. Thus, competitions tend to be used for group or area sales force motivation.

When establishing a sales force incentive scheme one must consider objectives, timing, scoring methods and prizes/rewards. Typical objectives of such a scheme may be:

(*i*)   the introduction of a new product line;
(*ii*)   the movement of slow selling items;
(*iii*)   to obtain wider territory coverage;
(*iv*)   to develop new prospects;
(*v*)   to overcome seasonal sales slumps;
(*vi*)   to obtain display; and
(*vii*)   to develop new sales skills.

The timing of the scheme may depend upon the size of the sales force, the immediacy of action required and the nature of the objectives to be achieved. An incentive programme runs on average for between two and six months.

Scoring, or measuring performance, may be simply based upon value or unit sales. In order to overcome territorial differences, quotas may be established for individual regions, areas or salespeople. Points, stamps, vouchers, etc., may be awarded on the achievement of a pre-stated percentage of quotas or levels of sales, and continue to be awarded as higher levels are achieved. These tokens, etc., may then be exchanged for merchandise, cash, etc., by the recipient. Frequently catalogues are supplied giving a range of merchandise for the salesman or his family to choose from. Vouchers for redemption or exchange in retail stores are also used as prizes or rewards.

During a scheme additional bonus points may be awarded for the attainment of more specific short-term objectives such as increased sales of a particular product, increased number of new customers, training and display objectives. In this way a long-running scheme can be kept active and exciting for participants.

Another form of sales force motivation is the award of recognitions in the form of a trophy or 'salesperson of the year' award.

It is not the purpose of this chapter to examine the detailed operation of sales incentive schemes as this is covered later in the sales management section (Part Four). The remainder of this chapter is an extension of the broad aspects of segmentation discussed in section 6.2. The first topic to be considered is that of selling to industrial/commerical/public authority purchasers.

6.4 INDUSTRIAL/COMMERCIAL/PUBLIC AUTHORITY

These categories are grouped together because the selling approach to each is similar and the behavioural patterns exhibited by each conforms to organisational buyer behaviour (discussed in Chapter 2).

There are a number of characteristics in these types of market that distinguish them from consumer markets.

6.4.1 FEWER CUSTOMERS

Institutions and businesses purchase goods either for use in their own organisations or for use in the manufacture of other goods. There are consequently few potential purchasers, each making high-value purchases.

6.4.2 CONCENTRATED MARKETS

Industrial markets in particular are often highly concentrated, a good example being the textile industry in the United Kingdom which is centred in Lancashire and Yorkshire. An industrial salesperson who sells into one industry may deal with only a few customers in a restricted geographical area.

6.4.3 COMPLEX PURCHASING DECISIONS

Buying decisions often involve a large number of people, particularly in the case of a public authority where a purchasing committee may be involved in a major purchase.

Many industrial buying decisions involve more than the buyer and in some cases the technical specifier, production personnel and finance personnel are involved. This can lengthen the negotiation and decision-making process. Salespeople must be able to work and communicate with people in a variety of positions and be prepared to tailor their selling approaches to satisfy individual needs, e.g. specifiers will need to be convinced of the technical merits of the product, production people will want to be assured of guaranteed deliveries and buyers will be looking for value for money.

For technically complicated products, selling is sometimes performed by a sales team, with each member of the team working with his or her opposite number in the buying team, e.g. a sales engineer works with engineers in the buying company.

6.4.4 LONG-TERM RELATIONSHIPS

A life policy insurance or encyclopaedia salesperson makes a sale, and probably never meets the customer again. However the nature of selling in industrial, commercial and public authority settings is that long-term relationships are established and both parties become dependent upon each other, one for reliable supplies and the other for regular custom.

There is thus a tendency to build up a strong personal relationship over a long time, and slick high-pressure selling techniques are unlikely to be of much help. A more considered approach which involves the salesperson identifying the needs of his or her individual customers and then selling the benefits of the product in order to satisfy those needs is more likely to be successful. The ability of salespeople to deal with complaints and provide a reliable after-sales service is very important.

6.4.5 RECIPROCAL TRADING

This is an arrangement whereby company A purchases certain commodities manufactured by company B and vice versa. Such arrangements tend to be made at board or director level and are usually entered into when there is a financial link between the companies, such as companies within the same group of companies (sometimes referred to as intergroup trading) or between companies whose directors simply want to formalise an arrangement to purchase as much of each other's products as possible.

Such arrangements can be frustrating for salespeople and buyers alike, because they deter free competition; the buyer does not like to be told from where he or she must purchase, just the same as the salesperson does not relish the thought of having a large part of his or her potential market permanently excluded because of a reciprocal trading arrangement.

6.4.6 TYPES OF PRODUCTION

This relates mainly to industrial sales. The type of production operated by the firm to whom the salesperson is selling can often determine the type of selling approach to be used. Basically, types of production can be as follows.

(*i*) JOB (OR UNIT OR SPECIFICATION) PRODUCTION. An item is produced to an individual customer's requirements. It is difficult to forecast demand in industries with this type of production. Product examples are ships, tailor-made suits and hospital construction.

(*ii*) BATCH PRODUCTION. A number of products or components are made at the same time, but not on a continuous basis. Like job production, batches are normally made to individual customer requirements, but sometimes batches are produced in anticipation of orders. Product examples are books, furniture and clothes.

(*iii*) FLOW (OR MASS OR LINE) PRODUCTION. There is continuous production of identical or similar products that are made in anticipation of sales. Product examples are motor cars, video recorders and washing machines.

(*iv*) PROCESS (OR CONTINUOUS) PRODUCTION. The production unit has raw materials coming into the manufacturing process and a finished product emerging at the end of the process. Examples are chemicals, brewing and plastic processes.

Clearly, a salesperson selling in a combination of these settings will have to adopt a different approach for each. With flow production he or she will have to anticipate model changes in order to ensure that the firm is invited to quote at the outset, and then follow up this quotation in the expectation of securing an order which will be fulfilled over the life of the product. If the salesperson is unsuccessful at this stage, then he or she may not have the opportunity of selling to the firm again until the next model change (and even then it is difficult trying to dislodge established suppliers).

It is also important to realise that a number of flow production producers are moving towards a 'just-in-time' (JIT) system of production. Here, reliability of quality and delivery is of prime importance because the producer works on minimal stock-holding of raw materials. Long-term relationships with suppliers are prevalent in these situations. 'Zero defects' are the goal that suppliers must strive to achieve in terms of quality.

With job production, losing an order is not quite so critical because, providing the firm is being correctly represented, it should be invited to quote for the next order and perhaps be successful then. Naturally, losing an order is a serious matter, but with job production it normally means waiting a short period before being asked to quote again for a different job, whereas with flow production it might be two years before the model is changed and the opportunity is provided to quote again (by which time the buyer might have forgotten the existence of the salesperson!).

6.5 SELLING FOR RESALE

Selling for resale includes selling to retailers (some of whom own their own retail establishments and many of whom belong to groups) and selling to wholesalers. Much buying in this type of trade is centralised, and in many cases the potential buyer visits the seller (unlike industrial selling when the seller normally visits the buyer). A look at the changing patterns of retailing since the end of the World War Two will illustrate how selling methods have been revolutionised.

Before examining these changing patterns of retailing, we must first categorise the different types of selling outlet.

(*i*) MULTIPLES. These are classed as belonging to a retail organisation with ten or more branches, each selling a similar range of merchandise. Examples are book/newspaper chains, clothing chains and meat chains.
(*ii*) VARIETY CHAINS (sometimes called VARIETY MULTIPLES). These are similar to multiples except that the qualifying number of stores is five and they sell a wider range of merchandise. Examples are mainly to be found in the grocery field.

(*iii*) COOPERATIVE SOCIETIES. These are owned and controlled by the people who shop there and each society is governed by a board of directors elected from its own members. Anybody can be a member by purchasing one share. The movement can be traced back to 1844 when it started in Rochdale. Its principles are:
- open membership;
- democratic control (one man one vote);
- payment of limited interest on capital;
- surplus arising out of the operation to be distributed to members in proportion to their purchases; this was originally distributed through dividends, later it was paid through trading stamps but is now being increasingly abandoned in favour of lower prices;
- provision of education;
- cooperation amongst societies, both nationally and internationally.

(*iv*) DEPARTMENT STORES. These are stores that have five or more departments under one roof and at least twenty-five employees. Stores sell a wide range of commodities, including significant amounts of household goods and clothing.

(*v*) INDEPENDENTS. As the term implies, these traders own their own retail outlets. There are however slight variations, the first being where the independent belongs to a retail buying association. This is an informal grouping whereby retailers (usually within a specific geographical area) group together to make bulk purchases. A more publicised arrangement

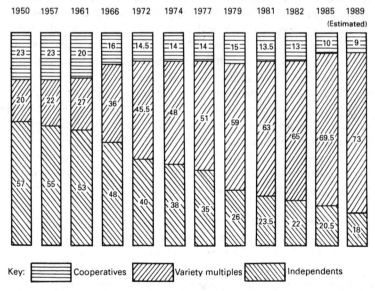

Fig 16   Shares of grocery market held by different types of retailer (selected years). All figures are percentages and were obtained from A. C. Nielsen Co.

is when a wholesaler or group of wholesalers invite retailers to affiliate to them and agree to take the bulk of their purchases from them. Such arrangements are termed voluntary groups (individual wholesaler sponsored) or voluntary chains (group wholesaler sponsored). Participating independent retailers have an identifying symbol, in addition to their customary title. Such retailers voluntarily agree to abide by the rules of the group or chain, which includes such matters as accounting procedures, standard facilities and group marketing/promotional schemes.

(*vi*) MAIL ORDER. Mail order has expanded significantly in recent years; the most popular type of trader in this section is the mail order warehouse, which carries a large range of goods. Such business is conducted through the medium of glossy catalogues held by appointed commission agents who sell to their families and friends. Mail order is also carried out by commodity specialists dealing in such items as gardening produce, military surplus and hi-fi. They tend to advertise in the appropriate specialist hobbies press and through the medium of direct mail. This type of business has expanded a lot in recent years, largely as a result of the expansion of the Sunday colour supplements. Many companies have been established that deal in more general ranges of goods and who use mainly such colour supplements to advertise their commodities. Some department stores also offer postal services and sometimes provide catalogues.

The success of the variety multiples has meant that manufacturers have had to reappraise their sales channels as it has meant a concentration of purchasing power into fewer hands. In the fast-moving consumer goods field, manufacturers have become increasingly involved in controlling the distribution of their products and have become involved in merchandising activities to support their 'pull' marketing strategies. This has meant heavy advertising expenditures, and the concurrent merchandising activities at point-of-sale have been necessary to ensure that the goods are promoted in-store to back up advertising. As a result of this, large manufacturers operating a 'pull' strategy have been able to exercise control over their distributive intermediaries; such intermediaries could only dismiss demand created through advertising and branding at the risk of losing custom. This control has meant lower margins for retailers, and manufacturers being able to dictate the in-store location of their particular products. The weight of advertising put behind major brands has given these manufacturers influence over their distributive outlets.

Although there was initially some resistance on the part of manufacturers to the development of the variety multiples, they eventually found it to their advantage to deal directly with them. This was because they purchased in bulk, often for delivery to a central depot and placed large orders well in advance of the delivery date, thus enabling the manufacturer to organise production more efficiently.

The implications for selling as a result of these developments have been that salespeople of fast-moving consumer goods are no longer compelled to sell the products in the old-fashioned 'salesmanship' sense, as advertising has already pre-sold the goods for them. Selling to the variety multiples is more a matter of negotiation at higher levels whereby the buyer and the sales manager negotiate price and delivery and the salespeople merely provide an after-sales service at individual outlets. Sometimes the salespeople carry out merchandising activities like building up shelf displays, providing window stickers and in-store advertising, although sometimes these duties are carried out by a separate merchandiser or team of merchandisers, particularly when some form of demonstration or product promotion is required.

Wholesalers of course have suffered during the post-war period, and many have gone out of business because their traditional outlet (the independent) has also suffered. In fact this is why wholesalers established voluntary groups or chains, in order to meet the challenge of the variety multiples and offer a similar type of image to the public. However, this seems to have largely failed, perhaps because of inferior purchasing power and because wholesalers must try to make their independent retailing members behave like variety multiples, using voluntary means. The wholesaler's only sanction against non-cooperating members is to expel them from the group, whereas in the case of the variety multiples a recalcitrant manager can be quickly removed.

The post-war years have witnessed the growth of large-scale retailing, including a growth in the size of retailing establishments, first to supermarkets, then to superstores and eventually to hypermarkets. The pattern of shopping has also changed in that the shopper has, for most goods, been prepared to dispense with the personal service of the shopkeeper, and self-service and self-selection have been readily accepted in the interests of lower overheads and more competitive prices. There has been a growth in mass marketing because increased standards of living have meant that products which were once luxury goods are now utility goods and required by the bulk of the population, e.g. cars, foreign holidays, televisions and telephones. Because supply normally exceeds demand for the bulk of consumer goods, there has been a massive increase in advertising and other forms of promotion in an attempt to induce brand loyalty; the faster-moving forms of consumer goods are pre-sold to the consumer by means of 'pull' promotional strategies. Thus the retailing scene has been one of dynamic change which has affected ways in which salespeople now operate.

6.6 EXHIBITIONS

Exhibitions are not strictly speaking sales settings because the prime objective is not to sell from display stands. Their main function is to build up goodwill and pave the way for future sales. They do, however, cover all branches of selling and cover most types of goods, and thus merit separate attention.

Exhibitions are often regarded as a luxury item in a company's marketing budget, and exhibition stand personnel often look upon manning an exhibition stand as an easy option to their normal duties. A study was undertaken by one of the authors in 1977 to investigate how trade exhibitions could be used more effectively as part of a communications programme, and the summary of the results of this study forms the remainder of this section (Lancaster and Baron, 1977).

Characteristics of a good exhibition were deemed to be:

(*i*)   a wide range of products;
(*ii*) a large number of competitors;
(*iii*) a good amount of information on the products shown should be available beforehand)emphasising the importance of pre-exhibition mailing);
(*iv*) a large number of nre products;
(*v*)   nearness to the buyer's home base; and
(*vi*) good exhibition hall facilities.

Characteristics of a good exhibitor were deemed to be:

(*i*)   exhibiting a full range of products, particularly large items that cannot be demonstrated by a travelling representative;
(*ii*) stand always manned;
(*iii*) well-informed staff stand;
(*iv*) informative literature available;
(*v*)   seating area or an office provided on the stand; and
(*vi*) refreshments provided.

Use of trade exhibitions is on the increase and firms increasingly need to establish a more scientific method of managing this function as it requires an understanding of how an exhibition stand communicates itself to the public. Setting exhibition objectives and measuring results are therefore important, as is the identification and comprehension of the elements within the exhibition effort. There is a need for the establishment of a managerial system to plan, coordinate and control the exhibition mix. Before a function can be managed, one must understand how it works and Fig. 17 suggests how the exhibition communication process works.

Different communication problems exist for different types of product, including materials, services and small or large, simple or complex machinery.

With materials the selling feature or unique selling proposition (USP) may be communicated quite simply or through a low-communication medium, e.g. the written word. The USP of a large piece of complex machinery can possibly only be communicated by the potential customer viewing the machinery working. The different methods of communicating the USP of different types of product are termed communication strata; a product with a simple USP can be communicated through a low communication stratum, whereas a product with a complex USP can best be communicated through a high communication stratum.

Having selected the stratum needed to put across the USP, the other methods of communication used must be organised to complement the selected stratum.

For example, if trade exhibitions are selected as the ultimate communication medium, all other marketing inputs, e.g. sales force and media advertising, must be coordinated with the programmed trade exhibition. If strata 5 or 6 (see Fig. 17) are needed, there are three communication media that can be used, i.e. trade exhibitions, demonstration centres or the salesperson taking the product into the firm.

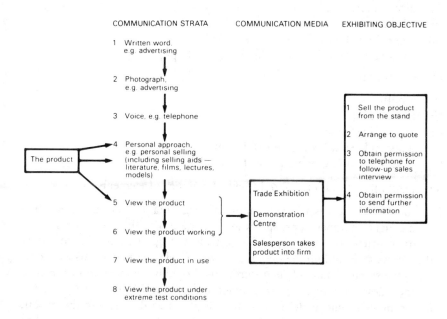

Fig 17   A model of the exhibition communication process.

In the management of any function, the setting of objectives is vital; without this, there is no basis for planning, coordination, control or measurement of results. Such objectives can be enumerated as follows.

(*i*) Define the market with which it is intended to communicate by region, by product or by any other segmentation method.

(*ii*) Define the value of potential purchases. Is the exhibition effort to be aimed at potentially small or large users?

(*iii*) Define the status of contact at which to aim, e.g. purchasing manager, managing director, etc. High status contacts cannot normally be attracted to small exhibitions – they may wish to speak to top management or require personal invitation plus entertainment.

(*iv*) Define the preference toward company products. Is the exhibition effort to be aimed at present customers? The danger here is that stand personnel's time can be taken up talking to the converted, whereas the objective should be to seek to interest potential customers.

(*v*) Define the communication level at which to aim:

- the ultimate (to sell the product from the stand);
- to obtain permission to quote;
- to obtain permission to telephone for a follow-up sales interview;
- to obtain permission to send further information.

Methods used to attract visitors to a particular stand include:

(*i*)   direct mail;
(*ii*) telephoning;
(*iii*) a personal sales call before the event;
(*iv*) an advertisement in the technical or trade press.

Once there, attractions can include:

(*i*)   a buffet;
(*ii*) give-aways;
(*iii*) advertising material;
(*iv*) films and seminars at the exhibition;
(*v*)   attention-gaining exhibits on the stand.

The exhibition stand itself should have a number of elements.

(*i*) Products on show will depend upon the target market. The more products, the higher number of prospects will be interested, although a balance has to be struck so as not to provide so wide a range as to make it confusing.

(*ii*) Literature should not be on a self-service display. When a prospect comes to the stand looking for literature, this should be an ideal opportunity for the salesperson to establish contact and obtain details of the prospect.

(*iii*) Graphics should include at least a display board featuring the product literature. Such aids make the stand look more attractive. Models of the item being marketed are useful when the product being sold is too large or bulky to be physically displayed.

(*iv*) An office or interview room can take up a lot of expensive display space. An alternative is to demonstrate the product and then ask the visitor to a nearby seating area to conduct the interview.

(*v*) Refreshment facilities on the stand are good attractors, and from the results of the study this was deemed to be a major drawing force.

(*vi*) An area should be designated for storage of coats, briefcases, literature, materials, etc., to avoid clutter and distractions from the main aim of the exhibition.

(*vii*) An expensive, eye-catching stand can be a double-edged weapon. It might attract visitors, but the study indicated that visitors' attitudes towards such ostentation were that it would be reflected in the price of the products.

The stand should be planned as early as possible by drawing up a checklist of everything required, checking limitations on stand design, drawing up a checklist of stand services required and a progress chart for the preparation of all products and exhibits, including their manufacture, transportation to the exhibition, assembly and dismantling.

Exhibition stand personnel must be able to communicate the USP of the products and have a sound commercial and technical knowledge. They may come from a variety of backgrounds such as sales, marketing and technical and should be briefed upon a number of areas beforehand:

(*i*) Objectives of the exhibition and set procedures to be used in achieving these objectives.
(*ii*) Features of the stand, who else is on the stand and the geography of the stand in the exhibition complex. Who is the exhibition stand manager?
(*iii*) How to approach stand visitors and how to interview them and how to deal with irrelevant visitors.
(*iv*) Tips on physical appearance before manning the exhibition stand.

Thus it has been shown that with professional pre-planning and management, exhibitions can be a powerful sales tool and not the expensive luxury that many companies regard them to be.

6.7 TELEPHONE SELLING

This sales technique is under-developed in the United Kingdom and telephone sales solicitation is largely confined to the non-consumer sectors. However, over recent years there has been a growth in such activity, largely through the medium of television.

What originally began as 'ordering by telephone' has evolved into what is termed *telemarketing*. This is a concept which can be described as any measurable activity that creates and exploits a direct relationship between supplier and customer through the interactive use of the telephone. *Direct marketing* is also an extension of telephone selling and this involves selling direct to the purchaser through mail order, television, radio, newspaper or magazine advertisements.

An illustration of such activity is where record collections are promoted (usually around Christmas time) through a series of single simple advertisements. Such records are usually a 'collection' and feature a particular theme (e.g. country & western or easy listening) and the advertisement states that the collection is not available in the shops. Simple methods of ordering are mentioned at the time of the advertisement with special emphasis on a local or freephone facility which asks the respondent to telephone and quote his or her credit card number, name and address. Other forms of ordering and payment are, of course, also quoted (e.g. letter and cheque) but the emphasis is upon 'instant' (i.e. do it now) response through the medium of the telephone.

In North America, sales prospects are solicited through the medium of the telephone for relatively expensive products like cars, freezers and home improvements. Telephonists work from prepared scripts designed to give different selling approaches according to the circumstances of the prospect, these circumstances being established before the sales talk. The idea is to 'smooth the way' for a salesperson's call following the telephone call. Success rates are low, but it is a very cost effective method and eliminates a lot of 'cold canvassing' by salespeople. It is a psychologically unrewarding task for the person soliciting over the telephone, and this is reflected in the vernacular term applied to the location from which such solicitation takes place – 'the boiler room'.

Insofar as the UK is concerned, very little of this activity takes place at end consumer levels, but its use has increased in industrial markets in support of sales, especially in relation to the following:

(*i*) Intial contacts with potential customers with a view to a follow-up sales call. Such contacts can be obtained from trade directories, visitors to an exhibition stand, members of a particular group (e.g. professional body or attendees at a conference);

(*ii*) Stock replenishment for established cutsomers when an enquiry can be made about a re-ordering possibility. In such cases, buyers might be often quite indifferent as to where the order goes (especially where there is no particular price advantage and the products are similar) and quite often a telephone call can obtain an order.

When one thinks that it is so easy to simply discard direct mail, it is more difficult to ignore a telephone call, especially if the message is 'personalised'. Thus the medium of the telephone as an ancillary to selling is invaluable.

The Bell Telephone System of American has published a seven step guide to telephone selling, with the objective of encouraging telephone users to utilise this method of contact. The guidelines are:

1   Identify yourself and your company.
2   Establish rapport. This should come naturally, since you should have already researched your potential client and his or her business.
3   Make an interesting comment (to do with cost savings, a special offer or something similar).
4   Deliver your sales message. Emphasise benefits over features and use a sales vocabulary (e.g. your production people will like it because it helps to overcome 'down time' through waiting for the material to set).
5   Overcome objections. They are never outright rejections, but rather excuses for not purchasing now.
6   Close the sale. (e.g. Can I send you a sample now, or would you like to place an order straight away?)
7   Summarise the order – arrange for a sales call or the next telephone call. Express your thanks.

As has been mentioned, this system of sales solicitation is used very rarely for end customers and only sparingly in industrial markets, but in North America it has reached a position where there are many complaints about such telephone calls being classed as an 'invasion of privacy'. They are called 'junk telephone calls' (akin to 'junk mail') and the problem has become exacerbated through machines that play pre-recorded taped messages to recipients. Such messages are relayed through automatic dialling machines to random or pre-selected telephone numbers and deliver a sales message without human intervention.

Whether or not such machines will eventually appear in the UK is open to conjecture, but clearly, if taken to extremes, such methods of communication will become counter-productive.

6.8 SELLING SERVICES

Just like a tangible product, a service must satisfy the needs of buyers. However, their benefits are much less tangible than a physical product in that they cannot be stored or displayed and satisfaction is achieved through activities (e.g. transportation from one place to another rather than say a seat on a train).

Services can come in many forms and some of the more obvious examples include:

1 Transportation – air, sea, rail and road.
2 Power – electricity, gas and coal.
3 Hotels and accommodation.
4 Restaurants (although here the product is more tangible).
5 Communications – telephone and fax.
6 Television and radio services.
7 Banking.
8 Insurance.
9 Clubs – social, keep fit, sporting and special interests.
10 Repair and maintenance.
11 Travel agencies.
12 Accounting services.
13 Business consultancy – advertising, marketing research and strategic planning.
14 Architectural.
15 Cleaning.
16 Library.
17 Public (local) authority services and undertakings – disposal of refuse and repair of roads.
18 Computing services.
19 Stock-broking services.

There are, of course, many more and they can be applied to both consumer and industrial users. The selling approach to each category will tend to differ, depending upon customer needs, just as selling approaches differ when considering physical products.

In the UK, the service sector has grown tremendously over the past decade or so, largely because manufacturers have attempted to reduce labour intensive tasks. In addition, more women work full-time, and the division of responsibilities between men and women is breaking down into more equitable shares. This has put pressure on the service sector to provide services that can perform tasks that have hitherto been seen as the province of being provided in the home (e.g. more eating out in restaurants and more holidays – often two per year – because of increased disposable income).

Better technology, too, has assisted in the development and provision of a more comprehensive range of services (e.g. banks offer credit cards, 'instant' statements, quicker decisions on loans and longer term services like mortgages). Building Societies also provide a broader range of services and have moved into areas traditionally viewed as the province of the banks, more so after the recent 'liberalisation' of their activities through the Financial Services Act (1987). In addition to an expansion of existing services in the financial sector, many more services are now available (e.g. professional drain clearing through the franchise operation 'Dynorod').

Public services have become more marketing orientated and have to be seen to be more accountable to their 'publics' (e.g. the police service which is now more public relations conscious than in the past). Local authorities, too, spend the money that is raised through poll tax. The public is beginning to question more closely how this money that they have contributed is being spent. Thus, local authority departments have to be seen to be spending money wisely as they are more publicly accountable. They have to communicate to their public and explain how the services they provide are of value.

Special characteristics of services include:

(i)   Intangibility.
(ii) Difficulty of separating production from consumption in that many services are consumed as they are produced.
(iii) They are not as 'standard' as products and are thus more difficult to assess (in terms of value).
(iv) It is not possible to 'stock' services, unlike products.

With the above background in mind, the task of selling services is perhaps more difficult than that of selling products because of their more abstract nature. A distinguishing feature is that those who provide the service are often the ones who sell that service. Thus, providers of services must be more highly trained in sales technique and sales negotiation forms an important part of such interaction. It is important, too, that close attention is paid to image building (e.g. banks and insurance companies must be seen to be stable, reliable institutions, but with a friendly, non-intimidating attitude – an image which banks in particular have spent a lot of money fostering over the past decade).

6.9 PUBLIC RELATIONS

6.9.1 NATURE AND ROLE OF PUBLIC RELATIONS

Public relations covers a wider field than selling or, indeed, marketing. Its application is much wider and encompassing the entire organisation and its various external and internal 'publics'.

Its role, however, is increasingly important as an ancillary to selling both in the receiving and giving senses. Selling needs public relations to assist it in its everyday operation and selling is often called upon to disseminate a public relations message. Since the first edition of this book was written, there has been a general recognition of the strategic role of public relations; no longer is it viewed as a means of 'covering up' when something has gone wrong. It has a positive role to play in an organisation, and that role is particularly emphasised in this chapter.

The public relations practitioner has to conduct activities which concern every public with which the organisation has contact. The specific nature of such groups will vary according to circumstances.

Jefkins (1989) identifies seven basic publics:

(*i*)   The community.
(*ii*)   Employees.
(*iii*) Government.
(*iv*)   The financial community.
(*v*)   Distributors.
(*vi*)   Consumers.
(*vii*) Opinion leaders.

Definition

The task of defining the exact nature of PR is difficult. Many definitions exist, each one emphasising a slightly different approach and each one attempting to arrive at a simple, yet brief and accurate, form of words. The difficulty in developing a single acceptable definition reflects the complexity and diversity of the subject. We will look at two definitions:

> 'PR practice is the deliberate, planned and sustained effort to establish and maintain mutual understanding between an organisation and its public.'
> (Institute of Public Relations [IPR])

The essential features of this definition are firstly that PR practice should be *deliberate*, *planned* and *sustained* – not haphazard (like responding to say accidental pollution of a river). Second, *mutual understanding* is necessary in order to ensure that the communication between the organisation and its 'publics' is clear (i.e. the receiver perceives the same meaning as the sender intended).

An alternative definition is given by Frank Jefkins, an acknowledged UK authority on the subject:

'PR consists of all forms of planned communication, outwards and inwards, between an organisation and its publics for the purpose of achieving specific objectives concerning mutual understanding.'

This modified version of the IPR definition adds two dimensions:

(*i*) 'Public' becomes 'publics', since PR addresses a number of audiences.
(*ii*) The inclusion of 'specific objectives' makes PR a tangible activity.

Communication is central to PR. The purpose of PR is to establish a two-way communication process to resolve conflicts by seeking common ground or areas of mutual interest. This is, of course, best achieved by word of mouth and is why the role of selling as the communication medium is so potentially important for PR to be successful.

If we accept the Jefkins definition, then we must also accept its further implication − 'that PR exists whether an organisation likes it or not'. Simply by carrying out its day-to-day operations, an organisation necessarily communicates certain messages to those who interact with it. Everyday opinions are formed about the organisation and its activities. It is thus necessary that PR orchestrates these messages in order to help develop a *corporate identity* or *personality*.

Corporate identity

The concept of corporate identity or personality is inextricably linked to PR. All PR activities must be carried out within the framework of an agreed and understood corporate personality. This personality must develop to reflect the style of the top management, since they control the organisation's policy and activities.

A corporate personality can become a tangible asset if it is managed properly and consistently. However, it cannot be assumed that all managers will consider the role of personality when they make decisions. A PR executive thus needs to be placed so that he or she is aware of all issues, policies, attitudes and opinions that exist in the organisation that have a bearing upon how it is perceived by the organisation's publics.

The use of the word 'personality', rather than 'image', is deliberate. An image is a reflection or an impression which may be a little too polished or perfect. True PR is deeper than this. To use a common denigrating quote of a 'PR job', this implies that somehow the truth is being hidden behind a glossy or false facade. Properly conducted, PR emphasises the need for *truth* and full information.

The public relations executive, as a manager of the corporate personality, can only sustain in the *long term*, an identity that is based upon reality.

What public relations is *not*

Misunderstanding and ignorance as to the nature of PR has led to confusion about its role. Certain distinctions are now clarified:

*PR is **not** free advertising*
(*i*) Advertising complements selling. PR is informative, educational and creates understanding through knowledge.
(*ii*) PR is not free. It is time consuming and costs money in terms of management expertise.
(*iii*) Editorial space and broadcasting time are unbiased and have more credibility than advertisements.
(*iv*) Every organisation, consciously or unconsciously, has PR.
(*v*) PR involves communications with many groups and audiences, not just potential customers.

*PR is **not** propaganda.* Propaganda is designed to indoctrinate in order to attract followers. It does not necessarily call for an ethical content, so facts are often distorted or falsified for self-interest. PR seeks to persuade by securing the willing acceptance of attitudes and ideas.

*PR is **not** publicity.* Publicity is a result of information being made known. The result may be uncontrollable and either good or bad. PR is concerned with the behaviour of an organisation, product or individual that leads to publicity. It will clearly seek to control behaviour in such a way as to attempt to ensure that the publicity is good.

6.9.2 OBJECTIVES OF PUBLIC RELATIONS

PR is used in order to create a better environment for the organisation and its activities. Some of the objectives may be to:

- attract sales enquiries,
- reinforce customer loyalty,
- attract investors,
- attract merger partners or smooth the way for acquisition,
- attract better employees,
- dissolve or block union problems,
- minimise competitor advantage whilst you catch up,
- open a new market,
- launch a new product,
- reward key people with recognition,
- bring about favourable legislation.

In order to achieve such objectives, PR is viewed as part of the total marketing communications strategy, the principal part of which is the selling function. At any point in a marketing exercise there can be PR activity, for the simple reason that PR is concerned with human relations and is a two-way process.

There is a PR element in every facet of marketing (e.g. a salesperson who exaggerates, cheats or lets down customers is a PR liability).

Manufacturers have to get 'closer' to people. In order to reach the different groups, each with separate interests, they must employ the techniques of press relations, house journals, seminars, works visits, private demonstrations, exhibitions, videos and other aids. Moreover, they have to consider those who influence opinion, sales channels and all communication media that express ideas and news.

6.9.3 CORPORATE PUBLIC RELATIONS

This is concerned with group image and is based on a long-term, carefully planned programme designed to achieve maximum recognition and understanding of the organisation's objectives and performance which is in keeping with realistic expectations.

The main medium for corporate PR is prestige advertising (e.g. ICI's 'pathfinders' which presents to the public a progressive image of the huge conglomerate). Another medium is house-style (e.g. a specific 'logo' like the woolmark sign devised by the International Wool Secretariat and displayed on hats and uniforms worn by the people they sponsor). Sponsorship is important for such sporting activities as: golf, football, cricket and motor racing. Sponsorship can also include partial funding for, and the resultant publicity of, such events as concerts and community projects.

6.9.4 EFFECTIVE PUBLIC RELATIONS

Effective PR depends on:

(i)   Setting specific objectives that are capable of evaluation.
(ii) Fully integrating the PR function into the organisation.
(iii) Selecting the right personnel to carry out the PR function.

We shall now examine each in more detail.

Objective setting. This is an essential requirement of PR practice. Bowman and Ellis (1982) state:

'If a PR programme is to be effective, then it is vital that its objectives be defined; that means of achieving them shall then be determined . . . and that progress, success and failure be reviewed.'

Although it is sometimes difficult to decide how an objective can be measured, an obvious objective can be cited in terms of increased sales, although it is sometimes difficult to determine whether such an increase in sales was due to PR activity or to some other marketing activity.

Crisis PR tends to dictate its own objectives. If information is to be prevented from reaching the press, then the yardstick that determines success or failure is whether that information reaches the press or not! If the objective is to maintain the company's reputation, then some attempt must be made to define 'reputation' in useful terms such that it can be measured and evaluated.

A traditional method of measuring PR activity is in terms of column centimetres gained from press coverage. This method does not, however, account for the quality of such coverage. Furthermore, the value of editorial cannot be quantified against equivalent advertising cost because of the greater credibility of editorial.

As PR matures, the call for more objectivity is likely to become greater. As Worcester and English (1985) state:

> 'Just as it is now difficult to conceive of marketing without measurement, a PR agency seeking to change the perception of its clients . . . will begin by quantifying the scale of the problem . . . and the effect of its activities over time.'

Integration. The integration of the PR function into the organisation is important. It should be decided whether PR should act in a 'technician' or 'policy-making' role, the implication being that a technician simply carries out top management orders whereas the policy-maker inputs into corporate strategic plans. Modern thinking favours the latter role because every decision has PR implications. If PR is not involved in policy formation, then top management is implicitly assuming the PR mantle.

The role that is suggested for PR is a far-reaching one, involving communication with large numbers of people. This requires cooperation with other organisational functions. PR must then be a reasonable autonomous unit so that it can serve all departments equally. A staff function should be positioned so that it can funnel its services to the organisational levels who may be the public face of the organisation to outside groups. The importance of PR at lower hierarchical levels cannot be over-stated, (e.g. from the way the secretary answers the telephone to the attitude of the company's delivery person).

The extent of PR responsibility has to be established initially by senior management and this can be achieved by objective-setting and well-defined job analyses. PR as a staff function exists to serve and facilitate line functions. Such lack of PR authority is desirable since it minimises conflict and ensures that the emphasis is upon cooperation and consultation between line and staff. It also recognises that day-to-day business and executive authority is vested in line management. It does, however, mean that it is essential that PR has direct access to the board in order that PR programmes can be sanctioned and executed with full backing from top management.

Selection. The selection of the 'right' personnel is especially important for potential PR practitioners. The practice of PR covers such a wide diversity of tasks that flexibility is very important. The Institute of Public Relations (IPR) recognises:

'There is no single set of ideal qualifications and no formal path into the profession.'

The IPR even states that formal qualifications are not necessary for PR personnel. It may be that PR as a profession has 'come of age' because Stirling University introduced a Master's degree in Public Relations in 1988 and Dorset Institute of Higher Education introduced a Batchelor's degree in 1989.

Practitioners have identified a number of skills and attributes necessary to be successful including:

(*i*)   Sound judgment.
(*ii*) Personal integrity.
(*iii*) Communications skills.
(*iv*) Organisational ability.
(*v*)   Strong personality.
(*vi*) Team player.

The traditional importance of media relations has resulted in a strong journalist contingent in the PR profession. However, some find it hard to adapt as the required writing style is different as are planning horizons and work routines. As the wide range of qualities and skills quoted above illustrate, relevant experience can be obtained from almost any background; personality is really of far more importance, together with a sense of empathy and the ability to be adaptable. It goes without saying that an ability to write and speak fluently is vital.

6.9.5 THE USE OF PUBLIC RELATIONS CONSULTANCIES

In some situations, it is more cost effective to use a PR consultancy, especially in areas where the organisation is inexperienced (e.g. the City or Parliament). Quite often larger companies find that a better interaction comes from an in-house PR department and an external specialist. Consultancies are an integral part of the PR industry and they do possess certain advantages of experience, independence and specialist skills that may not be evident internally.

External PR activities can be grouped as follows:

(*i*) Freelance writers/consultants – who are generally technical authors able to produce PR feature articles.
(*ii*) PR departments of advertising agencies, which can vary from a small press office handling product publicity to augment an advertising campaign, to a large comprehensive PR department not unlike the agency setup itself.
(*iii*) PR subsidiary of an advertising agency, where there is a desire to permit a fuller development of PR activity on the part of the advertising agency and indeed whose clients will provide a useful source of potential business. Its association with an advertising agency can have benefits through shared services such as art studios and production.
(*iv*) Independent PR consultants usually specialise in a particular class of

business, and clients can take advantage of this for ad hoc, or short-term assignments. Such consultants specialise in charities and appeals, the theatre, finance, agriculture, building, shipping, travel, fashion, etc.

(v) PR counsellors are people who advise, but do not carry out the PR work.

6.10 CONCLUSIONS

This has been a relatively lengthy chapter of necessity and it has placed sales settings in their respective contexts. It has been shown that different selling approaches must be adopted, depending upon the situation in which one is selling.

Segmentation has been discussed and its importance illustrated; once effective segmentation has been achieved, a company can concentrate its promotional effort on a particular target market.

Sales promotions relate to all types of sales setting, and their growth and importance have been shown in respect of consumer markets, trade markets and as an aid to sales personnel motivation.

Two relatively modern areas have been investigated – those of telephone selling as a technique and the selling of services because of societal changes that have taken place over recent years.

Finally, public relations has been looked at in some detail, because this area has expanded most over recent years and its relationship to the selling function is a very direct one as the sales force is increasingly being called upon to carry out PR activity.

Unlike other chapters, two practical exercises follow – one deals with a sales setting problem (Argent Distributors Ltd) and the other deals more specifically with public relations (Quality Chilled Foods Ltd).

The next chapter is concerned with international selling. Although this is perhaps another example of a sales setting, it is treated separately because of its diversity and ever-increasing importance, especially in view of 1992 European Community legislation and changes as they will affect the selling function.

PRACTICAL EXERCISE – ARGENT DISTRIBUTORS LTD

The company markets washing machines and dryers which it imports from a medium-sized Italian manufacturer. The selling franchise arrangement has operated quite successfully for the past eight years, and Argent Distributors have grown at a steady pace during this period, as can be seen from the sales turnover figures.

Argent Distributors Ltd sales (£000)

1980	1981	1982	1983	1984	1985	1986	1987	1988	1989
135	1,238	1,464	1,824	2,936	3,542	4,162	4,948	5,340	5,338

The Italian manufacturer seems to be happy with the arrangement because, being a medium-sized manufacturer, it is considered that it would be too expensive to set up their own distribution facilities in the United Kingdom, and Argent Distributors seem to have performed a reasonable selling job on their behalf.

The selling operation within the United Kingdom is essentially direct to the end user, and the machines undercut equivalent popular makes of machine by 10 to 15 per cent. Householders are thus tempted to purchase this less well-known brand more upon the basis of price than comparative performance. Advertisements are placed in the press, and potential purchasers are invited to telephone or fill in a coupon for further details. All such potential customer inquiries are followed up with a visit from a sales representative.

Sales representatives are employed on a low level of basic salary plus commission, and they are given the sales leads from the head office on a weekly basis. These sales leads are closely monitored from the head office and, if the salesperson consistently falls below the average success rate of converting leads into orders, then he or she is dismissed. Such leads are usually obtained through responses from advertisements placed in the press.

The selling process essentially follows a set pattern that the salesperson learns from a manual. It is designed to suit every type of circumstance and to overcome every type of objection the potential customer might place in the way of the salesperson. Before a salesperson is allowed in the field, he or she must pass a test in the presence of the field sales manager. Basically, the test is designed to cover every selling circumstance and is set to ensure that the knowledge has been successfully acquired. Upon successful completion, the salesperson is then entrusted to sell the washing machines and dryers unaided.

Sales representatives are engaged on a self-employed basis. They are supplied with a demonstration kit of a washer and dryer plus a small van painted with the company logo. The van is maintained by the company, but the representative pays for the petrol (on the premise that it can be offset against tax and it is also a bigger inducement to make a sale). The basic salary in 1989 was £5,500 per annum, rising by £500 per annum for every year of service to a maximum of £8,500. Commission boosted these earnings, and during 1989 the lowest earning salesman achieved £5,500 basic plus £6,700 commission. He was subsequently dismissed for not turning sufficient enquiries into sales. The highest earning salesman had been with the company for seven years and his earnings were £8,500 basic plus £26,850 commission in 1989. The average basic plus commission in 1989 was £16,925. Out of this, petrol and subsistence expenses had to be met.

The company believed in survival of the fittest and during 1988/9 turnover in salespersons was just under two years on average; four years previously the turnover period had been nearly three years.

For the first time in the company's history, sales had actually fallen from those of the previous year. It was felt that this had been actuated by some bad (and in the company's opinion, unfair) publicity. One of the company's washing machines had been featured on a well-known consumer affairs television programme, and some of the selling tactics used by Argent Distributors' salespersons were deemed to be rather suspect. In addition, it was concluded that once the sale had been made, the company no longer retained an interest by way of an adequate after-sales service. In some instances, parts were not available for more than four weeks after the machine had broken down.

The company viewed this fall in sales seriously, and was also aware of a growing disaffection amongst the sales staff. It had been content to leave the service arrangements to a network of service engineers who serviced other makes of machine as well as those provided by Argent Distributors (on the premise that one machine is very much like another) and Argent Distributors carried and provided the stock of spare parts that were unique to their machines. They also used this network of service engineers to provide the backup for the warranty work during the first year of the machine's use. It was expected that these service engineers would have sufficient parts from their own stocks to do simple repairs, and the theory was that major parts could be provided from Argent Distributors' warehouse within 48 hours. However, on some of the older machines, stocks of major component parts were not kept and had to be ordered from Italy; hence the instances of four-weeks-plus deliveries of certain components that was highlighted on the television programme. The sales force had found that many potential customers were using the sales objection of 'Is this the machine that you cannot provide parts for?' Although they had been told to counter this objection with the fact that this was a single instance or two of older machines and new machines could be serviced almost immediately, this did not altogether convince a potential customer and it was felt that many sales had been lost.

Discussion questions

1 What advice would you proffer to Argent Distributors Ltd to:
   (i)   counter their fall in sales;
   (ii) offer a better spares/after-sales service;
   (iii) remotivate their sales force.
2 What are the dangers of such a distribution arrangement to:
   (i)   the Italian manufacturer;
   (ii) Argent Distributors Ltd.
3 What is the implication to a company using such a non-traditional distribution channel as this for the sale of its goods?
4 What are the advantages and disadvantages of employing salespersons on such a 'high risk', low salary plus commission basis?
5 In which areas of operation and marketing is it more costly, and in which is it less costly, when adopting this direct type of distribution arrangement?

6   Are the sales figures put forward in the case study really as good as implied? In what other form(s) could the sales statistics have been more meaningfully presented?

EXAMINATION QUESTIONS

1   How important is the concept of segmentation in the area of selling?
2   How has the changing face of retailing since the late 1960s affected the role of selling for fast-moving consumer goods?

PRACTICAL EXERCISE – QUALITY CHILLED FOODS LIMITED

The company manufactures a range of up-market chilled foods in a market that covers the counties of Norfolk, Suffolk, Essex, parts of Cambridgeshire and parts of North East London. The region consists of more than 10 million people. The company's customers are quality delicatessens and some of the smaller 'non-chain' supermarkets.

The following report has been published in the *East Anglian Times*, a newspaper that more or less covers the area in which the company's products are sold. This paper is an evening paper and has a very high readership.

Listeria bacteria has been found in a high percentage of chilled foods throughout East Anglia. This information comes from a report published by Essex County Council and it is confirmed by Norfolk and Cambridgeshire County Councils.

The report says that the virulent bacteria – which is particularly dangerous to children, elderly people and pregnant women – has been found in food such as cooked chickens, cooked meats and pates in supermarkets and stores. The report is to be studied in more detail later in the month by Essex authority's environmental health sub-committee.

It has been drawn up following a widespread survey in the towns of Chelmsford, Southend and Colchester. At the same time similar surveys have been conducted in Ipswich and Cambridge, and although these results are not fully confirmed, their respective county councils state that their findings are likely to be similar to the findings from Essex.

It concludes: 'The relativley high percentage of commercial chilled foods which were positive gives cause for concern – not least because the large majority of these foods were ready to eat without further cooking or reheating.'

The Chief Environmental Health Officer for Essex said: 'The report is hardly a shock – it confirms a similar Government finding of last year.'

Quality Chilled Foods have asked you, a public relations consultant, to advise them what to do in relation to their retail customers in particular and the public in general. The company has absolute proof that none of their products fall into this category, because their chilling process is unique and has in-built safety checks to ensure against this kind of eventuality.

Prepare your advice in the form of a report, with special reference to the role which could be played by the sales force.

EXAMINATION QUESTION

Using appropriate illustrations explain how PR assists the sales function.

7 International Selling

INTRODUCTION

The key objective of this chapter is to summarise the most important facets of international selling. In a chapter of this length it is not possible to produce a comprehensive guide to the practice of international selling and exporting and indeed this is not the objective. It is, however, appropriate to explore some of the key steps in international selling and to examine some of the issues and problems which stem from these.

A number of the key areas outlined in the chapter, for example the selection and use of agents and product policy, are sufficiently involved and complex, not to say important, to warrant separate treatment. Companies contemplating entering overseas markets will need, and are advised to seek or develop, specialist knowledge and expertise in these areas.

It should not be felt that selling overseas is such a specialist and complex area that the uninitiated must for ever be excluded, or that membership can only be purchased at the expense of having very costly specialist services. Some sales managers feel that selling abroad is impossibly difficult, but those who try it feel that it is no more difficult than selling to the home market.

One thing for certain is that selling abroad is 'different'. Whether it is more difficult than selling only to the domestic market is a debatable point, but success depends to a large extent on the attitude and approach of the firm and the personal qualities of the salespeople – not every salesperson is suited to such a task from the point of view of understanding and empathy with the foreign market concerned. Whilst it is hoped that this text as a whole will contribute to the development of the personal qualities necessary for successful salesmanship, this chapter concentrates specifically on those aspects of international selling with which a firm either exporting or contemplating the same should be familiar.

Every year companies that have never been involved in selling abroad join the important, and often highly profitable, league of exporters or licensors and some even establish joint ventures or subsidiary companies in overseas countries. As will be seen, one of the problems for the United Kingdom economy is that, despite government exhortations for companies to become involved in selling overseas, many executives remain apprehensive because of the mystique with which the subject often surrounds itself. We shall now attempt to dispel some of this mystique by examining some of the more important economic aspects of international selling.

7.2 ECONOMIC ASPECTS

Many goods that we purchase are imported, and everywhere we read that industrialists are striving to increase exports. Successive governments have in their turn exhorted, threatened and promised in order to persuade the business community to become involved in foreign markets and export more. As far as the United Kingdom is concerned there is one major and very simple reason for this – exporting is necessary for our economic survival.

It is perhaps unfortunate, but true, that the United Kingdom is *not* self-supporting. Much of our raw materials and our food must be purchased in world markets and imported. In turn, if we are to be able to pay for these commodities, we must export. The ledger for these transactions is represented by the balance of trade accounts which show the difference between our overseas earnings and overseas expenditure. In fact the difference between our export earnings and our import expenditure (including 'invisibles', dealt with later) is often referred to as the 'balance of payments'. We shall now take a more detailed look at what is meant by this term.

7.2.1 THE BALANCE OF PAYMENTS

Goods passing from one country to another have to be paid for; trading between countries thus involves the creation of debts between countries. Over a period of, say, one year a country will add up how much it has paid or still owes for goods imported from foreign countries. In the same way, the country will add up how much has been paid or is still owed from overseas countries for goods exported to them. When the amount exported exceeds the amount imported the country is said to have a favourable balance of trade or a trade surplus. If the import of goods exceeds exports then the country is said to have an adverse balance of trade or a trading deficit.

Payments for actual physical goods are not the only items involved in international trade. Debts also arise between countries because of services performed by one country for another. Because one cannot actually see such services they are referred to as 'invisible' exports or imports. For example, the UK performs insurance services for other countries and the premiums are payments due from those countries to the UK. Payment for shipping services, income from tourism, banking services and interest payments from international loans are other examples of invisibles.

To find how a country stands in respect of international trade, i.e. its balance of payments, we must compare the country's total exports (visible and invisible) with its total imports (visible and invisible). In the long term, a country's payments for imports and receipts for exports must balance.

If a country finds itself in deficit it can really only do one of two things to put matters right.

(i) Reduce expenditure on imported foreign goods, reduce expenditure overseas on such items as defence and foreign aid and attempt to discourage its citizens from travelling overseas to stop money being spent abroad.

(ii) The country can sell more goods and services overseas to increase foreign revenue. It can encourage foreign tourists to spend their money or it can encourage foreign investment which will provide income.

Whilst the first alternative can be effective to some extent, there is a limit to which expenditure of this kind can be reduced. It is therefore to the second alternative – selling goods and services overseas – that countries must look if they are to maintain and improve their living standards and avoid a balance of payments crisis. We shall look briefly at the issues involved to fully understand these points.

A country that has a balance of payments surplus may receive payment from the debtor's foreign exchange reserves, receive the balance in gold, leave the money in the debtor country and use it to purchase goods and services in the future, or lend the debtor country the money to pay off the debt and receive interest on the loan in the meantime. In the same way, a country that has a deficit on its balance of payments will either have to run down its foreign exchange reserves, pay over gold, borrow the money to pay off the debt from other countries or hold money, in terms of credit, that the creditor country can use to purchase goods and services in the future.

A more technical explanation is that in essence the balance of payments is an accounting record, with information from various sources being entered on the basis of double entry book-keeping. If there is a deficit on the current account, i.e. if we import more goods and services than we export, this deficit must be matched by a surplus on the capital account to make the account balance. The capital account records purchases and sales of assets such as stocks, bonds, land, etc. There is a capital account surplus, or a net capital inflow, if our receipts from the sale of stocks, bonds, land, bank deposits and other assets exceed our payments for our own purchase of foreign assets.

If the government is to achieve a balance in the accounts in a current account deficit, it means either borrowing from abroad or reducing the government's stocks of gold and/or foreign exchange reserves. These borrowings and/or reductions are entered in the capital accounts as a positive figure and hence counteract the negative entry represented by a current account deficit, and hence the books balance.

As the reader will appreciate, a country can fund a continuing current account deficit only if it has limitless reserves of gold and foreign exchange or unlimited foreign borrowing power. In the long run, persistent current account deficits are difficult and costly to sustain and are damaging to an economy. Total exports must pay for total imports, and if a country's exports fall then imports will also fall unless the deficiency in exports can be made good in the ways specified. We can now understand the importance to a country of keeping up the volume of exports.

7.2.2 UNITED KINGDOM SHARE OF INTERNATIONAL TRADE

The United Kingdom's share of exports by the main manufacturing nations has declined dramatically in recent years. On the other hand some of our major competitors such as Japan and Western Germany have increased their share. The problems this has given rise to are compounded when one examines our import record. On the import side there has been a disturbing trend comprising two related factors:

(*i*) the tendency for real imports per unit of real gross domestic product to increase;
(*ii*) the rising share of manufactured goods accounted for by imports.

The effect of such trends on British manufacturing industry has been very serious.

In the later 1960s and 1970s the UK experienced an imbalance in the balance of payments. In fact the cost of physical imports has exceeded the value of exported products for over a century. This has been undesirable, but not of critical importance because our income from invisible exports has made good the difference. However, for a variety of reasons, income from invisible exports has failed to keep pace with expenditure on physical imports, resulting in an overall deficit throughout this period. It is only relatively recently that the imbalance has been corrected and this has been mainly due to oil from the North Sea, resulting in import savings and export earning. Over the past two years, however, we have even seen this 'bonus' eroded and the UK monthly balance of payments is again in constant deficit. Matters have not been helped by the disastrous fire in the Piper-Alpha field which put a lot of potential production out of commission for a number of months. Measures to correct this imbalance largely consisted of a manipulation of interest rates upwards in order to take the steam out of the economy and stem consumer spending (largely on imported consumer durables). However this resource cannot last for ever, and when the oil runs out the UK could well be faced with similar problems again.

Whatever the reasons for the current state of affairs, selling overseas has been, and always will remain, one of the keystones of our national prosperity. Not only is it in the national interest but it is in the interest of every industry, company, employer and employee.

7.2.3 FURTHER ECONOMIC FACTORS

It is appropriate to consider briefly some of the more important developments in world trade over the past fifteen years or so. It is difficult to comment on the general effect of these developments as different industries and individual companies have been affected in different ways. Some companies feel that they have had a beneficial effect on their trading situation, while others feel that their competitive position has been seriously undermined.

The European Community (EC)

The Common Market, or more accurately the European Economic Community (EEC) – later called the European Community (EC) – was legally established on 25 March 1957 with the signing of a treaty between the governments of France, Western Germany, Italy, the Netherlands, Belgium and Luxemburg. Since then, the ranks of 'Europeans' have been swelled by the accession of Ireland, Denmark, Greece, Spain, Portugal and, of course, the United Kingdom. Currently, Austria and Turkey have applied to join.

The initial objective of the treaty was to remove within 12 years (i.e. by 1969) all restrictions on the free movement of goods and services and individuals by removing taxation differentials, frontier controls and other forms of restriction. Since those early days, the movement towards this goal has been very slow for economic and political reasons. In fact, it was this political aspect that kept the United Kingdom out of the EC for many years. The UK was not seen to be a true 'European' – a contention which many would say holds true today – and it tends to view the EC as an economic, rather than as a political union.

By 1982 (the EC's 25th birthday) the momentum for a Single European Market had come to a virtual standstill. Many non-tariff barriers remained. The free movement of goods was hindered by varying taxation systems, public procurement restrictions (to only include tenders from domestic providers) and different technical and consumer protection standards. For example, at the time of writing rates of value-added tax differ widely between individual countries (Belgium has rates of 6 per cent to 17 per cent to 19 per cent to 25 per cent to 33 per cent; the UK has a single rate of 15 per cent; Greece has rates of 6 per cent, 18 per cent and 36 per cent and Denmark's single rate is 22 per cent). Much controversy is caused by Luxemburg's low rates of 6 per cent and 10 per cent, because Belgians simply shop 'over the border' and fill up their cars with cheap petrol.

A turning point came in 1984 when Jacques Delors (former French finance minister) assumed the presidency of the EC. He developed the concept of an open market within the Community to create the largest single market in the Western world. Although there was essentially nothing 'new' in what he said, his statement came at the end of the economic recession of the late 1970s and early 1980s, during which time member states had turned economically 'inwards', defending their national markets against European competition.

A programme for removing all remaining obstacles to trade by 31 December 1992 was drawn up by Lord Cockfield, EC Commissioner in charge of the internal market portfolio. The programme was presented to the Heads of Government at a summit meeting in Milan in June 1985 and eventually the Single European Act came into force in July 1987. This Act listed 300 measures which would have to be completed if the single market philosophy was to proceed to schedule. In order to hasten the decision making process, the power of veto was removed and these resolutions could be passed by a 'qualified majority'. These 300 initial proposals have subsequently been reduced to 279 by the withdrawal of certain proposals and the grouping of others into single proposals.

The main features of the Single European Act (SEA) were:

- the establishment of a Single European Market by the end of 1992;
- products approved in any one EC country can be freely marketed within the EC;
- progressive opening up of government and public body contracts to all EC contractors on an equal basis;
- more competitive and efficient Europe-wide services in telecommunications and information technology;
- removal of 'red tape' on road haulage and shipping services between member countries should be provided on equal terms, and more competition on air routes with lower overall fares;
- banks should be free to provide banking and investment services anywhere within the EC; insurers will have greater freedom to cover risks in member countries;
- restrictions on the movement of capital will be abolished;
- there will be a harmonisation of national laws on patents and trade marks;
- professional qualifications in one country will be acceptable throughout the EC.

There are, of course, many other features, but for our purposes these are the most significant ones.

A pamphlet produced by the Department of Trade and Industry (The Single Market – an action checklists for business, May 1989, HMSO) perhaps best sums up how companies can take advantage of the single market in terms of protecting their existing markets and developing new markets. This is quite poignant, because other members of the EC have more of a European 'mentality'. They tend to regard each others' markets as their own 'home' markets, whereas UK companies still tend to regard selling to EC countries as exporting. This is perhaps borne out by the fact that since the UK joined the EC with its current population of 320 million people, it has always operated with a net deficit on its balance of trade with its European partners. The pamphlet recommends that companies should ask a number of key questions in relation to their businesses.

- How has the market changed our business?
- Should we become a European business, looking upon Europe as our primary market rather than just the UK?

- Would becoming a European business alter the scale of the targets in our plans?
- In what ways will we be vulnerable to more competition in our present markets?
- Should we form links, merge or acquire business to strengthen our market presence, broaden our range of products and services and spread our financial risk?
- Is our management and structure appropriate to exploit new opportunities or defend our position?
- What training, in languages and other skills, do we need to be ready for the single market?
- Who in our firm is going to be responsible for deciding how to make the most of the Single Market?

To a certain extent the pamphlet states the obvious, but it does at least focus thinking in a formal manner to the issue of 1992. More specifically, it recommends that in the field of *selling* the company asks five key questions. The solution to each of these key questions is proffered through a list of suggestions:

1   How do you reach the customers?
- Investigate the trade structure such as wholesalers and retailers;
- identify buying points;
- find out about buying procedures, terms and practices, such as the preferred currency of invoicing;
- consider how far you need to know the local language;
- examine different selling approaches, including brokers and agents;
- find out how your competitors are using advertising, promotion and trade discounts.
2   How can you sell into this market?
- Consider regional test marketing;
- establish your sales targets;
- decide on your total sales and promotion budget;
- decide on your selling organisation.
3   What sales literature is necessary?
- Assess suitability of existing material for European markets;
- consider the need to redesign to appeal to new customers;
- arrange translation where necessary.
4   How should you advertise?
- Examine your existing advertising;
- assess differences in national media availability and costs;
- decide on your advertising budget.
5   How will you provide after-sales service?
- Consider relative merits and costs of direct provision or subcontracting.

At a more general level, by the terms of the Treaty of Rome that first initiated the EC in 1957, member countries are independent of their national governments and are not able to accept instructions from them. Their proposals are subject to the official sanctions of the (European) Council of Ministers and the democratically elected members of the European Parliament. This means that many of the decisions which ultimately affect UK industry are outside the direct control of the UK government and in many areas of trade, negotiations are carried out on our behalf by the EC as a whole. Much of this rankles with the present Conservative UK government and the Prime Minister openly criticises the 'nightmare' of a socialist European superstate run from Brussels. At the Conservative Party conference in October 1988 Mrs Thatcher stated: 'We haven't worked all these years to free Britain from the paralysis of socialism only to see it creep in through the back door of central control and bureaucracy from Brussels'. Whether one agrees or disagrees with this contention is immaterial. The point being made is that although it is ultimately envisaged that the EC will be similar to the USA with each member country being akin to a state and it even being billed as the 'United States of Europe', is it a reality when one considers differences in attitude, culture, language and even religion? It will indeed be difficult to envisage an homogeneous pan-European marketing programme not unlike that of the USA. Clearly, 1992 will pose many opportunities (and threats) to companies within the EC, but it is felt that things will not change overnight; it will be more of a slow transitionary period and it could well take decades before we see an integration similar to that in the USA today.

Finally, it has been postulated by Charles Betz of the European consultancy organisation Carré Orban and Paul Ray International that each European country will adopt a particular expertise as follows:

West Germany will specialise in high technology engineering;
The Netherlands will concentrate on service industries (e.g. storage and distribution of petrochemicals);
Belgium will form the hub of the community through Brussels and theirs will be a bureaucratic role;
France will become more technical;
Switzerland will remain outside the EC and will be the financial centre and act as the neutral protector of money;
Austria has much potential and could play a major role as the bridge between the EC and Eastern European countries;
Greece and Turkey will become cheap manufacturing bases producing goods for the Middle East and North Africa;
Italy and Spain will be the 'winners' as they have reasonable levels of readily available, cost-effective labour;
Portugal has low labour costs and is basically an agrarian economy, making it a natural country from which to sell winter-grown vegetables to the more affluent Northern countries;

Denmark has traded its Scandinavian independence for an ability to trade within the EC and should do well for innovative designs;

Ireland will hopefully solve its political problems with the North and its low labour costs will put it in a good position to compete in manufacturing and assembly;

United Kingdom will show leadership in financing the consolidation of industries across national boundaries.

This is, however, one expert's conjecture, but clearly there will be some movement towards specialisation by individual member countries of the EC.

OPEC

Another far-reaching economic factor that has affected world trade was the decision in November 1973 by the Organisation of Petroleum Exporting Countries (OPEC) to increase the price of oil. This has had such far reaching implications for the Western world that it deserves mention here.

The main effects of increases in the price of oil have been twofold. The first is that the increases have caused an unprecedented imbalance in the international monetary system, resulting in an immense payments surplus for oil producers and an ensuing loss of world liquidity. One of the more important consequences of this action – a consequence, incidentally, that we are still feeling the effects of – has been that demand for UK goods has been reduced not only in the UK but also in the other major industrialised oil importing nations. In short, the unprecedented growth in world trade referred to earlier has been all but curtailed.

Secondly, the increase in world oil prices has been responsible, if only in part, for the increase in prices of many of the products of Western economies. The consequences of these price increases are of course varied and complex; there is no doubt, however, that they have not made the job of existing and would-be future UK exporters any easier.

One positive feature of this transfer of world liquidity to the oil exporting countries has been the corresponding increase in demand for the world's products by these countries. To some extent this rate of growth has slowed slightly due to political developments in the Middle East. Non-oil countries have responded to this problem by producing more energy-efficient machinery (especially cars). In addition, the ending of the Iran/Iraq conflict has meant that there is now more oil on world markets and the price of oil has tended to fall over the last few months. There is thus now an excess of supply over demand which augurs badly for the UK as its North Sea oil is realatively expensive to produce and this has put certain marginal oil fields out of production.

GATT

Perhaps one of the most important developments of the last few years has been a steady but widespread trend towards protectionism.

The greater part of world trade is subject to the General Agreement on Tariffs and Trade (GATT). Basically GATT is a complex agreement, but its most important features can be summarised in four fundamental principles.

(*i*) NON-DISCRIMINATION. Each member country agrees that any tariff concession or trade advantage granted to one country, whether or not a member of GATT, shall be granted to all member countries.

(*ii*) CONSULTATION. Member countries are required to meet under GATT auspices to discuss any trade problems that may arise.

(*iii*) TARIFF NEGOTIATION. That tariffs should be open to negotiation is the idea that originally inspired GATT. The hope was that these negotiations would be aimed at reducing and eventually removing customs duties.

(*iv*) TRADE LIBERALISATION. The overriding aim of GATT, and from which the principles described above derive, is the continuing liberalisation of world trade. With this aim in mind, import quotas and licensing requirements, restrictions which nations have traditionally used to limit the volume and types of imports entering their countries, are prohibited. The idea is that temporary protection shall be afforded to each nation's domestic industry exclusively through the customs tariff.

There is no doubt that the effect of GATT over most of the postwar years has been to remove some of the protection afforded to national markets. As a result the GATT agreements have been responsible – at least in part – for the considerable growth in world trade referred to earlier. Recently this liberalisation of trade has been checked, or at least slowed, by a whole series of actions. It is well known that there has been widespread acceptance of restrictive trade measures falling outside the formal GATT rules, e.g. voluntary export restraints and anti-dumping legislation.

The Director-General of GATT has suggested that, excluding agricultural products, the volume of international trade so affected now represents more than 5 per cent of the total volume of world trade and is expanding steadily.

The continuing need to export

There is little doubt that the world economy is experiencing basic changes in the composition and direction of international trade, the terms of trade and in the size, direction and character of capital movements. In recent years the UK has moved from being heavily reliant on oil imports to self sufficiency. Related to this, our balance of payments accounts showed a surplus until the 1980s when they fell back into deficit again. Despite this, the imperative need to export our manufactures remains as strong as ever. Whilst these changes pose a formidable challenge to exporters, it can only be hoped that the response they evoke will be conducive to the well-being and prosperity of all.

Although increased exports of goods and services is in the national interest, individual firms have more selfish objectives, and the most positive inducement to them to sell overseas is the existence of potential profitable opportunities.

However there are other factors that an individual firm must consider and these are discussed in the next section.

7.3 INTERNATIONAL SELLING AND THE INDIVIDUAL COMPANY

Whilst the fact that our national economic prosperity depends upon selling overseas is not without relevance to individual companies, there are a number of more pressing reasons why companies benefit from selling overseas. Broadly, there are three reasons.

(*i*) TRADE DUE TO NON-AVAILABILITY OF A PARTICULAR PRODUCT. Such trade is clearly beneficial when a country is able to import a commodity it could not possibly produce itself. For example, some countries need to import coal because there are no indigenous supplies. The UK has to import rubber because it cannot be grown here. It may be that a product or process is protected by a patent and can only be produced if a firm purchases the patent right or enters a licensing agreement.

(*ii*) TRADE DUE TO INTERNATIONAL DIFFERENCES IN COMPETITIVE COSTS. The basis for international trade between countries can be explained in terms of the economist David Ricardo's theory of comparative costs. Quite simply, this theory states that countries will gain if each country exports a product in which costs of production are, comparatively, lower and imports a product in which its costs of production are, comparatively, higher. Although this principle of comparative costs is applied mainly in connection with international trade, one can see it in operation in all forms of production. It is a similar concept to the benefit of the division of labour, in that benefits are to be gained, not by persons doing what they can do best, but by persons doing what they can do *relatively* better than other people. The more productive country would still benefit from specialisation in those goods it produces best, and should then import those goods it is comparatively worse at producing.

(*iii*) TRADE DUE TO PRODUCT DIFFERENTIATION. In a number of industries each firm's product has some point of difference that differentiates it in some way from the products manufactured by other firms; differentiation may be in terms of quality, design or even an intangible difference such as customers' perceived image of the product. This latter factor is very much in evidence in relation to cars; this explains why the UK both imports cars from, and exports cars to, other countries.

It is important to note that the decision to export and import in a free market economy is not made by the country as a collective unit. It is made by individual firms who hope to benefit through foreign trade. We have looked at three broad economic reasons why individual firms may become involved in selling overseas, but there are other reasons that are more situation specific.

(*i*) To become less vulnerable to the effects of economic recession, particularly in the home market and/or market fluctuations.

(*ii*) Loss of domestic market share due to increased competition.

(*iii*) To take advantage of faster rates of growth in demand in other markets.

(*iv*) To dispose of surplus or to take up excess capacity in production.

(*v*) Loss of domestic market share due to product obsolescence. Products that become technically obsolete in the more developed economies may still be 'appropriate technology' in less advanced economies. For example, the old type of fly paper has been replaced by aerosol fly killers, but fly paper is relatively inexpensive and is still very much in demand in developing countries.

(*vi*) To achieve the benefits of long production runs and to gain economies of scale. If the firm can expand its production it will lead to a reduction in average cost and hence a reduction in price, not only in the overseas market but also in the home market, which may lead to further domestic market expansion.

(*vii*) The firm has special expertise or knowledge of producing a product that is not available in a foreign market.

(*viii*) Finally, simply the existence of potential demand backed by purchasing power. This is probably the strongest incentive of all.

So far we have looked at some of the main economic factors concerned with selling overseas. The coverage does not claim to be exhaustive and, indeed, entire texts have been written upon the economics of international trade. However it is hoped that this has given the reader an appreciation of some of the issues involved.

At the beginning of the chapter it was stated that selling overseas was 'different' to selling in the home market. Whilst economic factors are important, only non-economic factors can explain the different patterns of consumption of two different countries with similar per capita incomes. Selling overseas is a cultural as well as an economic phenomenon, and it is to the important area of cultural influences in overseas markets that we now turn.

7.4 CULTURAL FACTORS IN INTERNATIONAL SELLING

In essence, culture is a distinctive way of life of a people, not biologically transmitted but learned behaviour that is passed on from one generation to the next, evolving and changing over time. A society organises itself in such a way that people adhering to cultural norms are rewarded whilst those that deviate are 'punished', to a greater or lesser degree depending upon the culture. As a society's needs change and evolve, so will the cultural norms change and certain old patterns of behaviour will no longer be rewarded whereas new patterns will. In this way, society sustains itself and produces the type of behaviour and responses it needs to survive.

This reward and punishment principle of culture is important for selling overseas. The culture in which a person lives affects his or her consumption patterns and affects perceptions of specific products and the meaning attached to them. Because of this, only certain types of products and selling practices that the individual perceives as normal and acceptable to his particular culture will be acceptable. It follows that overseas salespeople need to understand how culture functions in individual overseas markets in order that the selling approach can be tailored accordingly. In order to be able to offer value to the market, a salesperson must understand the value system of the foreign market and this means a knowledge of the influence of cultural factors.

Culture includes both abstract and material elements. Abstract elements include values, attitudes, ideas and religion. These are learned patterns of behaviour that are transmitted from one generation to another. Material elements of the culture are levels and type of technology and the consumption patterns within that society.

An understanding of the way a society organises its economic activities and the type of technology used is important for selling overseas. It stands to reason that a firm would find difficulty selling advanced microelectronic machinery to a culture with a primitive agriculturally-based economy. In such a case 'appropriate' technology will have a greater chance of being accepted.

We shall now explore some of these abstract and material elements within cultures in the knowledge that in some countries factors like religion have inhibited the acceptance of Western materialism and industrialisation.

7.4.1 AESTHETICS

A non-material cultural factor which may have an influence on the development of overseas markets is aesthetics. This refers to a culture's ideas concerning beauty and good taste, together with an appreciation of colour and form. The exporter must be aware of the positive and negative aspects of its designs, its packaging, advertising, etc. The company needs to be sensitive to local preferences and tastes, and such things as company logos should incorporate local preferences.

Colour is important, the most quoted example being that black represents mourning in the West, whereas in Eastern countries the colour of mourning is white. This has obvious implications for pack design. Music is also important, particularly when used in advertising and promotion. Many non-Western cultures use a type of music, not used in the West, which has symbolic meaning to the members of the culture; an attempt should be made to understand this symbolism and turn it to positive selling advantage.

7.4.2 RELIGION

Material culture and aesthetics are outwards manifestations of a culture, and these give an indication of how consumers in a particular culture behave. However, the firm selling overseas needs an understanding of why they behave in that way. The religion of a culture can give insights into its members' behaviour.

There is not space here to give a detailed account of all religions, nor is it the purpose of this text to do this. Clearly such matters are a specialist business and one should take detailed local advice before making any decisions. For illustrative purposes, two of the largest religions – Hinduism and Islam – are now discussed.

Hinduism is followed by 85 per cent of India's population and is more a way of life than a religion. An understanding of the tenets of Hinduism is thus necessary for an understanding of the Indian culture. Important doctrines of Hinduism include the caste system, the joint family, the veneration of the cow and the restriction of women. Any product or selling activity which offends the tenets of Hinduism would have small chance of success because such views are deep rooted in the Indian culture.

Islam takes the Koran as its ultimate guide, and anything not mentioned in the Koran is likely to be rejected by the faithful. An important element in Islamic belief is that anything that happens proceeds from the divine will. This belief restricts any attempt to bring about change because to attempt to change may be a rejection of, or contrary to, what Allah has ordained. Thus, firms entering overseas markets must bear this in mind when introducing new products or services.

A company must, therefore be aware of religious differences in its foreign markets and be prepared to make adaptations where necessary, both in selling operations and in the products themselves.

7.4.3 EDUCATION

Analysing educational information for relevant markets gives the firm an insight into the nature and sophistication of consumers in different countries. It must be remembered that in some countries many of the population are not formally educated in the three Rs, although they may be very educated in the ways of their culture.

In attempting to market a new product in a foreign country, the firm is itself trying to educate consumers as to the uses and benefits of the product. The success of this sales communication will be constrained by the general level of education within the culture. If consumers are largely illiterate, then the firm's advertising, packaging and labelling will need to be adapted. Complex products that need written instructions may need to be modified to meet the educational level and skills of the particular culture.

7.4.4 LANGUAGE

The language of a particular culture is also an important factor. For example, a literal translation by someone not familiar with its deeper cultural meaning may result in serious mistakes. If the brand name is standardised worldwide in English it may be found to have an unfavourable meaning in some countries, or it may not be pronounceable in other countries that lack certain letters of the alphabet. A good example of the latter is Signal toothpaste which was called Shield toothpaste. A now famed example of the former (and we understand that it is now denied by Rolls Royce) is that the Rolls Royce Silver Shadow was nearly called the Silver Mist which would have been most unfortunate when selling to the German market.

7.4.5 SOCIAL ORGANISATION

Social organisation also differs between cultures. The primary kind of social organisation is based on kinship, and in many less-developed nations this takes the form of a very large extended family. A company operating in such a society must realise that the extended family means that the decisions on consumption are taken in a larger unit and in different ways. A firm selling overseas may find difficulty determining the relevant consuming unit (e.g. is it the family, the household or an individual?).

In many Asian and African countries, social organisation is in tribal groupings which may be a clue to effective market segmentation. Social class is more important and more rigid in many foreign countries, e.g. the Indian caste system. The selling firm must be aware of the cultural variations in social organisation when targeting sales efforts on to a particular social segment of the population.

7.4.6 POLITICAL

Culture includes all activities which characterise the behaviour of particular communities of people, including legal, political and economic factors. Nationalism and dealings with governments are often considered to be the major problems facing a firm trying to sell overseas. Most governments play either participating or regulatory roles in their economies. In India, for example, certain sectors of the economy are reserved exclusively for government enterprise. In Communist countries, firms can only deal with state trading organisations and the only customer is the government.

Government legislation and economic policy may affect a firm's pricing and credit policy and often there are regulations concerning products, promotions, etc. Factors such as nationalism, international relations, political stability and the level of capitalism and democracy in the foreign country will all have an impact on the overseas sales strategy (see Chapter 3).

7.4.7 GENERAL ATTITUDES AND VALUES OF A CULTURE

In some cultures selling and trade in general have low social approval; a company selling overseas may thus have difficulty in recruiting appropriate sales personnel and difficulty selling the products through the channel of distribution. Many Eastern cultures put spiritual values before material values.

Different cultures also have different 'time values'. A much quoted example is in Latin American cultures, where sales representatives are often kept waiting a long time for a business appointment; in our culture this would be unorthodox, and at best it would be seen as being very bad mannered. A delay in answering correspondence in the UK usually indicates that the matter has low priority. A similar delay in Spain could mean something altogether different because there close family relatives take absolute priority and, no matter how important other business is, all non-relatives are kept waiting. In the West we are used to business deadlines, but in many Middle Eastern cultures a deadline is taken as an insult, and such business behaviour may well lose the overseas salesperson business.

The concept of space has a different meaning to different cultures. In the West the size of an executive's office is often an indication of his status. In the Arab world this is not so; the managing director may use the same office as the general clerks, so the salesperson must be careful how he speaks to people! In the West, business agreements are carried out at a distance, say six feet or more. In the Middle East and Latin American countries, business discussions are carried out in very close proximity, involving physical contact, which many Western salespeople find strange.

In the West, business is discussed over lunch or at dinner in the businessman's home. In India, to discuss business at home or at any social occasion is a violation of hospitality rules. In the West we rely on the law of contract for all business agreements, but in a Moslem culture a man's word is just as binding. In fact a written contract often violates a Moslem's sensitivities because it challenges his honour.

Subcultural influences must not be overlooked, because these are sometimes the dominant force in the country. Examples are:

(i) nationality groups, e.g. French and English speaking Canadians;
(ii) religious groups, e.g. Protestant and Catholic groupings in Northern Ireland;
(iii) geographical areas, e.g. the North and South of England may be thought of as separate markets for many products;
(iv) racial groups, e.g. South Africa, where government policy still means strict delineation at the time of writing;
(v) social stratification, e.g. the caste system in India.

7.4.8 CULTURAL CHANGE

A company following the marketing concept overseas, i.e. trying to satisfy the needs and wants of target markets at a profit, must keep abreast of changes in the cultural environment which affect people's attitudes and values, and hence, indirectly, their needs and wants of products and services. In our own society, for example, our cultural values towards debt have changed. Debt has lost its stigma and is now a part of everyday life, with the universal acceptance and use of credit cards. Our society's moral values have also changed and we are more liberal and tolerant of such matters as entertainment. Thus the products and services demanded have reflected this change in cultural values.

A firm must, therefore, be aware that its products may face obsolescence in overseas markets, not necessarily because of any technical advance, but because of cultural change.

Not only are a firm's existing products vulnerable to cultural change, but it may miss new, lucrative opportunities by not being informed of changes in culture. The impact of culture is particularly important if the company is dealing with a foreign culture seeking rapid industrialisation. It is, therefore, necessary for a company operating in this type of environment to monitor trends and adapt as necessary. Not only must the firm contemplating selling overseas be versed in the economics, law and politics of a foreign country, but it will also have to understand the more subtle, less tangible, meanings, values and languages of the culture itself.

7.5 ORGANISATION FOR INTERNATIONAL SELLING

The organisation required to implement international sales operations can be complex. Decisions have to be made on how to arrange the interface between manufacturing and sales, and in the area of delegating responsibility for international operations. Each of these problems can have alternative solutions and an optimal decision must be tailored for each individual firm. Whatever the form of organisation for overseas selling, it is important that there should be a senior manager charged, if only in part, with the responsibility for exporting. This manager should be able, through his or her position, to advice and influence colleagues at the highest level.

In choosing how to organise for international selling there is a broad division into indirect and direct methods. Some of the more common forms of overseas sales organisation are described in this chapter. The choice of organisation will depend upon a number of factors; the proportion of total turnover accounted for by overseas business, the nature of the product, the relative advantages and disadvantages of each form of organisation. What is important is that there is no single rigid uniform approach to the task. The keynote should always be flexibility and adaptability.

We shall first consider the indirect approaches to international selling.

7.5.1 TYPES OF INTERMEDIARY AND THEIR SELECTION

It has been estimated that agents and distributors alone, acting on behalf of overseas companies, handle over half of the world's overseas trade. The term 'intermediary' is used to describe all those persons and organisations providing the service of representation between sellers and buyers.

Few manufacturers are able to cover a market adequately and satisfactorily without the service of some form of intermediary. The decision faced by firms as to which intermediary to use, and the policies to be adopted at this point, are critical to the firm's future in the market.

Agents

An agent is a firm or individual acting on behalf of another. This is one of the main forms of overseas representation. The most common form of agency is where the agents, acting as independent operators, obtain orders on behalf of the exporter on a commission basis and the exporter acts as principal. Agents also work on behalf of purchasers and some specialise in certain tasks, e.g. transport and distribution, advertising and market research.

Care should be exercised in appointing the right agent, and any company entering overseas markets should satisfy itself as to the agent's reputation and financial position. The agent may have other interests, and the firm should ensure that these interests do not conflict with its own. Agents are often key figures in a firm's overseas operations and success overseas will depend on the ability and commitment of the agent. Care therefore needs to be exercised in the choice of an agent and such organisations as the British Overseas Trade Board and banks will advise and assist in their selection.

In assessing the suitability of an agent, the principal will need clear answers to the following.

(*i*) When was the agency founded?

(*ii*) What other interests does the agency have, i.e. what other agencies are held?

(*iii*) Does the agent provide the required coverage for your market?

(*iv*) What is the agent's standing in the business community of the market in terms of professional integrity and reputation, reliability, etc.?

(*v*) Is the agent the type of person or company that will fit in with the way your company carries out its business? Will you be able to work with the agency?

(*vi*) Does the agent possess the resources necessary to carry out the task adequately, i.e. financial resources, transport, offices, warehouses and human resources?

(*vii*) Is the agent able to provide technical support or after-sales service arrangements if this is necessary?

This list is not exhaustive and more specific details may be necessary depending on the market, the industry and the type of product. Once a suitable agent has been found, progress should be carefully monitored. Agents are usually appointed for a trial period at first, with extensions to the contract after that.

The training of agents is important to indirect selling in overseas markets, particularly if the products are technically complex. Without proper product knowledge and technical appreciation of the product range, the agent will be ill-equipped to conduct negotiations with professional buyers who may be experts in their field. Training may have to take place at the principal's manufacturing plant and such training should form a compulsory part of any agreement. Training may need to be a continuous activity, with periodic updating sessions and refresher courses, especially if the firm is involved in new product development or if technology is changing rapidly.

Sales meetings and conferences in the principal's own country can be used for training purposes and these can be used as a forum for tackling specific problems and for discussing future promotional strategies. Such meetings will also have a social function, bringing agents together for a few days to exchange ideas, discuss common problems and be made to feel part of the company.

Once the correct agent has been found, the right kind of working relationship must be nurtured. Many companies feel that the appointment of a good overseas agent is an alternative to involvement in the market themselves. This is *not* so and the principal has to be actively involved; if the relationship is to be successful then it must be based upon partnership and cooperation. The principal should also visit the agent in the market as this will give the agent a sense of value, importance, belonging and encouragement. It also keeps the agent well informed of developments in the principal's country and of the principal's products. The principal will gain valuable market information on competitive actions, the overseas business environment and feedback on promotions and new products. All of this will lead to a better understanding of the dynamics of the overseas market and an improvement in the overall sales strategy.

The principal can also give assistance to the agent by helping in the commercial negotiations between the agent and important customers, helping with special discounts or credit arrangements in order to secure business. Frequency of visiting abroad by the principal will depend on the importance of the particular market, the competence of the agent and the distance from the home base. Important markets should be visited more frequently, particularly if technical assistance or after-sales service is required.

In many cases, agents feel insecure because companies often regard them as being a temporary method of servicing overseas markets. Once the market expands and matures, many companies dismiss their agents and enter direct selling or open a subsidiary company. Therefore the very success of an agent can sometimes mean his downfall. In anticipation of this eventuality, agents sometimes collect a large number of agencies, resulting in a diffusion of effort and possible conflict of interests. This problem can be overcome by negotiating a long-term arrangement once the agent has proved himself, or by inserting a gradual run-down clause into the agency agreement. In the latter case, the agent can often make a valuable contribution to, say, the setting up of a new overseas subsidiary company, or even become managing director of the subsidiary. Thus, fair treatment of agents and ex-agents cultivates a reputation as a good and fair employer and this, in turn, will probably be reflected in future dealings in that country.

Distributors

The distributor acts in a different capacity to that of an agent because he is the actual buyer and seller of the goods, whereas the agent works principally on commission. Like an agent, a distributor will usually be a local firm or individual and a specialist in the requirements of the local market. He should be familiar with the business practices of the area, the structure of the market, local customs and be aware of the various sociocultural factors pertaining to the market.

A distributor differs from an agent in the following ways.

(*i*) He will be able to finance his own stockholding of goods.

(*ii*) He will usually be able to purchase in larger quantities, thus saving on delivery costs.

(*iii*) Acting as principal, he will be commercially and legally responsible for all business transactions in the market.

(*iv*) He is an entrepreneur, and accepts risks involved in the purchase and re-selling of goods such as local falls in demand and currency fluctuations.

(*v*) In some cases he may provide an after-sales service.

A frequent complaint from companies using distributors is that, because they are independent businesses acting independently, they can decide the final selling price to the customer. If price is thought to be a significant factor in the product's success, then the manufacturer should only deal with distributors who are willing to agree a mark-up and selling price with the manufacturer.

As with agents, it is important for the manufacturer to develop a good working relationship with the overseas distributor as commitment to the commercial relationship is needed from both sides. Although the distributor actually purchases goods from the manufacturer to resell on his own account, he is much more than just another customer. The manufacturer is relying on the distributor to achieve their objectives, but the manufacturer must remember that the distributor has objectives and interests of his own. It is, therefore, in the firm's own interest to give the distributor as much technical and sales assistance as possible. Similar to agents, distributors can be used in an information gathering capacity to report on trends and developments in the market place.

A decision will also have to be made whether to use a number of smaller local distributors or a small number of large national distributors. Using a number of small distributors has the advantage of good coverage, and is advantageous where there are regional differences in culture or business practices. However, large national distributors give economies of scale as goods can be shipped in bulk.

In some cases it may be desirable to have an exclusive agreement with the distributor, otherwise he might offer competitors' products to customers if they offer a higher margin. If such an exclusive arrangement is agreed, then it should also ensure that the distributor does not sell competing goods.

Licensing

Licensing is another alternative open to a firm that is contemplating an indirect venture into overseas markets. It does, of course, assume that the company has some unique product or process (preferably protected by patent) that an overseas company will want to manufacture. This is a particularly good way of entering and remaining in more distant markets, or in any market where it is difficult or impossible to export finished goods. In such markets, direct selling or control of agents or distributors might be impractical, or it may be the case that import duties or other non-tariff barriers might present obstacles to exporters.

The costs of setting up a manufacturing subsidiary might be prohibitive or the foreign country might be politically unstable. Licensing avoids the danger of the firm's overseas assets being expropriated and, in some situations, repatriation of profits is sometimes difficult for a manufacturing subsidiary. Where the product is bulky and expensive to transport relative to its value, licensing might be the only way to produce that good at a competitive price. If a firm has a good product idea, but is short of capital to expand and exploit the commercial opportunity itself, licensing allows the earning of at least some profit, or more precisely, royalty, without having to commit scarce financial resources.

The main problem is that if one has a licensing arrangement with a company in a politically sensitive area then, for one reason or another, royalties due might not be paid. This is one of the dangers of licensing and obviously the licensee will have to be chosen with great care. There are two possible suggestions to try to overcome this type of situation. One is to ensure that the licensing arrangement means the acceptance of certain component parts from the licensor and if there are problems in payment then components can be withheld. The other suggestion is that where the product under licence is technically advanced it is likely that it will be continually improved through innovation; the sanction here is that if there are royalty payment problems then the latest innovation can be withheld. However, these suggestions indicate a negative aspect of licensing and the vast majority of such arrangements are successful. The obvious answer is to choose a licensee of undoubted integrity in a politically stable country (the only problem is that in such a situation there there are probably more lucrative export arrangements than licensing!).

Assuming that a licensing arrangement is agreed, then regular checks must be made as to the quality of the licensee's finished products and defined quality standards should be part of the licensing agreement.

Export houses

The use of export houses is an alternative to the manufacturer having his own export department. Export houses are usually home-based organisations which carry out some or all of the overseas activities in place of the manufacturer, often using their own agents, distributors or other intermediary. They are a useful alternative for small companies whose overseas operations are limited, not warranting the expense of direct involvement. They are also used by larger firms who are only marginally involved in smaller markets, or use export houses until such markets have expanded sufficiently to warrant their own overseas operation.

A manufacturer can delegate some or all of his overseas operations to an export house or he may delegate parts of the actual selling task to the export house. Thus, export houses offer flexibility, and they offer a range of services, including the following.

(*i*) Export factoring – handling finance and credit arrangements on behalf of the manufacturer.

(*ii*) Factory representation – a sales supervisor supervising the sales activities of distributors or dealers on behalf of the manufacturer.

(*iii*) Market intelligence gathering in overseas markets.

(*iv*) Handling export procedures and documentation.

(*v*) Help in selecting agents, distributors and dealers.

(*vi*) Confirming orders – paying the manufacturer on confirmation of an order from an overseas buyer and receiving commission, although here the export house is not actually paying the manufacturer but merely confirming liability for payment.

Having looked at the services export houses have to offer, we shall now look at a number of reasons why a manufacturer might want to use one.

(*i*) Lack of resources to carry out overseas operations by the manufcturer.

(*ii*) When overseas selling operations are only small scale and it would not make economic sense to carry out such operations oneself.

(*iii*) Where the export house has particular expertise in a country or an industry.

(*iv*) Where the manufacturing company is predominantly production orientated and lacks the marketing expertise.

There are, however, a number of disadvantages, the main one being lack of direct contact with the market. The manufacturer may also experience difficulty in monitoring developments and changes in the overseas market and adapting to these changes in good time.

Having examined the indirect approaches to selling, we shall now look at the more direct methods.

7.5.2 DIRECT METHODS OF OVERSEAS SELLING

Subsidiary companies

The subsidiary may be a selling or manufacturing organisation or both. The selling subsidiary usually replaces agents and distributors with the company's own permanent staff. In certain cases it is possible for a firm to start its own sales organisation with little investment. The usual way, however, is to start by using an agent, then opening its own sales office with a limited number of staff and, once profits start to show, allow the unit to become self-sufficient and expand ultimately into manufacturing.

The above is, however, a generalisation and sales subsidiaries may require a larger investment than many companies can afford, especially where an after-sales service has to be offered and where the stocking of a large volume of spare parts is necessary. Manufacturing subsidiaries range from simple assembly plants to complete production units.

A simple assembly plant subsidiary is particularly useful where the product is bulky and freight costs are high. By using local assembly, the final cost of transport may be reduced as it is often more economical to ship containers of parts for assembly than to ship the finished bulky manufactured product. In addition, local employment is created and this promotes goodwill towards the company, which in itself assists in developing markets further.

Reasons for establishing overseas manufacturing subsidiaries differ from company to company, but the following factors are important.

(i) PRODUCTION CAPACITY. Where overseas markets are expanding, a firm may find problems in serving the market from the home base.

(ii) NON-TARIFF RESTRICTIONS. Where such restrictions exist, the setting up of a subsidiary may be the only way around them. Many foreign governments give grants and incentives to firms to set up manufacturing bases in their country and their purchasing strategy favours goods made at home. In some cases restrictions placed against imports may take the form of complex (and unnecessarily prohibitive) safety or packaging regulations.

(iii) COSTS. Where labour and manufacturing facilities are often quite economical in overseas countries and setting up a manufacturing base saves transportation costs.

(iv) EXPLICIT IMPORT RESTRICTIONS. Where these exist, the setting up of a manufacturing subsidiary may be the only way to enter or stay in the market.

When establishing a subsidiary, local legal and taxation regulations must make it possible to set up a profitable subsidiary and allow the parent company to extract profits from the country. It may be prudent for a firm to gain experience in the market through agents and distributors before venturing directly into setting up a manufacturing subsidiary. Many firms employ the staff of a previous agent or distributor to form the basis of the new company.

Although it may seem that the establishment of a foreign subsidiary exposes a firm to many of the risks which licensing minimises, a venture of this kind may offer the greatest potential. Not only may local employment and production be beneficial for the reasons mentioned, but the parent company can offer the subsidiary the wealth of its business experience and resources. Other advantages are that employees working direct for a company are often better motivated than those of an intermediary and it is easier to control a subsidiary because it is under the parent company's direct control. The main disadvantage is that political or economic instability within the country may cause problems outside the control of the parent company.

Joint ventures

A joint venture is where usually two, but sometimes more, firms manufacture and sell products on a joint basis. As such it can be an indirect as well as direct method of exporting, depending upon the arrangement. It is quite common in the transport, construction and high technology sectors of business.

Such agreements have financial benefits as the cost of development is shared, but friction and disagreement can sometimes arise between members of the agreement.

Direct selling

Despite the strengths already outlined of using intermediaries, some companies find that selling direct from the home country to overseas markets offers more advantages. Direct selling requires the firm to take full responsibility for establishing contact with potential customers.

Direct selling provides a degree of control that is impossible to achieve through intermediaries over such matters as price, credit, after-sales service, etc. The chief disadvantage is that more frequent travel is involved, and a lack of a permanent presence in the market can cause problems. The firm may find difficulty keeping abreast of developments in the market and will have to rely on customers to provide market information. Customers may also view this lack of permanent presence as a lack of definite commitment to the market. Firms supplying technically complex products that require technical service and advice often place a sales engineer in the market on a semi-permanent basis, which does tend to obviate the lack of commitment criticism somewhat.

The following are guidelines as to where direct selling is most appropriate.

(*i*) BUYER SPECIFIED WORK. Where individual orders are large and custom made it may be necessary for the manufacturer and purchaser to get together to discuss each job as a unique contract.
(*ii*) CONTINUOUS SUPPLY. Once set in motion this requires only the periodic visit to negotiate such matters as price changes. Such contracts are normally able to run smoothly without a permanent overseas presence.
(*iii*) PRODUCTS ARE TECHNICALLY COMPLEX WITH A CLEARLY DEFINED MARKET. Here problems can be discussed directly between the supplier and user.
(*iv*) GEOGRAPHICAL PROXIMITY. Countries in Western Europe can sometimes be serviced direct from the UK because of good communication facilities.

(*v*) FEW CUSTOMERS BUT LARGE OR HIGH VALUE ORDERS. In such situations time and expense involved travelling abroad is sometimes small compared with the size and value of the potential order.

In selling direct to a customer overseas, there is the opportunity to build up close relationships with individual customers, based upon trust, commitment and understanding. A close interactive commercial relationship is beneficial, particularly if the exporting company is unfamiliar with the market. Speaking the language of the country is more important in direct selling than if the firm is dealing through an intermediary. If the salesperson is to build up a close personal relationship with his or her customers, he must understand the cultural, religious and business practices of the country. There may be many mental barriers to a foreign buyer placing an order with an overseas salesperson, and patience will be required to break down these barriers. Thus, emphasis must be placed upon gradual acceptance rather than the expectation of instant success. This involves careful planning in building up contacts and nurturing them and not taking the first 'no' for an answer.

7.6 A SPECIFIC STUDY IN INTERNATIONAL SELLING – JAPAN

It was stated at the beginning of this chapter that the objective was not to provide a comprehensive guide to international selling and exporting. The general case for exporting for the good of the economy and for the good of individual companies has been covered, together with an overview of organisational and cultural issues. The specific type of information that is of direct use to a potential exporter is that which follows in respect of exporting to Japan. This information has been taken from an article (Saunders and Hon-Chung, 1984) in the *Journal of Sales Management* for which the first author was editor.

Successful selling to Japan requires patience and a sensitivity to customs and business practices not altogether appreciated by Westerners. Business in Japan is still conducted in a traditional Confucian manner where civility, politeness and the search for constructive relationships are of the essence, and successful business follows the establishment of such relationships.

In many ways the Japanese do not respond in the same way as Westerners. For the most part, the Japanese keep their emotions under control, and culture demands that a person of virtue will not show a negative emotion when shocked or upset by sudden bad news. This ideal of an expressionless face in situations of great anxiety was strongly emphasised in the *bushido* (way of the warrior) which was the guideline for *samurai* and the ideal for many others. Furthermore, not only are negative emotions suppressed, but the control of an outward show of pleasant emotions in public is also rarely relaxed in Japan. Women tend to cover their mouths while laughing, and males show true merriment (and true anger) mainly after hours when their culture allows them greater freedom of behaviour while drinking alcohol. Thus the poker-faced ideal is very common in public settings in Japan. The moral of these observations is that one must develop a sensitivity to the reactions of the Japanese because of the difficulty of telling how they are reacting.

Another noteworthy aspect is that shame is intolerable in Japan. This means that one should never put one's Japanese counterpart in a position that will force him to accept blame for a project going wrong, being delayed, etc. This characteristic has important implications for two elements of the sales process: handling objections and the close. The Japanese may avoid explicit objections because politeness demands that the seller does not lose face. Similarly, an attempted close may put the Japanese in a position where they are concerned for the seller's loss of face if the answer is to be negative. The deft footwork associated with the persuasion approach to selling clashes with the Japanese character and is completely opposed to the spirit of Japanese negotiations.

In some countries it is considered socially acceptable to compliment someone directly on his business accomplishments or the accomplishment of his company, but in Japan anything in the way of a compliment is made indirectly. Instead, say, of complimenting someone directly on his taste and sophistication, the Japanese practice is often to approach this particular problem indirectly, and pick out some aspect of the room which reflects the other person's taste and sophistication and comment on that.

With regard to business correspondence, Japanese companies may fail to answer written enquiries concerning possible business relationships. This does not necessarily mean a lack of interest. There can be a number of reasons for a slow response. Decision-making tends to be much slower and this is often the reason for such slowness. Most Japanese companies are also accustomed to being able to talk face to face with suppliers and it is the usual way of conducting business in Japan.

Personal introductions are commonly executed by a third party rather than through say the medium of a telephone call requesting a meeting. The person making the introduction will explain to the person one wishes to meet approximately what subjects are to be discussed, what company one comes from and one's position within that company. Because there will usually be a common understanding between the two Japanese, the Japanese businessman whom one wishes to meet will generally be more favourably disposed to hearing one's opinion than if one walks in without an introduction.

The key to a successful business relationship in Japan is a successful personal relationship and nowhere in the world are business and personal relationships so intertwined. However, such friendship only opens the door; thereafter the hard reality of the benefits to be gained and the risks to be run will take over. Friendships in Japan take more time to form, are deeper and last longer than those in the West and often these obligations extend to business relationships. For example, during a recession, a large firm will commit itself to its suppliers and subcontractors for continued orders to tide them over. The lesson of these observations is that one must be prepared to operate within this two tier business structure; establish friendship first and then move to the second stage of actual business negotiations.

To Westerners, Japanese business seems formal and ritualistic. To a degree this is true, but business relationships do no more than reflect the formality of relationships generally. As in all societies, ritual is particularly important when meeting someone for the first time. It is used to establish and signal that one has identified initial relationships. The first meeting is also a time when transgressions are most likely to cause lasting damage.

One of the most powerful forms of non-verbal communication is dress. The usual dress for Japanese businessmen is a dark suit, a white shirt and dark tie. However, most Japanese businessmen acquainted with foreigners have come to expect a certain variety within reasonable limits in the dress of foreign businessmen. It is not, therefore, expected that one should imitate the Japanese mode of dress. However, one should avoid extremes in dress which may cause uneasiness. For example, loud clothing will create the disturbing feeling among the Japanese businessmen that the foreigner has perhaps failed to take them as seriously as he might have, by failing to observe that the common practice in dress in Japan is some degree of formality.

At the beginning and end of every meeting, the Japanese businessman will bow very formally to the members of the other side in the negotiations. This is generally observed at the first meeting and to a somewhat lesser extent at subsequent meetings. Most Japanese with experience in dealing with Westerners will be expecting to use a handshake rather than a bow. The appropriate strategy is perhaps to wait to determine whether the Japanese businessman is prepared to offer his hand for a handshake or whether he is going to bow. The question of whether the non-Japanese should imitate the bow of the Japanese is controversial within Japan itself. Generally, a nod of the head or a slight bow is considered acceptable for the non-Japanese. One should be aware that reciprocal bowing behaviour is dependent on the status relationship of participants; the inferior must begin the bow, and his bow is deeper, while the superior determines when the bow is complete. When participants are of equal status, they must both bow the same way and begin and end the bow at the same time.

One of the most obvious differences between Japanese and Western business practices is the use of business calling cards or *meishi*. These are exchanged on every occasion where one businessman meets another. The prime purpose is to enable the recipients of the cards to know the other's status so that not only do they bow correctly, but also use the proper form of language. Japan is a hierarchical society and the Japanese are very status conscious in that they use different forms of language and bow in different manners according to the status relationship with another individual. Business cards also serve the function of not having to memorise instantaneously the names and positions of one's business counterparts and they provide a record for future reference.

Such cards are a standard pattern and size, so that they will fit in the Japanese filing systems. They must have square corners for males and round corners for females. The typical business card that the non-Japanese businessman should have will have the Japanese translation of the individual's name on one side, along with his company, its address and the person's title. The other side will have the same information in English (which is the most common foreign language used in Japanese business).

The exchange of business cards is a very important part of the process of introduction in Japan. For this reason, cards should be exchanged one at a time and with some care. The courteous method is to present it, Japanese side up, with the printing facing the receiver.

One of the peculiarities of these business cards is that there is no single standard set of English translations for the ranks and positions in Japanese companies. As mentioned earlier, Japan is a very hierarchical and status-conscious society, so an understanding of the ranks in business is very important. Table 3 (Japanese External Trade Organisation, 1976) translates some of the more common Japanese business titles.

Table 3. *Translations of common Japanese business titles*

Japanese title	Description and/or usual translation
No title	New graduate, aged 23–33
Kakaricho	Manager, aged 34–43
Kacho	Section chief, aged 44–47
Bucho	Bureau chief, aged 48+, senior manager
Torishimariyaku	Director
Fuku Shacho	Vice-president (more senior director)
Shacho or Daihyo Torishimariyaku	President (managing director)
Kaicho	Chairman

The basic titles in a Japanese firm are usually very clear, and the level of the position within a company, as indicated by the title, is usually closely related to the age of the individual. This system of ranking and responsibility, corresponding closely with age and years of service in the company, is one unique characteristic of Japanese organisations.

While the details of negotiations may be left to a representative in Japan, the managing director of the foreign firm (or some other high official in the company) should establish an initial contact with his equal in the Japanese firm. This is terms the *aisatsu* or the greeting. The purpose of this *aisatsu* is to establish a presence.

The Japanese term *hai* is literally translated as 'yes', although it can also mean 'I see' or 'I understand' and does not necessarily mean agreement. Furthermore, the Japanese are very reluctant to give a direct 'no' answer, because Japanese culture emphasises harmony rather than confrontation. Instead of the answer 'no', one is more likely to hear something non-committal such as 'Let me think.'

One must, therefore, learn to read the negative response signs such as hesitancy or an unwillingness to be more specific.

Postponements of negotiations are common in Japan, largely because decision-making follows a prescribed process called the *ringi* system. This means that a proposal must be circulated among various sections and departments that will be affected by the proposal, with much discussion and correction ensuing. The *ringisho* (request for a decision) goes back and forth and eventually a consensus is achieved among the interested parties, with the president giving his final approval.

During negotiations long periods of total silence are common. This is because the Japanese like time to think over what has been said and what alternatives are open to them when they next speak. Silence is also part of the Japanese communication procedure and they tend to rely heavily upon non-verbal communication. Westerners often find such silences embarrassing and feel obliged to say something unnecessary to relieve the supposed tension. The best way to handle such silences is to exercise restrain and outwait the silence.

Japanese businessmen have little confidence in detailed contracts which attempt to provide for all possible contingencies. Their preference is for broad agreements and mutual understanding. Contracts are drawn up with an eye to flexibility and a contract is often considered an agreement to enter into a general course of conduct rather than something fixing precise terms. The Japanese like to negotiate each issue as it arises and there is an assumption that each party is prepared to make substantial accommodations to the other. This should not be interpreted as an attempt to violate the contract, but rather the desire of the Japanese to allow both sides the ability to adjust to unforeseen circumstances. One should not expect to obtain a detailed contract, but once a commitment is made it is for the long term. Japanese firms prefer long-term reliable and exclusive business relationships and they tend to turn to established channels to develop new business initiatives.

Because of the consciousness of using the correct level of language in a conversation or discussion, any interpreter one engages may unconsciously modify statements going from English to Japanese and back to English again, according to the rank of the people involved. For example, if a senior official of a Western company is speaking with a high-level Japanese manager, the interpreter will feel in an inferior position to both of them. The statement that the senior official intends to have translated verbatim for his Japanese counterpart may end up as being something quite different.

Entertainment in Japan plays a major role in establishing personal and business relationships. Unlike the West, business luncheons are a rarity and evening entertainment almost never takes place in the home. The typical pattern is for the Japanese businessman to eat at a restaurant in the evening and thereafter go to a bar or cabaret. Such evenings are for cementing business relationships rather than for discussing specific aspects of business.

The personal skills necessary to conclude negotiations successfully in Japan do not come naturally to the Westerner. What is perhaps even more disturbing is the inappropriateness of much sales training to the Japanese situation. Many skills such as reading body language are culture bound. The persuasion approach to selling seems diametrically opposed to the Japanese character and perception of the role of negotiations.

7.7 CONCLUSIONS

This chapter has examined international selling. The broad economic aspects were first discussed, including balance of payments and the United Kingdom's share of international trade. Britain's entry into the European Community was examined, together with the effects of the General Agreement on Tariffs and Trade.

The advantages to the individual company entering international selling were discussed and this was followed by aspects of how different cultures affect the sales approach. More specifically, this included aesthetics, religion, education, language, social organisation and political factors.

Different types of organisation for international selling were considered, including agents, distributors, licensing and export houses under indirect methods. Direct methods included subsidiary companies, joint ventures and direct selling. This was concluded by a specific description of the problems involved in selling to Japan.

The next chapter considers the legal and social aspects of selling which then concludes the section on the sales environment.

PRACTICAL EXERCISE – QUALITY KRAFT CARPETS LTD

This company was founded in 1981 by William Jackson and John Turner in Kidderminster, a town in the UK with a tradition of carpet-making going back hundreds of years. Carpet manufacture and related activities had been the major provider of employment in the area up until the late 1960s. However, since that date, the carpet industry, like many other areas of British textiles, faced problems and decline.

Paradoxically, it was this decline that brought Quality Kraft Carpets into existence. William Jackson had been production manager with one of the largest carpet manufacturing firms in the area, with a worldwide reputation for quality carpets. John Turner had been a loom tuner (a maintenance engineer) responsible for maintaining over one hundred carpet looms for another large company. Jackson had been made redundant as a result of a drastic decline in orders and Turner's company had gone into liquidation. Both of them were very good friends, and since their respective demises had come together they decided to start their own small company, specialising in the product they knew best – traditional, woven, good quality, Axminster carpets.

Because so many firms in the area were either closing down or cutting back production, there was a steady supply of textile machinery being sold very cheaply by local auctioneers. By pooling their respective resources, plus help from the bank, they were able to acquire a 15-year lease on a small factory and purchase enough equipment to enable them to commence production.

Their policy was to weave best-quality carpets made of 80 per cent wool and 20 per cent nylon. The market was good-quality carpet shops and the contract market, especially hotels, restaurants, offices and large stores. They made a conscious decision not to deal with the new carpet superstores, largely because profit margins would be so low in that their bulk purchasing power made them able to demand low margins. In addition, these carpet superstores predominantly sold cheaper carpets, mainly tufted synthetic carpets purchased from North America. It was contended that purchasers looking for a good-quality carpet would go to a conventional carpet shop and not to a carpet superstore which they considered was more applicable to the lower end of the market.

At the time of setting up the main problems facing UK carpet manufacturers were the depressed state of the economy and the fact that imports of carpets were taking an increasing share of a diminishing market. Thus, the recession made carpet purchasing a lower priority matter for those who already had carpets and the attitude was to make them last longer.

Nowadays, imports account for over 20 per cent of the UK carpet market and this percentage is increasing. The main imports are synthetic tufted carpets, mainly from North America but increasingly from EC countries – Belgium followed by Western Germany and Holland. Nylon carpet is basically oil based, which gave the Americans a significant advantage until 1980 because of the cheapness of their oil. However, since then their oil prices have increased and the strength of the US dollar has made their exports to the UK less competitive.

Despite the apparently depressing picture for UK manufacturers, the UK carpet industry is still the largest in the world, particularly the high-quality woven carpet sector. The UK has always been a net exporter of carpets and its reputation for quality has worldwide acclaim.

Since Quality Kraft Carpets commenced, its total sales have been as follows:

Quality Kraft Carpets Ltd sales (£000)

1981	1982	1983	1984	1985	1986	1987	1988	1989	1990
510	820	1,280	1,760	2,300	2,900	2,100	2,000	1,970	1,950

These sales are to two distinct markets:

(*i*) direct to quality retailers;
(*ii*) the contract market.

The percentage of sales accounted for by each of these market segments is given below:

Percentage of sales to each segment

	1981	1982	1983	1984	1985	1986	1987	1988	1989	1990
Retail	76	70	66	63	60	60	58	56	52	52
Contract	24	30	34	37	40	40	42	44	48	48

At the 1986 level of demand the company was operating at full capacity, but today it has an excess of manufacturing capacity. The company has not laid off any employees, but overtime has been cut out and some work that was given to outside contractors, e.g. final 'shearing' up of carpets, is now done in the company. An interesting facet of contract sales is that much of it is for customised carpet, often incorporating the customer's company logo in the design.

The company now feels that the industry is likely to remain depressed and foreign competition in the UK market is likely to increase further. The company has not attempted to sell its products abroad, but feels that if it is ever to expand again, then overseas markets are the only feasible method. William Jackson and John Turner had a long discussion about exporting, as they were both inexperienced in such matters, and they listed the strengths and weaknesses of Quality Kraft Carpets in order to arrive at a decision as to which would be the most appropriate overseas market to enter. Their conclusions were as follows.

(*i*) WEAKNESSES.
- Small and relatively new without the reputation of a long-established firm.
- Management has no knowledge of selling overseas and, although educated by experience, has little knowledge of finance, economics, languages, etc., which are of help when selling overseas.
- The more popular types of tufted carpets are not manufactured.
- The company cannot compete on price in the volume markets because of outdated equipment and small purchasing power.
- Although products are first class, they are expensive.
- The company does not directly employ such specialists as designers, but operates on a freelance/contractual basis.

(*ii*) STRENGTHS.
- Expertise in the manufacture of good-quality conventionally-woven Axminster carpets.
- The company is small and flexible and can easily cope with new trends in designs.
- Proficiency is increasing in contract work and staff have specialist knowledge of such one off tasks. Much repeat business is coming from satisfied contract customers.
- There is a loyal work force who have flexible working arrangements in that the workers can each carry out a number of different jobs without demarcation disputes.

– The company is reasonably profitable and it has very little long-term debt.
– The retail part of the business contains loyal customers with much repeat business.

After discussions with the bank and advice from the British Overseas Trade Board, it was decided that the USA offered most potential for the immediate future. The Middle East and Japan also showed promise in the medium term. It was also decided that they should concentrate on the contract market. These decisions were based upon the following criteria.

(*i*)   The USA is a growing market for best quality Axminster carpet.
(*ii*) Although the USA does manufacture some conventionally woven Wilton carpet, it does not manufacture much good-quality Axminster carpet.
(*iii*) In the contract market, quality seems to be more important than price and it would seem to be good for the company to concentrate on contract carpet sales.
(*iv*) Import tariffs into the USA from the UK are 9½% *ad valorem* (on top of the imported cost) for Axminster and 19½% for Wilton (the latter being higher to protect the USA producers). This gives an undoubted advantage for the export of Axminster carpets.
(*v*)   A market research survey conducted in the USA had indicated that their interior designers liked Axminster because of the fact that any pattern or logo could be woven into the design. Most contract carpet in the USA is tufted and printed which only makes mass production runs feasible. This printing process, although much cheaper, is inferior to the design being actually woven into the carpet as is the case with Axminster.
(*vi*) The pound is still at a relatively low value against the United States dollar, and this would make the product better value in the USA.
(*vii*) Advice from the British Overseas Trade Board has indicated that the UK has a high reputation in the USA for quality carpets, that they appreciate personal service and good delivery and that British carpet might be seen as a status symbol.

Quality Kraft Carpets Ltd decided that they would immediately enter the North American market, but did not want to commit too much money to the venture in case it failed. On the other hand, if it was successful, they were prepared to commit more resources.

Discussion questions

1   Draw up a short-, medium- and long-term sales strategy upon how Quality Kraft Carpets can enter, develop and remain in the United States market.
2   What form of representation would you recommend for this new market – or would you consider setting up a manufacturing subsidiary? Give reasons for your decision.
3   How might your various strategies change and what further considerations

would need to be made if, after initial success in the United States market, the Middle East and Japan offered good export opportunities?

4 What would be your marketing communications and sales promotional strategies for the company in the USA? More specifically, outline your sales 'message' and the type of media you would use to communicate this message.

5 What, if any, further research needs to be undertaken before attempting to export to the USA?

EXAMINATION QUESTIONS

1 Discuss the contention that there is no such thing as 'overseas selling'; it is merely an extension of selling to the home market.

2 How does the role of an export agent differ from the role of an export salesperson?

8 Law and Ethical Issues

Consumer protection by the law is very much a twentieth century phenomenon. Before that the prevailing attitude can be described by the phrase *caveat emptor* – let the buyer beware. Much of the legislation has been drawn up since 1970 when there was a recognition that sellers may have an unfair advantage compared with consumers when entering into a contract of sale. Some of the major laws controlling selling activity in Britain are:

(*i*)   Weights and Measures Acts 1878, 1963, 1979;
(*ii*)   Sale of Goods Acts 1893 and 1979;
(*iii*) Resale Prices Acts 1964, 1976;
(*iv*)   Restrictive Trade Practices Acts 1956, 1968, 1976;
(*v*)   Misrepresentation Act 1967;
(*vi*)   Trade Descriptions Acts 1968, 1972;
(*vii*) Unsolicited Goods and Services Acts 1971 and 1975;
(*viii*) Supply of Goods (Implied Terms) Acts 1973, 1982;
(*ix*)   Fair Trading Act 1973;
(*x*)   Hire Purchase Act 1973;
(*xi*)   Consumer Credit Act 1974;
(*xii*) Unfair Contract Terms Act 1977.

In addition to these Acts, consumers are protected by a range of codes of practice covering such activities as advertising, market research and direct selling. Trade associations such as the Association of British Travel Agents, the Society of Motor Manufacturers and Traders, and the Radio, Electrical and Television Retailers' Association have also drawn up codes of practice which have been approved by the Office of Fair Trading.

The consumers' interest is also protected by the Consumers' Association which campaigns for consumers and provides information about products, often on a comparative basis, which allows consumers to make a more informed, rational choice between products and brands. This information is published in their magazine *Which?* The National Consumer council was established in 1975 to represent the consumer interest at national level and to issue reports on various topics of consumer concern, e.g. consumer credit.

Since a Conservative government came to power in 1979, there has been a certain amount of reigning back in relation to consumer protection. The first indication of this was the dissolution of the post of Minister for Consumer Affairs and this was followed by the merging of Consumer Advice Centres with Citizens' Advice Bureaux. The feeling was that consumer protection had gone too far and it was time to give power back to manufacturers. However, more fundamental was the notion that market forces would keep 'good' manufacturers in business and force 'bad' ones out. Thus the age of the so-called 'consumerist movement' effectively lost its momentum at the end of the 1970s.

8.1 THE CONTRACT

All this activity is centred upon the contract entered into when a seller agrees to part with a good, or provide a service, in exchange for monetary payment.

A contract is made when a deal is agreed. This can be accomplished verbally or in writing. Once an offer has been accepted a contract is formed and is legally binding. Thus if a builder offers to build a garage for £1,000 and this offer is accepted, the builder is obliged to carry out the work and the householder is under an obligation to pay the agreed sum upon completion. Although contracts donot have to be in writing – except, for example, house purchase – to place an offer and acceptance in writing can minimise the likelihood of misunderstanding over the nature of the agreement which has been struck and provide tangible evidence in the event of legal action. Important in written contracts are the terms and conditions which apply. This aspect of the contract will now be considered, before an examination of some business practices, and the way in which they are controlled by law, is undertaken.

8.2 TERMS AND CONDITIONS

As the name suggests, terms and conditions state the circumstances under which the buyer is prepared to purchase and the seller is prepared to sell. They define the limit of responsibility for both buyer and seller. Thus both buyer and seller are at liberty to state their terms and conditions. Usually the buyer will state his on the back of his order form and the seller will do so on the reverse of his quotation form. Often a note is typed on the front of the form in red ink: 'Your attention is drawn to our standard terms and conditions on the reverse of this order.'

Typical clauses incorporated into the conditions of a purchase order include the following.

(*i*) Only orders issued on the company's printed order form and signed on behalf of the company will be respected.

(*ii*) Alterations to orders must be confirmed by official amendment and signed.

(*iii*) Delivery must be within the specified time period. The right to cancel is reserved for late delivery.

(*iv*) Faulty goods will be returned and expenses charged to the supplier.

(*v*) All insurance of goods in transit shall be paid for by the supplier.

(*vi*) This order is subject to a cash discount of 2½ per cent, unless otherwise arranged, for payment within twenty eight days of receipt. Any payment made is without prejudice to our rights if the goods supplied prove to be unsatisfactory or not in accordance with our agreed specification or sample.

(*vii*) Tools supplied by us for the execution of this order must not be used in the service of any other firm without permission.

Careful drawing up of terms and conditions are essential in business since they provide protection against claims made by the other party should problems arise in fulfilment of the contract.

An example of a conditions of sale document for a seller is given in Fig. 18 below.

CONDITIONS OF SALE

These Conditions apply except so far as they are inconsistent with any express agreement entered into between the Seller and the Buyer before the delivery.

1 Where the Seller delivers in bulk it is the Buyer's responsibility

    (a) to provide a safe and suitable bulk storage which complies in all respects with all relevant regulations made by H.M. Government or other competent authority.

    (b) to ensure that the storage into which delivery is to be made will accommodate the full quantity ordered and in the case of Petroleum Spirit to procure certification to this effect and also to the effect that the connecting hose is properly and securely connected to the filling point. In this regard the Buyer is referred to the regulations currently in force relating to the storage and use of petroleum spirit.

    (c) in the case of highly inflammable products and where otherwise applicable, strictly to observe any regulations laid down by H.M. Government or other competent authority in respect of the avoidance of smoking, naked lights, fires, stoves or heating appliances of any description in the vicinity of the storage and the fill, dip and vent pipes connected thereto.

The Buyer will indemnify the Supplier against any damages, claims, expenses or costs which may arise as a result of the Buyer's non-observance of these conditions.

2   It is a condition of every bulk sale that the quantity shown by any measuring devices employed by the Seller shall for the purpose of accounts be accepted by the Buyer as the quantity delivered but the Buyer may be represented at the taking of these measurements in order to verify them if he so desires. The Seller cannot accept any responsibility whatever for discrepances in the Buyer's tanks, dip rods or other measuring devices.

3   Prices include any Government Tax (other than Value Added Tax) in force at the time of supply. Any variation in the rate of existing tax, or any additional taxation, is for Buyer's account.

4   All products supplied are chargeable at the price ruling on the day of despatch irrespective of the date of the order or the amount of cash sent with order.

5   In the event of missing consignments, short delivery or damage the Seller can only investigate the circumstances if
   (a)   In the case of damage the Buyer notifies the Railway or other Carrier and the Seller of the damage immediately upon receipt of the damaged goods, such notices to be in writing and quoting the invoice number.
   (b)   In the case of non-receipt or short delivery the Buyer notifies the Seller in writing of non-receipt or short delivery. Such notice, quoting the invoice number should be sent within 21 days of date of despatch.

6   Acceptance of goods will be treated as acceptance of the Seller's conditions.

Fig 18   Example of conditions of sale document.

8.3 BUSINESS PRACTICES AND LEGAL CONTROLS

8.3.1 FALSE DESCRIPTIONS

Unscrupulous salespeople may be tempted to mislead potential buyers through inaccurate statements about the product or service they are selling. In the UK the consumer is protected from such practice by the Trade Descriptions Act 1968. The Act covers descriptions of products, prices and services and includes both oral and written descriptions.

Business are prohibited from applying a false trade description to products and from supplying falsely described products. The false description must be false to a material degree, and the Act also covers 'misleading' statements. Not only would a salesperson be contravening the Act is he described a car as achieving 50 miles per gallon when, in fact, it only achieved 30 miles per gallon, he would also be guilty of putting a false trade description if he described a car as 'beautiful' if it proved to be unroadworthy.

The Act also covers the display of prices. Section 11 of the Act states:

(1)   If any person offering to supply goods of any description gives, by whatever means, any false indication to the effect that the price at which the goods are offered is equal to or less than
a) a recommended price; or
b) the price at which the good or goods at the same description were previously offered by him; or is less than such a price by a specified amount, he shall be guilty of an offence.

(2)   If any person offering to supply any goods gives, by whatever means, any indication likely to be taken as an indication that the goods are being offered at a price less than that at which they are in fact being offered he shall be guilty of an offence.

This part of the Act was designed to combat the practice of displaying bargain prices by comparing the price with a recommended or usual price when, in fact, the latter was fictitious. A business must not display a price at which the goods have been previously offered for sale unless they have been on offer at that price for at least twenty-eight days during the preceding six months. Businesses have gone to extraordinary lengths to circumvent this rule. One method is to display the goods at a high price in one branch of a store so that they can be advertised nationally as being reduced during 'sale' time. In order to plug this loophole, the Price Marking (Bargain Offers) Order was drawn up. This prohibits references to a business's previous price unless it is charged on the same (or other identified) premises at least once.

Services are also dealt with in the Act. Reckless statements regarding the nature of services, accommodation or facilities are controlled by the Act. However, unlike the cases of product and prices, consumer protection departments need to prove that the false statement was deliberate. Also, the Act only appears to cover a situation as it exists now, not in the future. Thus, if a travel brochure advertises a hotel as having a discotheque, and holidaymakers complain later that year that when they took their holiday no discotheque existed, the travel operator is not committing an offence unless the discotheque did not exist when the brochure was published. Other difficulties have arisen. A travel operator was prosecuted under the Act because its brochure contained a picture of a hotel, beach and resort different to the one named, which was of a much lower standard. The operator successfully defended its case since the court accepted that the picture was only intended to give a general impression of the event and not an exact presentation.

8.3.2 FAULTY GOODS

The principal protection for the buyer against the sale of faulty goods is to be found within the Sale of Goods Act 1979. This Act states that a product must correspond to its description and must be of merchantable quality, i.e. 'fit for the purpose for which goods of that kind are commonly bought as it is reasonable to expect.' An example is a secondhand car which is found to be unroadworthy after purchase; it clearly is not of merchantable quality, unless bought for scrap! Finally a product must be fit for a particular purpose which may be specified by the buyer and agreed by the seller. If, for example, a buyer bought a car in this country with the expressed desire to use it in Africa, a retailer may be committing an offence if he agrees that the car is fit to be used when in fact, because of the higher temperatures, it is not.

The condition that products must correspond to their description covers both private and business sales, whereas the merchantability and fitness for purpose conditions apply to sales in the course of a business only. The latter two conditions apply not only at the time of purchase but for a reasonable time afterwards. What exactly constitutes 'reasonable' is open to interpretation and will depend upon the nature of the product.

In order to protect the consumer against faulty goods, some companies give guarantees in which they agree to replace or repair those goods should the fault become apparent within a specified period. Unfortunately, before the passing of the Supply of Goods (Implied Terms) Act 1973, these so-called guarantees often removed more rights than they gave. However, since the passing of the Act it is now unlawful for a seller to contract out of the conditions that goods should be merchantable and fit for their purpose. Buyers can now be confident that signing a guarantee will not result in them signing away their rights under the Sale of Goods Act 1979.

8.3.3 INERTIA SELLING

Inertia selling involves the sending of unsolicited goods or the providing of unsolicited services to people who, having received them, may feel an obligation to buy. For example, a book might be sent to people, who would be told that they had been specially chosen to receive it. They would be asked to send money in payment or return the book within a given period, after which they became liable for payment. Non-payment and failure to return the good would result in letters demanding payment, sometimes in quite threatening terms.

The growing use of this technique during the 1960s led to a campaign organised by the Consumers' Association demanding that legislation be enacted curbing the use of the technique. As a result the Unsolicited Goods and Services Act 1971 was passed, followed by the Unsolicited Goods and Services (Amendment) Act 1975.

These Acts have not prohibited the use of the technique but have created certain rights for consumers which makes the use of the method ineffective.

Unsolicited goods can be treated as a free gift after a period of six months from receipt if the sender has not reclaimed them. Further, if the recipient notifies the sender that they are unsolicited, the sender must collect them within thirty days or they become the property of the recipient. The thirty-day rule was felt to be a fair compromise between the rights of the recipient and the rights of the sender who may be the subject of a false order placed by a third party.

The practice of sending threatening letters demanding payment has been outlawed, as have the threats of legal proceedings or placing of names on a published list of defaulters.

Unsolicited services have also been controlled by law. For example, the practice of placing unsolicited entries of names of firms in business directories and then demanding payment has been controlled.

The law therefore gives sufficient rights to consumers effectively to deter the practice of inertia selling. Fortunately for the consumer the trouble and costs involved in using this technique nowadays outweigh the benefits to be gained.

8.3.4 PYRAMID SELLING

There are a number of variants of pyramid selling, but basically the practice involves the selling of consumer goods through a number of levels of distributors. Each distributor makes money by recruiting lower level distributors, thus forming the pyramid.

An individual or company acquires a stock of goods, for example, consmetics, and recruits a number of first-tier distributors, who pay a substantial sum of money for the franchise to sell the goods which are sold to them at a discount. These first-tier distributors then recruit second-tier distributors, who pay them an entrance fee plus a sum of money to cover the cost of goods which are sold at a lower discount. These second-tier recruits make their profit by persuading third-tier distributors to join the scheme, and so on. High-pressure selling, with potential recruits being invited to attend meetings where early entrants sell the idea by revealing the enormous profits they have made, is used to attract inexperienced and gullible newcomers.

One point of view is that recruits know the risks that they are taking in attempting to get rich quick, and the unsuccessful are simply paying the price of their own greed. However, the heavy losses which some participants incur, and the dubious practices associated with their recruitment, led to a belief that pyramid selling should be controlled by law.

This control was brought about by an amendment to the Fair Trading Act 1973 whereby it is an offence for promoters or participants to solicit or take payment from another person for the right to join such a scheme. Regulations have also been drawn up as a result of the powers contained in the Fair Trading Act which further protect the unwary. A seven-day cooling off period is enforced, during which a new participant can withdraw without loss. The organiser of the scheme must buy back goods from participants at 90 per cent of purchase price if the latter wishes to leave. No claims can be made regarding the expected level of income which can be earned. The identity of the organisers of the scheme, and the details of the operation of the scheme, must be included in the recruiting literature. The payment new distributors make for goods upon joining the scheme is limited, and all participants must be given a written contract.

The law has effectively eliminated pyramid selling in this country through the Act, and the regulations which stem from it. The losers are those people who joined such schemes before the enforcement of the Act, since no provision for compensation was made.

8.3.5 EXCLUSION CLAUSES

Another practice which some sellers have employed in order to limit their liability is the use of an exclusion clause. For example, a restaurant or discotheque might display a sign stating that coats are left at the owner's risk, or a dry cleaners might display a sign excluding themselves from blame should clothes be damaged. This practice is now controlled by the Unfair Contract Terms Act, 1977. A seller is not permitted to limit liability or contract out of his liability for death or injury arising from negligence or breach of contract or duty.

For other situations, where loss does not include death or injury, an exclusion clause is only valid if it satisfies the requirement of 'reasonableness'. This means that it is fair taking into account the circumstances prevailing when the sale was made. Relevant factors which are taken into account when making a judgment about 'reasonableness' are:

(*i*) the strength of the bargaining positions of the relevant parties;
(*ii*) whether the customer received an inducement to agree to the exclusion clause;
(*iii*) whether the customer knew or ought to have known of the existence of the exclusion clause;
(*iv*) whether the goods were produced to the special order of the customer;
(*v*) for an exclusion clause which applies when some condition is not complied with, whether it was practicable for the condition to be met.

8.3.6 BUYING BY CREDIT

Before 1974 obtaining consumer credit through a hire-purchase agreement was treated differently, under the law, to consumer credit by means of a bank loan. However from the consumer's point of view there is very little difference between paying for a good by instalments (hire purchase) or paying in cash through a bank loan which is itself repayable by instalments. The Consumer Credit Act 1974 effectively abolished this distinction. Almost all consumer credit agreements between £30 and £5,000 are termed regulated agreements. A notable exception is a building society mortgage.

An important consumer protection measure which resulted from the Act was that a lender should disclose the true interest rate in advertisements and sales literature. This true rate now appears in advertisements as the APR (annual percentage rate) and enables consumers to compare rates of interest charged on a common basis. Prior to this Act, cleverly worded advertisements and sales literature could give the impression that the scale of charges was much lower than was the true case.

Control of credit trading was achieved by a system of licensing which is placed in the hands of the Director-General of Fair Trading. This system was designed to ensure that only people with a sound trading record are able to deal in credit. Not only finance companies but also retailers who arrange credit in order to sell their products must have a licence. Exempt from the Act, however, is weekly or monthly credit. Thus, many credit card agreements are exempt since total repayment is often required at the end of each month.

People entering credit agreements are entitled to receive at least one copy of the agreement so that they are informed of their rights and obligations. A 'cooling off' period is provided for in the Act when the agreement is preceded by 'oral representations' (sales talk) and the agreement was not signed on business premises. This provision was designed to control doorstep selling through credit arrangements. A consumer who wishes to cancel must serve notice of cancellation within five days of the date of receiving the copy of the signed agreement.

8.3.7 COLLUSION BETWEEN SELLERS

In certain circumstances it may be in the sellers' interest to collude with one another in order to restrict supply, agree upon prices (price fixing) or share out the market in some mutually beneficial way. The Restrictive Trade Practices Act 1979 requires that any such trade agreement must be registered with the Director-General of Fair Trading, a post established under the Fair Trading Act 1973. If the Director-General of Fair Trading considers that the registered agreement is contrary to the public interest, he is empowered to refer it to the Restrictive Practices Court. If the Court agrees, the agreement may be declared void.

8.4 CONCLUSIONS

This chapter has examined some of the laws and organisations which have been established to protect consumer interests. Unfortunately the unscrupulous few have made it necessary to enact laws which provide consumer protection.

Central to the study of the sale is an understanding of a contract and its associated terms and conditions. Finally, a number of business practices and their related legal controls are described.

Part Four examines the issues and methods relevant to the management of a sales force.

PRACTICAL EXERCISE – KWIKSELL CARS LTD

John Perry spent £1,500 on a secondhand car bought from Roy Clarke, Kwiksell Cars' salesperson. He was rueing his decision. Perry had never bought a car before but believed that he was smart enough to tell a good car from a bad one. After several weekends of trying to buy a car from private sellers, he decided that to go to a dealer was the only sensible option left to him if he wanted to buy one quickly.

A four year old Austin Astrada 1100 in the forecourt of Kwiksell Cars had caught his eye as he travelled to work by bus. It was advertised at £1,800 and looked in good condition.

When Perry and his girlfriend visited Kwiksell Cars the following Saturday he was greeted by Roy Clarke, who asked him which car he was interested in and took him to see the Astrada. Clarke described the car as 'in lovely condition', the mechanics having been overhauled recently and the engine tuned. Perry was concerned about petrol consumption and was told that he could expect around 40 mpg around town, increasing to nearly 55 mpg on long runs. Perry was very impressed but he was a little worried about the car's capacity to pull his father's caravan. 'There's no problem there,' said Clarke. 'The Astrada might have a small engine but the carburettor has been souped up and it will cope with a caravan. No problem!'

Clarke asked Perry if he and his young lady would like a test drive. Perry agreed and found the car quite good on acceleration, although the engine was a bit noisier than his father's car. 'That's the souped up engine,' said Clarke. 'It makes it sound a bit racey, doesn't it?'

To Perry, the car looked like the solution to his long search but he knew that, as a cash purchaser, he might be able to negotiate a lower price.

'The car seems to suit my purposes but the price is a little higher than I would be prepared to pay.'

'Yes, but it's not often a car in this condition comes onto the market, sir,' retorted Clarke.

'What would you be prepared to knock off the price for a cash deal?' asked Perry.

'Usually, the maximum I am allowed to go is £200, but if you are prepared to pay a deposit now, with the remainder on, say, Tuesday when you collect the car, I'm willing to reduce the price to £1,500.'

Perry felt pleased with himself, and in front of his girlfriend, too! He agreed. He wrote a check for £500 and agreed to bring the balance in cash on the following Tuesday. Clarke asked him to sign a contract of sale and promised that the car and all the necessary documents would be ready by Tuesday.

Perry was pleased with his new purchase at first, but the following weekend when he was on a long run, Perry noticed a knocking noise coming from the engine. The car also appeared to be using much more petrol than he expected. He decided to buy a car guide from W H Smiths and check the petrol consumption figures. The guide stated that the Austin Astrada would achieve

30 mpg on the urban cycle and 40 mpg at a steady 56 mph. Perry was livid!

The knocking noise was still to be heard, so he took the car to his father's garage. The mechanic told Perry that the car's big ends were worn badly. It would cost £300 to be repaired. 'The engine's not souped up,' he said, 'it's kaput!'

'But I need the car next weekend; I'm going on holiday in my father's caravan,' said Perry.

'Well, I hope you're thinking of using your father's car,' said the mechanic. 'You'd blow the engine for sure with a car like the Astrada. It's only got an 1100 engine!'

Perry stormed into Clarke's office.

'I'm sorry you've had these problems but engine troubles are common with Astradas,' explained Clarke. 'I'd like to help but I did take you for a test drive.'

'You conned me!' shouted Perry.

'Not at all. You will see that the contract you signed clearly states that the responsibility to check for defects was the buyer's. That means that any faults which appear after sale are your responsibility to put right. You told me you knew a bit about cars. If you didn't you should have brought a mechanic with you. I knocked £300 off the price. That was to cover for any problems like this.'

Discussion question

1   Did Clarke break the law regarding the sale of the car? Which laws are relevant to this case?

EXAMINATION QUESTIONS

1   What is a contract? Of what significance are contracts in buyer-seller relationships?
2   Distinguish between pyramid selling and inertia selling. Do you believe consumers are adequately protected from these practices?

PART FOUR
Sales Management

9 Recruitment and Selection

THE IMPORTANCE OF SELECTION

In attempting to recruit and select a new sales representative, the sales manager finds himself in an unaccustomed role. Instead of being a seller he, for once, takes on the role of buyer. It is crucial that this transition is carried out effectively because future success of the sales force depends upon the infusion of high-calibre personnel. There are a number of facts which emphasise the importance of effective selection.

(*i*) There is wide variability in the sales effectiveness of salespeople. In 1979, the Institute of Marketing commissioned a study (PA Consultants, 1979) into sales force practice. In this study, the following question was asked of sales managers: 'If you were to put your most successful salesperson into the territory of one of your average salespeople, and made no other changes, what increases in sales would you expect after say two years?' The most commonly expected increased was 16–20 per cent, and one-fifth of all sales managers said they would expect an increase of 30 per cent or over. It must be emphasised that the comparison was between the top and *average* salesperson, not top and *worst* salesperson. Clearly, the quality of the sales representatives which sales managers recruit can have a substantial effect on sales turnover.

(*ii*) Salespeople are very costly. If a company decides to employ extra sales personnel, the cost will be might higher than just basic salary (and commission). Most companies provide a car if travel is required, and travel expenses will also be paid by the company. The special skills necessary to make a sale, rather than to receive an order, imply that training will be required. No company will want to incur all of these costs in order to employ a poor performer.

(*iii*) Other important determinants of success, like training and motivation, are heavily dependent on the intrinsic qualities of the recruit. Although sales effectiveness can be improved by training, it is limited by innate ability. Like other activities where skill is required, such as cricket, soccer and athletics, ultimate achievement in selling is highly associated with personal characteristics. Similarly, motivational techniques may stimulate the salesperson to achieve higher sales but they can do only so much. A lot will be dependent on the inborn motivation of the salesperson himself to complete a difficult sale or visit another prospect instead of returning home.

Sales managers are clearly faced with a difficult and yet vitally important task. However, many of them believe that the outcome of the selection process is far from satisfactory. In the Institute of Marketing survey, nearly half of the sales managers reported that fewer than seven out of ten of the salespeople they had recruited were satisfactory. How, then, should a sales manager approach the task of selection?

There are a number of stages in the recruitment and selection process. An understanding of each stage and the correct procedures to be followed will maximise the chances of selecting the right applicant.

(*i*) Preparation of the job description and personnel specification.
(*ii*) Identification of sources of recruitment and methods of communication.
(*iii*) Designing an effective application form and preparing a short-list.
(*iv*) Interviewing.
(*v*) Supplementary selection aids – psychological tests, role playing.

9.2 PREPARATION OF THE JOB DESCRIPTION AND SPECIFICATION

The production of an accurate job description should prove of little difficulty for the sales manager. He has intimate knowledge of what is required, having been a salesperson himself or herself and having been out on the road with his salespeople during training and evaluation exercises. Generally a job description will cover the following factors.

(*i*) The title of the job.
(*ii*) Duties and responsibilities – the tasks which will be expected of the new recruit, e.g. selling, after-sales service, information feedback, and the range of products/markets/type of customer with which he will be associated.
(*iii*) To whom he will report.
(*iv*) Technical requirements, e.g. the degree to which the salesperson needs to understand the technical aspects of the products he is selling.
(*v*) Location and geographical area to be covered.
(*vi*) Degree of autonomy – the degree to which the salesperson will be able to control his own work programme.

Once generated, the job description will act as the blueprint for the personnel specification which outlines the type of applicant the company is seeking. The technical requirements of the job, for example, and the nature of the customers which the salespeople will meet, will be factors which influence the level of education and, possibly, the age of the required recruit.

The construction of the personnel specification is more difficult for the sales manager than that of the job description. Some of the questions posed lead to highly subjective responses. Must the recruit have selling experience? Should such experience be within the markets that the company serves? Should he be within a certain age range? Is it essential that the salesperson hold certain technical qualifications? If the answer to all of these question is yes, then the number of possible applicants who qualify is reduced.

The danger is that applicants of high potential in selling may be excluded. Graduates at polytechnics and universities often complain that jobs which they are confident that they are capable of doing well are denied them because of the 'two years experience in selling' clause in the advertisements. The implications of this are that the job specification should be drawn up bearing in mind the type of person who would be *excluded* from applying if conditions are laid down with regard to such factors as previous experience. Is it really necessary or just more convenient since less training may then be required?

Another aspect of the personnel specification is the determination of qualities looked for in the new salesperson. This is a much more nebulous concept than the level of technical qualifications, age or previous experience. The qualities themselves may depend on the nature of the job, the personal prejudices of the sales manager (a good rule of thumb is that many managers favour people who are like themselves) or be based on more objective research which has been conducted into attributes associated with successful salespeople. A survey (Jobber and Millar, 1984) which investigated selection practice amongst sales manager in large UK companies produced a plethora of qualities deemed to be important. Figure 19 lists the top twenty characteristics and the percentage mentioning each.

Mayer and Greenberg (1964) produced a more manageable list. Extensive research amongst over 1,000 companies in the USA revealed only two qualities essential to selling – empathy and ego drive. *Empathy* is defined as the ability to feel as the buyer does; to be able to understand the customers' problems and needs. This is distinct from sympathy. A salesperson can feel and understand without agreeing with that feeling. The other basic determinant of sales success, *ego drive*, is defined as the need to make a sale in a personal way not merely for money.

Mayer and Greenberg claim that when an applicant has a large measure of both of these qualities he will be successful at selling anything. Their research led them to believe that sales ability is fundamental, not the product being sold:

> Many sales executives feel that the type of selling in their industry (and even in their particular company) is somehow completely special and unique. This is true to an extent. There is no question that a data-

processing equipment salesperson needs somewhat different training and background than does an automobile salesperson. Differences in requirements are obvious, and whether or not the applicant meets the special qualifications for a particular job can easily be seen in the applicant's biography or readily measured. What is not so easily seen, however, are the basic sales dynamics we have been discussing, which permit an individual to sell successfully, almost regardless of what he is selling.

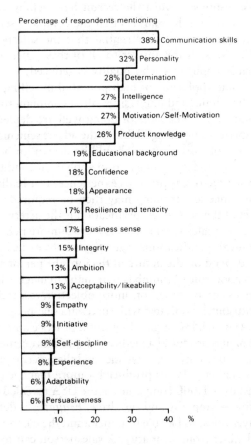

Fig 19   Important qualities in salespeople (Jobber and Millar, 1984)

Certainly, the evidence which they have provided, which groups salespersons into four categories (highly recommended, recommended, not recommended, and virtually no chance of success) according to the degree to which they possess empathy and ego drive, correlated well with sales success in three industries – cars, mutual funds and insurance. Their measures of empathy and ego drive were derived from the use of a psychological test, the multiple personal inventory, which will be discussed in the section covering psychological tests (see section 9.6.1).

In summary, a personnel specification may contain all or some of the following factors.

(*i*) Physical requirements, e.g. speech, appearance.

(*ii*) Attainments, e.g. standard of education and qualifications, experience and successes.

(*iii*) Aptitudes and qualities, e.g. ability to communicate, self-motivation.

(*iv*) Disposition, e.g. maturity, sense of responsibility.

(*v*) Interests, e.g. degree to which intereses are social, active, inactive interests.

(*vi*) Personal circumstances, e.g. married, single, etc.

The factors chosen to define the personnel specification will be used as criteria of selection in the interview itself.

9.3 IDENTIFICATION OF SOURCES OF RECRUITMENT AND METHODS OF COMMUNICATION

9.3.1 SOURCES

There are six main sources of recruitment:

(*i*) from inside – the company's own staff;

(*ii*) recruitment agencies;

(*iii*) educational establishments;

(*iv*) competitors;

(*v*) other industries;

(*vi*) unemployed.

Company's own staff

The advantage of this source is that the candidate will know the company and its products. The company will also know the candidate much more intimately than an outsider. A certain amount of risk is thereby reduced in that first-hand experience of the man's personal characteristics is available. However there is no guarantee that he has selling ability.

Recruitment agencies

Recruitment agencies will provide lists of potential recruits for a fee. In order to be entered on such a list, reputable agencies screen applicants for suitability for sales positions. It is in the long-term interests of the agencies to provide only strong candidates. The question remains, however, as to the likelihood of top salespeople needing to use agencies to find a suitable job.

Educational establishments

It is possible to recruit, straight from higher education, personnel who have, as part of their degree, worked in industry and commerce. All business study degree students in UK polytechnics have to undergo one year's industrial training. Some of these students may have worked in selling, others may have worked in marketing. The advantage of recruiting from universities and polytechnics is that the candidate is likely to be intelligent and may possess the required technical qualifications. It should be borne in mind that the applicant may not see his long-term future in selling, however. Rather, he may see a sales representative's position as a preliminary step to marketing management.

Competitors

The advantage of this source is that the salesperson knows the market and its customers, and the ability of the salesperson may be known to the recruiting company, thus reducing risk.

Other industries and unemployed

Both of these categories may provide applicants with sales experience. Obviously careful screening will need to take place in order to assess sales ability.

9.3.2 COMMUNICATION

Although some sales positions are filled as a result of personal contact, the bulk of recruitment uses advertisements as the major communication tool. Figure 20 shows how large companies attract applicants from outside the company. It is advisable to be aware of a number of principles which can improve the communication effectiveness of advertisements.

There is a wide selection of national and regional newspapers for the advertiser to consider when placing an advertisement. A major problem with such classified recruitment advertising is impact. One method of achieving impact is size. The trick here is to select the newspaper(s), check the normal size of advertisement which appears in it, then simply make your advertisement a little bigger than the largest. This should ensure a good position and its size will give the advertisement impact. This method assumes, of course, adequate funds, although compared with selecting a lower-quality salesperson, the extra cost to many companies is small.

The other component of impact is the content of the advertisement, of which the headline is the most important ingredient simply because if it does not attract and is not read then it is very unlikely that *any* of the advertisement will be read. An inspection of any Friday night regional newspaper will highlight the lack of imagination employed in designing the average sales representative recruitment advertisement. There is plenty of scope, therefore, to attract

Percentage of respondents mentioning:

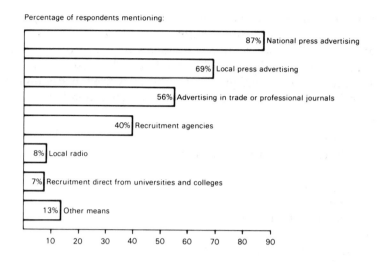

87%	National press advertising
69%	Local press advertising
56%	Advertising in trade or professional journals
40%	Recruitment agencies
8%	Local radio
7%	Recruitment direct from universities and colleges
13%	Other means

Fig 20   How companies attract applicants from outside the company (Jobber and Millar, 1984).

attention by being different. As in the case of size, look at the newspaper which is to be used and ask the question 'If I were contemplating changing jobs, what headline would attract my attention?'

Finally, if imagination is low and funds are high, it is worth considering employing a recruitment advertising specialist who will produce the advertisement and advise on media.

Whether the advertisement is produced by the company itself or by a recruitment specialist, it is important to ensure that all of the major attractions (not just features) of the job are included in the advertisement. This is necessary to attract applicants – the object of the exercise.

9.4 DESIGNING AN EFFECTIVE APPLICATION FORM AND PREPARING A SHORT-LIST

The application form is a quick and inexpensive method of screening out applicants in order to produce a short-list of candidates for interview. The questions on the form should enable the sales manager to check if the applicant is qualified vis-à-vis the personnel specification. Questions relating to age, education, previous work experience and leisure interests are often included. Besides giving such factual information, the application form also reveals defects such as the inability to spell, poor grammar or carelessness in following instructions.

The application form can reveal much about the person who is applying. Some applicants may be inveterate job-hoppers; others may have inadequate educational qualifications. Whatever the criteria, the application form will often be the initial screening device used to produce a short-list. Its careful design should, therefore, be a high priority for those involved in selection.

Four categories of information are usual on application forms.

(*i*) PERSONAL
- Name.
- Address and telephone number.
- Sex.
- Marital status.
- Children.
- Date of birth and age.

(*ii*) EDUCATION
- Schools: primary/secondary.
- Further and higher education: institutions, courses taken.
- Qualifications.
- Specialised training, e.g. apprenticeships, sales training.
- Membership of professional bodies, e.g. Institute of Marketing.

(*iii*) EMPLOYMENT HISTORY
- Companies worked for.
- Dates of employment.
- Positions, duties and responsibilities held.
- Military service.

(*iv*) OTHER INTERESTS
- Sports.
- Hobbies.
- Membership of societies/clubs.

Such an application form will achieve a number of purposes.

(*i*) To give a common basis for drawing up a short-list.
(*ii*) To provide a foundation of knowledge which can be used as the starting point for the interview.
(*iii*) To aid in the post-interview decision-making stage.

Having eliminated a number of applicants on the basis of the application form, an initial or final short-list will be drawn up depending on whether the interviewing procedure involves two or only one stage. At the same time, references will be sought for short-listed candidates.

9.5 THE INTERVIEW

The survey into the selection processes for salespeople of large UK companies (Jobber and Millar, 1984) identified a number of facts pertinent to the interview.

(*i*) Most companies (80 per cent) employ two-stage interviews.
(*ii*) In only one-fifth of the cases does the sales manager alone hold the initial interview. In the majority of cases it is the personnel manager or the personnel manager and the sales manager together who conduct the initial interview. This tends to be the case at the final interview also.
(*iii*) In 40 per cent of the cases the personnel manager and the sales manager together make the final choice, and in 37 per cent of the cases the sales manager only makes the final decision. In other cases, marketing directors and other senior management may also be involved.

These facts highlight the importance of the sales manager in the selection process and indicate that selection normally follows two interviews – the screening interview and the selection interview. Already, if he has followed the procedures described so far, he will have produced a personnel specification including some or all of the factors outlined above and repeated here for convenience.

(*i*)   Physical requirements, e.g. speech, appearance, manner fitness.
(*ii*)   Attainments, e.g. standard of education, qualifications, sales experience and successes.
(*iii*) Aptitudes and qualities, e.g. ability to communicate, empathy, self-motivation.
(*iv*)   Disposition, e.g. maturity, sense of responsibility.
(*v*)   Interests, e.g. identification of social interests, interests which are related to products which are being sold, active v. inactive interests.

The job specification will be used as a means of evaluating each of the short-listed candidates. In reality other, more personal considerations, will also play a part in the decision. A candidate which the sales manager believes would be difficult to work with or might be a troublemaker is unlikely to be employed. Thus, inevitably, the decision will be based upon a combination of formal criteria and other more personal factors which the sales manager is unable or unwilling to express at the personnel specification stage.

Having carried out the essential preparation necessary to form the basis of selection, what are the objectives and principles of interviewing? The overall objective is to enable the interviewers to form a clear and valid impression of the strengths and weaknesses of the candidates in terms of the selection criteria. In order to do this each applicant must be encouraged to talk freely and openly about himself. However, at the same time the interviewer(s) must exercise a degree of control in order that the candidate does not talk at too great length on one or two issues, leaving insufficient time for other equally important factors (possibly where the candidate is weaker) to be adequately discussed.

9.5.1 THE INTERVIEW SETTING

The interview setting will have a direct bearing on the outcome of the interview. A number of examples will illustrate this point.

(*i*) A room where the sales manager is likely to be interrupted by colleagues or telephone calls is not ideal for interviewing. If such a room has to be used, visitors and telephone calls should be barred.

(*ii*) A very large room with just two or three people occupying it may not have the intimacy required to obtain a free, natural discussion.

(*iii*) A large desk situated between candidate and interviewer, particularly if littered with filing trays and desk calendars, can have the psychological effect of distancing the two parties involved, creating too formal an atmosphere and inhibiting rapport. A more relaxed, informal setting away from the manager's work desk is likely to enable the interviewee to relax more easily. The use of a low table which interviewers and interviewee can sit around (rather than sitting face-to-face) is a common method for achieving this effect.

9.5.2 CONDUCTING THE INTERVIEW

Besides creating the right atmosphere by the judicious selection of the interview setting, the interviewers themselves can do much to help establish rapport.

What happens at the beginning of the interview is crucial to subsequent events. The objective at this stage is to set the candidate at ease. Most interviewees are naturally anxious before the interview and when they first enter the interview setting. They may feel embarrassed or be worried about exposing weaknesses; they may feel inadequate and lack confidence; and above all they may feel worried about rejection. This anxiety is compounded by the fact that the candidate may never have met his interviewers before and may thus be uncertain about how aggressive they will be, the degree of pressure which will be applied and the type of questions they are likely to ask. Some sales managers may argue that the salesperson is likely to meet this situation out in the field and therefore needs to be able to deal with it without the use of anxiety-reducing techniques on the part of the interviewers. A valid response to this viewpoint is that the objective of the interview is to get to know the candidate in terms of the criteria laid down in the personnel specification, or 'man profile' as it is sometimes called. In order to do this he must be *encouraged* to talk about himself. If sales ability under stress is to be tested, role playing can be employed as part of the selection procedure.

There are a number of guidelines which, if followed, should reduce anxiety and establish rapport.

(*i*) One of the interviewers (preferably the sales manager) should bring the candidate into the room, rather than the candidate being sent for through a secretary or junior administrator. This reduces status differentials and hence encourages rapport.

(*ii*) Open the conversation with a few easy-to-answer questions which, although not directly pertinent to the job, allow the candidate to talk to the interviewers and gain confidence.

(*iii*) Continuing in this vein, questions early in the interview should be, if possible, open-ended rather than closed. Open-ended questions allow the applicant scope for talking at some length on the topic, e.g. 'Can you tell me about your experiences selling pharmaceuticals?' Closed questions, on the other hand, invite a short answer, e.g. 'Can you tell me how long you worked for Beechams?' Some closed questions are inevitable but a series of them makes it difficult for the candidate to relax and gain confidence. Indeed, such questions may give the impression that the applicant is uncommunicative, when really the problem lies with the interviewer.

(*iv*) Interviewers should appear relaxed and adopt a friendly, easy manner.

(*v*) They should be courteous and appear interested in what the applicant says.

Having successfully established rapport and reduced anxiety, the interview will wish to encourage the candidate to talk about himself, his experiences, attitudes, behaviour and expectations. To do this the interviewer not only needs to develop the art of being a good listener but also needs to develop skills in making people talk. The skills required in the needs analysis stage of the selling process discussed in Chapter 4 may be used in an interview to good effect. Specifically, the interviewer can use the following techniques:

(*i*) the 'playback' technique;
(*ii*) the use of rewards;
(*iii*) the use of silence;
(*iv*) the use of probes;
(*v*) summarising.
(*vi*) the use of neutral questions.

The 'playback' technique

The interviewer repeats the last few words of the candidate's sentence in order to elicit the reason for what has been said. For example, the candidate might say 'I worked for XYZ Company for two years, but I didn't like it very much.' The interviewer follows with 'You didn't like it very much?' Candidate: 'No, the sales manager was always on my back, checking to see that I was making my calls.'

Use of rewards

Obvious interest in the candidate's views, experiences and knowledge shown by the interviewer confers its own reward. This can be supplemented by what can only be described as encouraging noises such as 'Uh uh' or 'Mmm, yes, I see.' The confidence which is instilled in the candidate will encourage further comment and, perhaps, revelations.

A further method of reward is through 'eye behaviour'. The subtle narrowing of the eyes, together with a slight nodding of the head can convey the message 'Yes, I see.' The correct use of such rewards comes only with experience, but their application is undoubtedly an aid in encouraging the candidate to talk freely.

The use of silence

Silence can be a very powerful ally of the interviewer. However, silence must be used with discretion, otherwise rapport may be lost and the candidate may raise his barriers to open expression.

Its most common use is after the candidate has given a neutral, uninformative reply to an important question. A candidate, eager to impress, will feel uncomfortable, interpreting silence as an indication that the interview is not going well. In such a situation he will normally attempt to fill the void, and it may be that the only way he can do this is by revealing attitudes or behaviour patterns which otherwise he would have been happy to have kept hidden. Alternatively, the pause may allow the candidate to formulate his thoughts and thus stimulate a more considered reply. Continuing with a follow-up question without a pause would have precluded this happening. Either way, extra potentially revealing information can be collected by the discriminate use of silence.

The use of probes

The salesperson who is adept at needs analysis will be well acquainted with the use of probes. In an interview, comments will be made which require further explanation. For example, the applicant might say 'The time I spent on a sales training course was a waste of time', to which the interviewer might say 'Why do you think that was?' or 'That's interesting, why do you say that?' or 'Can you explain a little more why you think that?' Such phrases are to be preferred to the blunt 'Why?' and are really alternatives to the 'playback' technique mentioned earlier.

A choice of phrases and techniques allows the interviewer to vary his approach to probing during the course of the interview. Although it may not always be possible to guarantee, probing of particularly embarrassing events such as the break up of an applicant's marriage (if thought relevant to job performance) or failure in examinations, should be left until the interview is well under way and should certainly not be the subject of scrutiny at the strart of the interview.

Summarising

During an interview, the interviewer will inevitably be attempting to draw together points which have been made by the applicant at various times during the interview in order to come to some opinion about the person under scrutiny. A useful device for checking if these impressions are valid in the subject's eyes is to summarise them and ask for corroboration.

After a period of questioning and probing the interviewer might say 'So, as

I understand it, your first period in sales was not a success because the firm you worked for produced poor quality products, inferior in terms of technical specifications compared to competition and you felt inexperienced, but your second job, working with a larger, more well-known company, was more satisfactory, having received proper sales training and having the advantage of selling a recognised high-quality product line. Would you say that this was a fair summary?' Having obtained agreement, the interviewer can then move to another area of interest or continue to investigate the same area with the certainty that there has been no earlier misunderstanding.

The use of neutral questions

A basic principle of good interviewing is to use neutral rather than leading questions. The question, 'Can you tell me about the sales training you received at your previous employer?' is likely to lead to rather different, less biased responses than 'I'm sure you learnt a lot from your sales training courses, didn't you?' Again, 'What do you feel about dealing with the type of customer we have?' is more neutral than 'I'm sure you wouldn't have any problems dealing with our customers, would you?'

Other considerations

There are other considerations which an interviewer is wise to bear in mind. First, he must not talk too much. The object is for most of the time spent interviewing to be used to evaluate the candidates. Second, part of the interview will be a selling task in order to ensure that the chosen applicant accepts. The balance between evaluation and selling is largely based upon judgment, and no hard and fast rules apply, but obviously the competitive situation and the strength of the candidate will be two factors which affect the decision.

Third, the interviewer must discreetly control the interview. A certain amount of time will be allocated to each candidate and it is the interviewers' responsibility to ensure that all salient dimensions of the candidate are covered, not only those about which the candidate wishes to talk. Some of the earlier techniques, used in reverse, may be necessary to discourage the candidate from rambling on. For example, the interviewer may look disinterested, or ask a few closed questions to discourage verbosity. Alternatively, the interviewer can simply interrupt with 'That's fine. I think we're quite clear on that point now,' at an appropriate moment.

Finally, the interviewer will need to close the interview when sufficient information has been obtained. Usually, the candidate is forewarned of this by the interviewer saying 'O.K., we've asked you about yourself, are there any questions you would like to ask me (us)?' At the end of this session, the interviewer explains when the decision will be made and how it will be communicated to the candidate and then thanks him for attending the interview. They both stand, shake hands and the candidate is shown to the door.

9.6 SUPPLEMENTARY SELECTION AIDS

9.6.1 PSYCHOLOGICAL TESTS

Although success at the interview is always an important determinant of selection, some firms employ supplementary techniques to provide a valid measure of potential. A number of large firms use psychological tests in this way. However, care has to be taken when using these tests and a trained psychologist is usually needed to administer and interpret the results. Further, there are a number of criticisms which have been levelled at the tests.

(*i*) It is easy to cheat. The applicant, having an idea of the type of person who is likely to be successful at selling, does not respond truly but 'fakes' the test in order to give a 'correct' profile. For example, in response to a question such as 'Who is of more value to society – the practical man or the thinker?' he answers 'the practical man' no matter what his true convictions may be.

(*ii*) Many tests measure interest rather than sales ability. The sales manager knows the interests of its successful salespeople and uses tests to discover if potential new recruits have similar interest patterns. The assumption here is that sales success can be predicted by the type of interests which a person has. This is as unlikely as discovering a new George Best by measuring the interests of young footballers.

(*iii*) Tests have been used to identify individual personality traits which may not be associated with sales success. Factors such as how sociable, dominant, friendly and loyal a person is have been measured in order to predict sales success. While some of these factors may be useful attributes for a salesperson to possess, they have failed to distinguish between high- and low-performing sales personnel.

Earlier in the chapter, reference was made to the use of the multiple personal inventory in order to predict the degrees of empathy and ego drive which a person possesses. Mayer and Greenberg have shown that sales success can be reasonably accurately predicted once these characteristics are known. The ideal is a person who possesses a high degree of both. A high degree of empathy (an ability to feel as the customer feels) and ego drive (the need to make a sale in a personal way) are usually associated with high sales performance. Plenty of empathy but little ego drive means that the salesperson is liked by his customers but sales are not made because of an inability to close the sale purposefully. A person with little empathy but much drive will tend to bulldoze his way through a sale without considering the individual needs of his customers. Finally, the person with little empathy and ego drive will be a complete failure. Too many salespeople, say Mayer and Greenberg, fall into this last group.

The test itself – the multiple personal inventory – is based on the forced choice technique. The subject picks those statements which are most like and least like himself from a choice of four. Two of these statements may be termed favourable and the other two unfavourable. Mayer and Greenberg claim that the test is difficult to fake, since the two favourable statements are chosen to be equally favourable and the two unfavourable ones are equally unfavourable. The subject, then, is likely to be truthful. Since it is very difficult to produce statements which are *equally* favourable or unfavourable, the cautious conclusion is that the forced choice technique minimises cheating rather than completely eliminating it. The test also overcomes the criticism that psychological tests measure personality traits which may not be correlated with performance. Mayer and Greenberg describe empathy and ego drive as the 'central dynamics' of sales ability and produce evidence that scores on these characteristics correlate well with performance in the car, insurance and mutual funds fields.

If the multiple personal inventory, or any other psychological test, is to be used as a basis for selection of sales personnel, a sensible procedure would be to validate the test beforehand. Research has shown that other personality tests correlate with performance and that different types of people do well in different selling situations. Randall (1975), for example, has shown that the type of person who was most successful selling tyres could be summarised as a 'grey man'. His characteristics were those of a humble, shy, tender-minded person of below-average intelligence, quite unlike the stereotyped extrovert, happy-go-lucky, fast-talking salesperson. The explanation of why such a person was successful was to be found in the selling situation. Being in the position of selling a brand of tyre that was not widely advertised and that had only a small market share, the salesperson had to hang around tyre depots hoping to make sales by solving some of the supply problems of the depot manager in meeting urgent orders. He was able to do this because his company provided a quicker service than many of its competitors. Thus, the personality of the man had to be such that he was prepared to wait around the depot merging into the background, rather than by using persuasive selling techniques.

This rather extreme example demonstrates how varied the sales situation can be. Contrast that situation with the skills and personality required to sell hi-fi equipment, and it becomes immediately apparent that successful selection should focus on matching particular types of people to particular types of selling occupations. Indeed Greenberg, since his earlier study, does seem to have moved position and recognised that successful selling depends on other personality dynamics 'which come into play depending on the specific sales situation' (Greenberg and Greenberg, 1976). Consequently different psychological tests may be required for different situations.

Validation requires the identification of the psychological test or tests which best distinguish between a company's above-average and below-average existing salespeople. Further validation would test how the predictions made by the test results correlate with performance of new recruits. Recent research has cast doubts on the general applicability of the empathy/ego drive theory of sales success, but certainly the multiple personal inventory could be one psychological test used in this validation exercise, although it must be carried out under the supervision of a psychologist.

Finally, it must be stressed that the proper place of psychological tests is alongside the interview, as a basis for selection, rather than in place of it.

9.6.2 ROLE PLAYING

Another aid in the selectoin of salespeople is the use of role playing in order to gauge the selling potential of candidates. This involves placing them individually in selling situations and assessing how well they perform.

The problem with this technique is that, at best, it measures sales ability at that moment. This may depend, among other things, on previous sales experience. Correct assessment of salespeople, however, should be measuring *potential*. Further, role playing cannot assess the candidate's ability to establish and handle long-term relationships with buyers and so is more applicable to those selling jobs where the salesperson/buyer relationship is likely to be short-term, and the sale a one-off. Role playing may, however, be valuable in identifying the 'hopeless case', whose personal characteristics, e.g. an inability to communicate or to keep his temper under stress, may preclude him from successful selling.

9.7 CONCLUSIONS

The selection of salespeople, while of obvious importance to the long-term future of the business, is a task which does not always receive the attention it should from sales managers. All too often, the 'man profile' is ill-defined and the selection procedure designed for maximum convenience rather than optimal choice. The assumption is that the right man should emerge whatever procedure is used. Consequently the interview is poorly handled, the smooth talker gets the job, and another mediocre salesperson emerges.

This chapter has outlined a number of techniques which, if applied, should minimise this result. Specifically, a sales manager should decide on the requirements of the job and the type of person who should be able to fulfil them. He or she should also be aware of the techniques of interviewing and the necessity of evaluating the candidates, in line with the criteria established during the personnel specification stage. Finally, he should consider the use of psychological tests (under the guidance of a psychologist) and role playing as further dimensions of the assessment procedure.

The next chapter examines two further key areas of sales management, motivation and training.

PRACTICAL EXERCISE – PLASTIC PRODUCTS LTD

Plastic Products Ltd is a company that produces and markets plastic cups, tea spoons, knives and forks for the catering industry. The company was established in 1974 in response to the changes taking place in the catering industry. The growth of the fast-food sector of the market was seen as an opportunity to provide disposable eating utensils which would save on manpower and allow the speedy provision of utensils for fast customer flow. In addition, Plastic Products has benefited from the growth in supermarkets and sells 'consumer packs' through four of the large supermarket groups.

The expansion of sales and outlets has led Jim Spencer, the sales manager, to recommend to Bill Preedy, the general manager, that the present sales force of two regional representatives be increased to four.

Spencer believes that the new recruits should have experience of selling fast-moving consumer goods since essentially that is what his products are.

Preedy believes that the new recruits should be familiar with plastic products since that is what they are selling. He favours recruiting from within the plastics industry, since such people are familiar with the supply, production and properties of plastic and are likely to talk the same language as other people working at the firm.

Discussion questions

1 What general factors should be taken into account when recruiting salesmen?
2 Do you agree with Spencer or Preedy or neither?

EXAMINATION QUESTIONS

1 Distinguish between the job description and the personnel specification. For an industry of your choice, write a suitable job description and personnel specification for a salesperson.
2 Discuss the role of psychological testing in the selection process for salespeople.

10 Motivation and Training

10.1 MOTIVATION

Creating and maintaining a well-motivated sales force is a challenging task. The confidence and motivation of salespeople are being constantly worn down by the inevitable rejections they suffer from buyers as part of everyday activities. In some fields, notably life insurance and double glazing, rejections may greatly outnumber successes; thus motivation may be a major problem. This is compounded by the fact that salesperson and supervisor are normally geographically separated, so that the salesperson may feel isolated, even neglected, unless management pays particular attention to motivational strategies which take account of his and her needs.

An understanding of motivation lies in the relationship between needs, drives and goals. 'The basic process involves needs (deprivations) which set drives in motion (deprivations with direction) to accomplish goals (anything which alleviates a need and reduces a drive)' (Luthans, 1981). Thus a need, resulting from a lack of friends, sets up a drive for affiliation which is designed to obtain friends. In a work context, the need for more money may result in a drive to work harder in order to obtain increased pay.

In this chapter both applied theory and practice will be evaluated in order to identify the means of motivating a sales force.

10.1.1 MOTIVATIONAL THEORIES

Motivation has been researched by psychologists and others for many years. A number of theories have evolved which are pertinent to the motivation of salespeople. These are the theories of Maslow (1943), Herzberg *et al.* (1959), Vroom (1964) and Likert (1961).

Maslow's hierarchy of needs

Maslow's classic hierarchy of needs model proposed that there are five fundamental needs which are arranged in a 'hierarchy of prepotency'. Table 4 shows this hierarchy.

Table 4. *Maslow's hierarchy of needs*

Category	Type	Characteristics
Physical	1 Physiological	The fundamentals of survival, e.g. hunger, thirst
	2 Safety	Protection from the unpredictable happenings in life, e.g. accidents, ill health
Social	3 Belongingness and love	Striving to be accepted by those to whom we feel close (especially one's family) and to be an important person to them
	4 Esteem and status	Striving to achieve a high standing relative to other people; a desire for prestige and a high reputation
Self	5 Self actualisation	The desire for self-fulfilment in achieving what one is capable of for one's own sake − 'Actualised in what he is potentially' (Maslow)

Maslow argued that needs form a hierarchy in the sense that, when no needs are fulfilled, a person concentrates upon his physiological needs. When these needs are fulfilled, safety needs become preponderant and become important determinants of behaviour. When these are satisfied, belongingness becomes important − and so on up the hierarchy.

Although Maslow's belief, that one set of needs only becomes important after lower order needs have been completely satisfied, has been criticised, the theory does have relevance to sales force motivation. First, it highlights the perhaps obvious point that a satisfied need is not a motivator of behaviour. Thus, for a salesperson who already receives a more than adequate level of remuneration, additional payments may have no effect on motivation. Second, the theory implies that what may act as a motivator for one salesperson may not be effective with another. This follows from the likelihood that different salespeople will have different combinations of needs.

Effective motivation results from an accurate assessment of the needs of the individual salespeople under the manager's supervision. The overriding need for one salesperson may be reassurance and the building of confidence; this may act to motivate him. For another, with a great need for esteem but a problem regarding work rate, the sales manager may motivate by displaying to his colleagues at a sales meeting his relatively poor sales performance.

Herzberg

Herzberg distinguished factors which can cause dissatisfaction but cannot motivate (hygiene factors) and factors which can cause positive motivation. Hygiene factors included physical working conditions, security, salary and interpersonal relationships. Directing managerial attention to these factors, postulated Herzberg, would bring motivation up to a 'theoretical zero' but would not result in positive motivation. If this was to be achieved, attention would have to be given to true motivators. These included the nature of the work itself which allows the person to make some concrete *achievement, recognition* of achievement, the *responsibility* exercised by the person, and the *interest value* of the work itself.

The inclusion of salary as a hygiene factor rather than as a motivator was subject to criticisms from sales managers whose experience led them to believe that commission paid to their salespeople was a powerful motivator in practice. Herzberg accommodated their view to some extent by arguing that increased salary through higher commission was a motivator through the automatic recognition it gave to sales achievement.

The salesperson is fortunate that achievement is directly observable in terms of higher sales (except in missionary selling, where orders are not taken, e.g. pharmaceuticals, beer and selling to specifiers). However the degree of responsibility afforded to salespeople varies a great deal. Opportunities for giving a greater degree of responsibility to (and hence motivating) salespeople include giving authority to grant credit (up to a certain value), discretion to offer discounts, and handing over responsibility for calling frequencies to the salespeople. The results of an experiment with a group of British salespeople by Paul, Robertson and Herzberg (1969) showed that greater responsibility given to salesmen by such changes resulted in higher sales success.

Herzberg's theory has been well received, in general, by practitioners, although academics have criticised it in terms of methodology and oversimplification (see Dessler, 1979). The theory has undoubtedly made a substantial contribution to the understanding of motivation at work, particularly in extending Maslow's theory to the work situation, and highlighting the importance of job content factors which had hitherto been badly neglected.

Vroom's expectancy theory

Basically this theory assumes that a person's motivation to exert effort is dependent upon his expectations for success. Vroom (1964) based his theory on three concepts – expectancy, instrumentality and valence.

(*i*) EXPECTANCY. This refers to a person's perceived relationship between effort and performance, i.e. to the extent to which a person believes that increased effort will lead to higher performance.

(*ii*) INSTRUMENTALITY. This reflects the person's perception of the relationship between performance and reward; for example, it reflects the extent to which a person believes that higher performance will lead to promotion.

(*iii*) VALENCE. This represents the value placed upon a particular reward by a person. For some individuals promotion may be highly valued, for others it may have little value.

Thus, according to the theory, if a salesperson believes that by working harder he or she will achieve increased sales (high expectancy), and that higher sales will lead to greater commission (high instrumentality) and higher commission is very important (high valence), a high level of motivation should result. The nature of the relationships in the sales setting are depicted in Fig. 21.

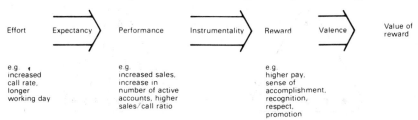

Fig 21   The Vroom expectancy theory of motivation.

Clearly, different salespeople will have different valences (values) for the same reward. Some might value increased pay very highly, while for others higher pay may have less value; for some the sense of accomplishment and recognition may be very important, for others much less so. Also, different salespeople may view the relationship between performance and reward, and between effort and performance in quite different ways. A task of sales management is to specify and communicate to the sales force these performance criteria, which are important in helping to achieve company objectives, and to relate rewards to these criteria. Further, this theory supports the notion that performance targets, e.g. sales quotas, to be effective motivators, should be regarded as attainable (high expectancy) by each salesperson, otherwise the first link in the expectancy model will be severed. Finally, this model provides a diagnostic framework for analysing motivational problems with individual salespeople and provides an explanation of why certain managerial activities can improve motivation. Training in sales skills, for example, can improve motivation by raising expectancy levels.

Likert

Unlike Herzberg, Maslow and Vroom, who developed 'general' theories of motivation, Likert (1961) based his theories on research which looked specifically at salesmen's motivation. His research related differing characteristics and styles of supervision to performance. One of the hypotheses he tested was that the sales managers' own behaviour provides a set of standards which, in themselves, will affect the behaviour of their salespeople. He found that there was a link. High performing sales teams usually had sales managers who themselves had high performance goals.

His research also investigated the methods used by sales managers in the running of sales meetings. Two alternative styles were compared (see Fig. 22). Sales managers who used the group method of leading sales meetings encouraged their team both to discuss sales problems which had arisen in the field and to learn from one another. Sales managers who monopolised the meeting discouraged interaction between salespeople and used the meeting as an opportunity to lecture them rather than to stimulate discussion. There was a strong tendency for higher-producing sales teams to use the group method.

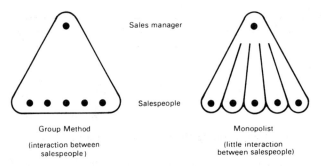

Fig 22   Methods of conducting sales meetings.

Several reasons can be put forward to explain this. First, it is likely that a problem faced by one salesperson has been met previously by another who may have found a way of overcoming it; for example, a troublesome objection to one salesperson may have been successfully dealt with by another. The group method of leading a sales meeting, then, encourages problem-solving and stimulates communication. Second, the more open style of meeting enables the sales manager to gain a greater understanding of the needs and problems of his sales force. Finally, the group method promotes a feeling of group loyalty since it fosters a spirit of cooperation.

The research conducted by Likert, then, suggests that, to produce a highly motivated sales force, the sales manager himself should have high performance goals and encourage analysis and discussion of salespeople's performance and problems through the group method of conducting sales meetings.

10.1.2 MOTIVATION IN PRACTICE

A study into sales force practice commissioned by the Institute of Marketing (PA Consultants, 1979) asked sales managers to rank eight factors (excluding salary, bonus or commission) which could be effective in stimulating their salespeople to better their usual performance. The results of this research are given in Fig. 23.

Figure 23 illustrates the importance of the manager/salesperson relationship in motiviation. Individual meetings between sales manager and salesperson were thought to be the most effective of the eight factors investigated. Sales contests and competitions were ranked only sixth in importance, although a more detailed

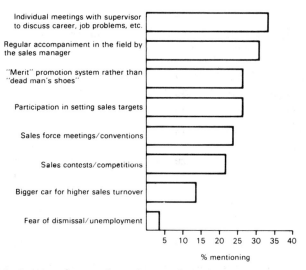

Fig 23   Motivating factors for salespeople.

analysis of the answers revealed that this form of motivation was ranked first among the consumer goods companies replying to the questionnaire.

More recent surveys by Shipley and Kiely (1988) and Coulaux and Jobber (1989) investigated factors which motivated industrial and consumer goods salespeople. In both surveys self-satisfaction from doing a good job was ranked as the top motivator; achieving targets and acknowledgement of effort were also highly ranked by both industrial and consumer salespeople. However, a major difference was the factor 'satisfy customer needs' with industrial salespeople ranking it second while their consumer counterparts ranked it only sixth. The difference between industrial and consumer products and customers probably explains the discrepancy with the former selling more technical products to customers with more complex needs (see Fig. 24 overleaf).

Some of these factors, along with financial incentives, will now be evaluated in terms of their potential to motivate.

Financial incentives

Most companies, whether they be selling consumer or industrial goods, pay commission or bonus to their salespeople. The most usual form of payment is the salary plus commission system since this provides a level of security plus the incentive of higher earnings for higher sales. However, in some instances salespeople are paid on a straight commission basis so that earnings are entirely dependent upon achievement.

There are a number of variants of the commission system, each depending on the outcome of the following decisions (Kotler, 1980).

(*i*) The commission base, e.g. sales revenue, or profits.

	Industrial			Consumer		
	Extremely strong	Moderately strong	Ranking[a]	Extremely strong	Moderately strong	Ranking[a]
Self-satisfaction from doing a good job	75	24	1	75	21	1
Satisfy customer needs	51	39	2	36	46	6
Achieve sales budgets	35	46	3	58	35	2
Acknowledgement of effort	36	43	3	50	37	4
Increase chance of promotion	89	29	5	58	31	3
Improve lifestyle	34	35	6	42	33	6
Meet family responsibilities	40	22	6	44	25	8
Make more money	38	22	7	46	33	5
Satisfy sales managers' expectations	24	32	8	29	35	9

Note: [a] Note that the ranking is based on the sum of responses to extremely strong and moderately strong motivator with double weighting to the former category.

Sources: Industrial – Shipley and Kiely 1988, Consumer – Coulaux and Jobber 1989

Fig 24   Motivational factors for salespeople in industrial and consumer goods markets.

(ii) The commission rate, e.g. a set percentage of all sales or different for various products.

(iii) The starting point for commission, e.g. the first sale, or at some predetermined sales level.

A commission system may thus comprise a given percentage, e.g. 1½ per cent of total sales revenue generated per salesperson, or a percentage, e.g. 5 per cent of sales revenue for all sales in excess of a sales quota. Some companies may construct more complicated commission systems whereby different products have varying commission rates. Higher rates may be paid on higher profit items, lines which are regarded as being harder to sell or products with high inventory levels. Thus the commission system can be used not only to stimulate greater effort in general but also to direct salespeople towards expending greater energy on those products the company particularly wants to sell.

Commission may work in motivating salespeople through providing a direct reward for extra effort (Vroom) and by giving recognition for achievement (Herzberg).

Setting sales targets or quotas

If a sales target or quota is to be effective in motivating a salesperson it must be regarded as fair and attainable and yet offer a challenge to him. Because the salesperson should regard the quota as fair, it is usually sensible to allow him to participate in the setting of the quota. However, the establishment of the quotas is ultimately the sales manager's responsibility and he will inevitably be constrained by overall company objectives. If sales are planned to increase by 10 per cent, then salespeople's quotas must be consistent with this. Variations around this average figure will arise through the sales manager's knowledge of individual sales personnel and changes in commercial activity within each territory; for example, the liquidation of a key customer in a territory may be reflected in a reduced quota. The attainment of a sales target usually results in some form of extra payment to the salesperson.

Meetings between manager and salespeople

These were highly regarded by sales managers in the motivation of their sales teams. Managers have the opportunity to meet their salespeople in the field, at head office and at sales meetings/conventions. They provide a number of opportunities for improving motivation.

First, they alllow the sales manager to understand the personality, needs and problems of each salesperson. The manager can then better understand the causes of demotivation in individual salespeople and respond in a manner which takes into account the needs, problems and personality of the salesperson. Second, meetings in the field, which may form part of an evaluation and training programme, can also provide an opportunity to motivate. Sales technique can be improved and confidence boosted, both of which may motivate by restoring in the salesperson the belief that performance will improve through extra effort. Third, group meetings can motivate, according to Likert, when the sales manager encourages an 'open' style of meeting. Salespeople are encouraged to discuss their sales problems and opportunities so that the entire sales team benefits from the experiences of each salesperson. This leads to a greater sense of group loyalty and improved performance. Finally, meetings between manager and salespeople provide the opportunity for performance feedback where weaknesses are identified and recognition for good work is given.

The study by Coulaux and Jobber (1989) found that almost half their sample of consumer salespeople wanted more meetings with their sales managers. Table 5 shows the topics which they would most like to discuss. Three-quarters of the salespeople said that they would like more opportunity to analyse job problems and try to find a solution with their sales managers. Sales targets were second on the list of issues which they would like to discuss.

The work by Herzberg highlights the importance of recognition as a positive motivator and Maslow suggests that many people have a need to be accepted. Thus what sales managers say to their salespeople can have both motivational and demotivational effects, by giving and/or taking away recognition and acceptance. Giving recognition and acceptance (by a pat on the back or praise for example) are called *positive strokes* and can act as a motivator, withdrawing recognition and acceptance (for example by criticising or ignoring the person)

Table 5. *Topics salespeople would like to discuss more with their sales managers.*

Matters	%
Analyse job problems and try to find solutions together	75
Sales targets	70
Job problems	68
Promotion	45
Job career	45
Remuneration	22
Review performance together	30
Personal problems	22

are called *negative strokes* and can act as both a motivator, or a demotivator depending on the circumstances. Such withdrawal can motivate when the salesperson is underperforming through lack of effort and that person has a strong desire for recognition and acceptance. However many managers can demotivate almost unknowingly by what they say and do. Outside factors such as domestic problems may cause managers to give out negative strokes to people who do not deserve them. Under such circumstances they can have a demotivational effect. Figure 25 gives a few examples.

Strokes	Physical contact	Psychological
Positive	Handshake Pat on the back	Praise, Smile, Appreciative glance
Negative	Push Slap	Criticism, Ridicule, Ignore, Sideways glance, Frown

Fig 25   Positive and negative strokes.

Promotion

Sales managers believe that a merit-based promotional system does act as a motivator. If the promotion is to a managerial position, there are grave dangers of promoting the company's best salesperson. The skills required of a sales manager are wider than those required of a salesperson. A sales manager must be able to analyse and control the performance of others, motivate and train them. These are skills which are not required to sell successfully.

If promotion is to be tied to sales performance, it is sensible to consider the creation of a dual promotional route. The first path follows the normal managerial career sequence. The other is created to reward outstanding sales success. An example of such a merit-based promotional ladder is:

Salesman   →   Senior Salesman   →   National Account Executive

Sales contests

Sales contest are a popular form of incentive for consumer sales forces. The purpose of the sales contest varies widely. It may be to encourage a higher level of sales in general, to increase the sales of a slow-moving product or to reward the generation of new customers. The strength of a sales contest lies in its ability to appeal to the competitive spirit of salespeople and to their need for achievement and recognition. As with other financial incentives, to be effective the contest must be seen to be fair and each salesperson must believe that he is capable of winning.

However, problems can occur. Contests can encourage cheating. In one company which used a sales contest to promote sales at a series of promotional events around the country with its dealers, salespeople 'stored up' orders achieved prior to the events in order to increase the apparent number of orders taken at the events. Also, contests, by pitching salesperson against salesperson, militate against the spirit of mutual help and cooperation which can improve sales force performance.

10.2 TRAINING

A recent study for the Learning International Organisation (1988) revealed seven sales challenges that organisations must meet in the 1990s if they are going to survive in the competitive marketplace:

(*i*) DISTINGUISH BETWEEN SIMILAR PRODUCTS AND SERVICES. Success in sales requires more than just having an exceptional product or service. The proliferation of 'me too' products is causing buyers to become confused. Excellent salespeople are needed to capitalise on the product differences that their offerings are better than the competitor's.

(*ii*) PUTTING TOGETHER GROUPS OF PRODUCTS TO FORM A BUSINESS SOLUTION. As customers requirements are continually becoming more complex, single product or service selling is becoming obsolete. Their needs can only be met by a 'package' of products or services. The salesperson will have to be highly trained to put together a package to satisfy these needs.

(*iii*) HANDLING THE MORE EDUCATED BUYING POPULATION. Today's customers are willing to work harder and take the time to shop around for what they need. They are also more aware of the product features, benefits, options and prices. Today's professional salesperson must thus work harder to close the sale.

(*iv*) MASTERING THE ART OF CONSULTATIVE SELLING. The salesperson now needs to understand the specific business issues and problems faced by customers. His role is to lessen the customers responsibility to discover their own needs, and show how the product and service being offered will fill these needs.

(v) MANAGING A TEAM SELLING APPROACH. In the future a team selling approach will have to be adopted to satisfy customer needs. The salesperson will have to draw on knowledge of technical staff, marketing staff, and experts in other product areas.

(vi) KNOWING THE CUSTOMERS' BUSINESS. Future sales will require in depth knowledge of the customer's business, with salespeople well-versed in the requirements of the market segment in which they sell. Relationship building with the customer is paramount and the customers' best interests are always placed at the forefront. Accurate marketing information is needed to provide each customer with the best possible service.

(vii) ADDING VALUE THROUGH SERVICE. When a product reaches a commodity status the salesperson's perceived value is diminished. They are reduced to 'order takers'. Companies must continue to build up their relationship with customers by adding value through services such as business consultations and on-going product support.

These challenges assume even greater importance with the prospect of a single European Market in 1992. For the first time there will be easy access to the European markets. Thus competition will increase, and it is only companies who are prepared to meet these challenges that will survive.

Producing the best available product or service is not enough; it has to be sold. If companies are to survive they must attach the utmost importance to training their field salesforce, not just pay lip service to the concept. Top management must be totally committed to training and authorise sufficient investment for this to occur. They must also accept that the benefits deriving from sales training may not be immediate; they take time to show through.

On the whole, insufficient attention is paid to training. Presumably it is believed that salespeople will learn the necessary skills on the job. This approach ignores the benefits of a training programme which builds a reference frame within which learning can occur and provides the opportunity to practise skills with feedback which is necessary to identify the strengths and weaknesses of performance. For training to succeed the salesperson must accept that there is a problem with his performance, otherwise he is unlikely to attempt to rectify the problem.

Another approach to the training problem of new salespeople is to send them out with an experienced salesperson to observe how selling is done. This, in itself, is insufficient for successful sales training. Its virtues are that the trainee may gain insights not only into techniques which appear to be successful in selling, for example, certain closing techniques, but also into the kinds of objections which are raised by buyers. However, its value is greatly enhanced if supplemented by a formal sales training programme conducted by an experienced sales trainer who is himself skilled in lecturing, handling role-playing sessions and providing constructive feedback in such a way that it is accepted by the trainee.

10.2.1 SKILL DEVELOPMENT

There are four classic stages to learning a skill. These are shown in Table 6.

Table 6. *Skills development*

Stage	Description
1 Unconsciously unable	Trainee does not think about skills
2 Consciously unable	Trainee reads about skills but cannot carry them out in practice
3 Consciously able	Trainee knows what to do and is reasonably proficient in individual skills but has difficulty putting them all into practice together
4 Unconsciously able	Trainee can perform the task without thinking about it; skills become automatic

The first stage defines the situation before a trainee decides to enter a career in selling. He is unable to carry out the skills and has not even thought about them. By reading or being told about the skills involved he reaches the stage of being consciously unable. He knows what he is supposed to do but cannot successfully perform any of the skills.

At the next stage (consciously able) the trainee not only knows what to do but is reasonably proficient at putting the skills into practice individually. He is like a learner driver who can engage gear, release the clutch, look in the mirror, gently press the accelerator and release the handbrake as a series of separate operations, but not in a coordinated manner which successfully moves the car from a standing start. The trainee may be able to make a presentation successfully, to handle objections and to close a sale, but he may be hopelessly adrift when he needs to handle objections, continue making the presentation and all the while look for signs to close the sale.

A successful training programme takes the trainee through this difficult barrier to the final stage (unconsciously able) when he can perform all of the skills at once and has the ability to think a stage in advance so that he has control of the selling situation. A car driver reaches this stage when he can coordinate the skills necessary to start, move and stop a car without thinking; the timing of gear changes and braking, for example, become automatic, without conscious thought. Similarly, the salesperson can open the interview, move through the stages of need identification, presentation and handling objections in a natural manner, and can alter his approach as situations demand, before choosing the right moment and most appropriate technique to close the sale.

When a salesperson becomes unconsciously able he or she is likely to be a competent salesperson although, like a driver, football player or cricketer, there will always be room for further improvement and refinement of his skills.

10.2.2 COMPONENTS OF A TRAINING PROGRAMME

A training programme will attempt to cover a combination of knowledge and skill development. Five components can be identified.

(*i*) The company – objectives, policies and organisation.
(*ii*) Its products.
(*iii*) Its competitors and their products.
(*iv*) Selling procedure and techniques.
(*v*) Work organisation and report preparation.

The first three components are essentially communicating the required level of knowledge to the salesperson. The first component will probably include a brief history of the company, how it has grown and where it intends to go in the future. Policies relevant to the selling function, for example how salespeople are evaluated, and the nature of the compensation system will be explained. The way in which the company is organised will be described and the relationship between sales and the marketing function, including advertising and market research, will be described so that the salesperson has an appreciation of the support he is receiving from headquarters.

The second component, product knowledge, will include a description of how the products are made and the implications for product quality and reliability, the features of the product and the benefits they confer on the consumer. Salespeople will be encouraged to carry out their own product analyses so that they will be able to identify key features and benefits of new products as they are launched. Competitors will be identified and competitors' products will also be analysed to spotlight differences between them and the company's products.

Some training programmes, particularly within the industrial selling area, stop here, neglecting a major component of a training programme – selling procedures and techniques. This component involves an examination of the factors analysed in Chapter 5 and will include practical sessions where trainees develop skills through role-playing exercises.

The final component of the programme – work organisation and report writing – will endeavour to establish good habits among the trainees in areas which, because of day-to-day pressures, may be neglected. The importance of these activities on a salesperson's performance and, hence, earnings will be stressed.

10.2.3 METHODS

The lecture

This method is useful in giving information and providing a frame of reference to aid the learning process. The lecture should be supported by the use of visual aids, for example, professionally produced overhead projector transparencies.

Trainees should be encouraged to participate so that the communication is not just one way. Discussion stimulates interest and allows misunderstandings to be identified and dealt with.

Films

These are a useful supplement to the lecture in giving information and showing how a skill should be performed. They add an extra dimension to a lecture by demonstrating how the principles can be applied in a selling situation. In terms of the stages of learning skills, lecture and films take the trainee up to the point of being consciously unable. They will show him what he is required to do, but he will lack the experience to put the theory into practice successfully.

Role-playing

This learning method moves the trainee into the stage of being consciously able to perform a skill. It allows the trainee to learn by his own successes and failures in a buyer-seller situation. Feedback is provided by other group members, the sales trainer and by audio-visual means.

Seeing oneself perform is an enlightening and rewarding experience and can demonstrate to the trainee the points raised by other members of the group. Without this dimension some trainees may refuse to accept a fault, for example, losing the buyer's interest, simply because in the heat of the selling discussion they genuinely do not notice it. Playback allows the trainee to see the situation through the eyes of a third person, and problems are more easily recognised and accepted.

Role-playing has its critics. Some say that trainees do not take it seriously enough and that by its very nature it is not totally realistic. Its main value is in teaching inexperienced salespeople the basic skills of selling in a less threatening environment than real selling. The selling process can be broken up into a series of activities, e.g. opening and need identification, sales presentation and overcoming objections, each of which requires a special set of skills. Role-playing can be used to develop each set of skills in a series of exercises which gradually build up to a full sales interview. A role-playing exercise designed to develop skills in need identification is given at the end of Chapter 5.

The degree of success achieved by role-playing is heavily dependent upon the skills of the sales trainer. When the trainees have at least a modicum of sales experience, it is good practice to allow them to devise their own sales situations based upon actual experiences. The briefs so produced are then exchanged between trainees so that each is presented with a situation which is new to them but which, at the same time, is realistic (Wilson, 1983).

Case studies

Case studies are particularly appropriate for developing analytical skills. Trainees are asked to analyse situations, identify problems and opportunities and make recommendations for dealing with them. They can be used, for example, in setting call objectives. A history of a buyer-seller relationship is given and the trainee is asked to develop a set of sensible objectives for his next visit.

In-the-field training

It is essential that initial training given to trainees is reinforced by on-the-job training. The experience gained by real-life selling situations plus the evaluation and feedback provided by his sales manager should mean that the salesperson moves solidly into the final stage of learning skills process – unconsciously able. The salesperson does the right things automatically, just as a driver can coordinate a set of skills necessary to drive a car without consciously thinking.

Although unconsciously able is the final stage in the learning process, it does *not* describe a finite position beyond which improvement cannot take place. Field training is designed to improve the performance of the experienced as well as the newer salesperson. In order to do this the sales manager needs to:

(*i*)   analyse each salesperson's performance;
(*ii*) identify strengths and weaknesses;
(*iii*) gain agreement with the salesperson that a weakness exists;
(*iv*) teach the salesperson how to overcome the weaknesses;
(*v*)   monitor progress to check that an improvement has been realised.

There may be a strong temptation during a sales interview for a manager to step in when it is obvious that the salesperson is losing an order. Whether he succumbs to this temptation will depend upon the importance of the order, but to do so will undoubtedly reduce the effectiveness of the training session. Ideally, the sales manager should use the situation as an opportunity to observe and evaluate how the salesperson deals with the situation. Stepping in may save the order but cause resentment on the part of the salesperson, who loses face with the customer. This may jeopardise future sales and damage the manager's relationship with the salesperson.

Generally, a salesperson will respect criticism which he feels is fair and constructive. To achieve a sense of fairness, the sales manager should begin the post-interview assessment session by listing the positive points in the salesperson's performance. He should then ask the salesperson to relate any aspects of the sales interview which could be improved upon. If the salesperson, himself, realises that he has a weakness, then the manager does not have the problem of convincing him that a difficulty exists.

It is inevitable that some weaknesses will not be exposed in this way and that the manager will have to explain them to the salesperson. However, since the manager has earlier praised other aspects of performance, the salesperson is unlikely to reject his manager's criticisms out of hand. Having gained agreement, the sales manager will then suggest methods to overcome the problem. Perhaps, he will take the role of the buyer and engage in a role-playing exercise to rehearse the way in which a problem should be dealt with before the next call, or he may simply instruct the salesperson and suggest that he applies what has been said at his next call.

10.2.4 EVALUATION OF TRAINING COURSES

A study by Stanford-Bewley and Jobber (1989) sought to identify the methods used to evaluate training courses among a sample of companies in service, consumer and industrial sectors. The results appear in Fig. 26. It appears that only 57% attempt to measure changes in sales volume which may occur as a result of the course. More popular were field visits with salespeople (78%) where the sales manager would subjectively gauge whether ability had improved as a result of the training course.

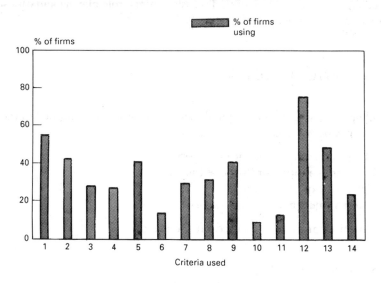

Key: Criteria used to evaluate training course

1. Change in sales net volume
2. Change in sales net value
3. Change in sales volume per call
4. Change in sales value per call
5. Number of new accounts gained
6. Number of old accounts lost
7. Order / Call rate
8. Order taken / Target
9. Coverage of territory
10. Length of time representatives spend with customer
11. Length of time representatives stay with company
12. Ability shown during field visits
13. Questionnaire at end of course
14. Questionnaire at some time in the future

(*Source:* Stamford-Bewley and Jobber, 1989)

Fig 26   Criteria used to evaluate training courses.

10.2.5 TRAINING SALES MANAGERS

Sales managers themselves require a formidable set of skills in order to perform their jobs efficiently, including:

(*i*) teaching skills;
(*ii*) analytical skills;
(*iii*) ability to motivate others;
(*iv*) communication skills;
(*v*) ability to organise and plan.

Not all of these skills are required to sell successfully. It is not surprising, then, that top salespeople do not always make the best managers. However it is possible to train sales managers to analyse and evaluate salespeople, identify motivational problems, suggest remedies, design appropriate compensation schemes, and train others in selling techniques. Courses are run by consultants and business schools which aim to create an awareness of the full range of sales management responsibilities and how to manage them. As with training salespeople, a mixture of lectures, discussion, films, role-playing and case studies is often used to develop managerial skills.

10.3 CONCLUSIONS

This chapter considers motivational theory and practice as applied to the sales area. A number of theories are examined:

(*i*) Maslow's hierarchy of needs theory;
(*ii*) Herzberg's motivator/hygiene theory;
(*iii*) Vroom's expectancy theory;
(*iv*) Likert's sales management theory.

Motivation in practice is focused on the use of:

(*i*) financial incentives;
(*ii*) sales quotas or targets;
(*iii*) meetings between salesperson and manager;
(*iv*) sales contests.

Sales training involves the development of a programme which develops selling skills. The components of a training programme, and the methods used, are examined before the skills required for sales management are outlined.

The next chapter explores two other management considerations – sales organisation and compensation.

PEN	Filling method	Price	Spare nibs	Spare cartridge costs	Nib size/type	Construction material (all with pocket clips)	Shape	Colours	Other features	
A	Capillary refillable	£15	£2.50	—	Medium/gold	All-metal "gold" finish	Round	"Silver"/"gold" tops	Barrel has to be unscrewed to refill with an easy grip feature; guaranteed for 2 years; screw cap; spare italic nib supplied; made in UK 	
B	Cartridge. 3 spare	£12	£1.50	£1 for 4	Medium/gold	Metal/plastic	Round	Black/"silver" top	Very slim enclosed nib; screw cap; guaranteed for 1 year; made in France 	
C	Cartridge. 2 spare	£10	£1.50	£1 for 4	Medium/steel	Metal/plastic	Round	Various/"silver" top	Bulky easy-to-hold style; screw cap; guaranteed for 1 year; made in Italy 	
D	Cartridge. 4 spare	£10	£1.30	£1 for 6	Fine/steel	Plastic with silver top	Round	Various/"silver" top	Superslim variety enclosed nib; screw cap; guaranteed for 2 years; made in France 	
E	Cartridge. 1 spare	£9	£2.00	£1 for 6	Fine/steel	Plastic	Triangular	Black/red/blue	Push-on cap; 1 year guarantee; made in W. Germany 	
F	Cartridge. 1 spare	£7	£4.00	£0.60 for 4	Broad/steel	Metalised plastic	Round	"Silver"	Choice of left/right-hand nib; push-on cap; guaranteed for 6 months; made in UK 	

Fig 27 Fountain pen features.

PRACTICAL EXERCISE – SELLING FOUNTAIN PENS

(The authors are grateful to Mr Robert Edwards, sales training manager, UKMP Department, ICI Pharmaceuticals, who devised this exercise, for permission to reprint it.)

This exercise can be used to develop the skills required for effective selling outlined in Chapter 5, i.e. need identification, presentation and demonstration, answering questions and handling objections and closing the sale.

The salesperson's profile is given below while the customer profile is given in Appendix 5 at the end of this book.

The salesperson should be given fifteen minutes to study the range of pens on sale.

The role play can be video-recorded and played back in front of the class to provide a focus for discussion.

Salesperson's profile

You are a salesman in a stationery department of a small store. For a few minutes a person of about 40 has been looking at your range of quality pens. The person comes up to you saying, 'I'm looking for a good fountain pen.'

You take the interview from this point. You have a display of six fountain pens (A–F) with the features shown in Fig. 27.

EXAMINATION QUESTIONS

1   It is impossible to motivate, only to demotivate. Discuss.
2   You have recently been appointed sales manager of a company selling abrasives to the motor trade. Sales are declining and you believe that a major factor causing this decline is a lack of motivation of your sales force. At present they are paid a straight salary, the size of which depends on length of service. Outline your thoughts regarding how you would approach this situation.

11 Organisation and Compensation

11.1 ORGANISATIONAL STRUCTURE

Perhaps the classical form of organising a sales force is along geographical lines, but the changing needs of customers and technological advances have led many companies to reconsider their sales force organisation. The strengths and weaknesses of each type of organisational structure will now be examined.

11.1.1 GEOGRAPHICAL STRUCTURE

An advantage of this form of organisation is its simplicity. Each salesperson is assigned a territory over which he has sole responsibility for sales achievement. His close geographical proximity to customers encourages the development of personal friendships which aids sales effectiveness. Also, compared with other organisational forms, for example, product or market specialisation, travelling expenses are likely to be lower.

A potential weakness of the geographical structure is that the salesperson required to sell the full range of his company's products. They may be very different technically and sell into a number of diverse markets. In such a situation it may be unreasonable to expect the salesperson to have the required depth of technical knowledge for each product and be conversant with the full range of potential applications within each market. This expertise can only be developed if the salesperson is given a more specialised role. A further related disadvantage of this method is that, according to Moss (1979), salespeople in discrete geographical territories, covering all types of customer, are relatively weak in interpreting buyer behaviour patterns and in reporting about changes in the operational circumstances of customers compared with salespeople organised along more specialised lines.

11.1.2 PRODUCT SPECIALISATION STRUCTURE

One method of specialisation is along product lines. Conditions which are conducive to this form of organisation are where the company sells a wide range of technically complex and diverse products, and where key members of the decision-making unit of the buying organisations are different for each product group. However, if the company's products sell essentially to the same customers, problems of route duplication (and hence higher travel costs) and customer annoyance can arise. Inappropriate use of this method can lead to a customer being called upon by different salespeople representing the same company on the same day. When a company contemplates a move from a geographically-based to a product-based structure, some customer overlap is inevitable, but, if only of a limited extent, the problem should be manageable.

11.1.3 CUSTOMER-BASED STRUCTURES

Market-centred structure

Another method of specialisation is by the type of market served. Often in industrial selling the market is defined by industry type. Thus, although the range of products sold is essentially the same, it might be sensible for a computer firm to allocate its salespeople on the basis of the industry served, e.g. banking, manufacturing companies, retailers, given that different industry groups have widely varying needs, problems and potential applications. Specialisation by market served allowed a salesperson to gain greater insights into these factors for his particular industry, as well as to monitor changes and trends within the industry which might affect demand for his products. The cost of increased customer knowledge is increased travel expenses compared with geographically determined territories.

Account-size structure

Some companies structure their sales force by account size. The importance of a few large customers in many trade and industrial markets has given rise to the establishment of a 'key account' sales force. The team comprises senior salespeople who specialise in dealing with large customers who may have different buying habits and may demand more sophisticated sales arguments than smaller companies. The team will be conversant with negotiation skills since they are likely to be given a certain amount of discretion in terms of discounts, credit terms, etc., in order to secure large orders. The range of selling skills required is therefore wider than for the rest of the sales force, who deal with the smaller accounts. Some organisations adopt a three-tier system, with senior salespeople negotiating with national accounts, ordinary salespeople selling to medium-sized accounts, and a telephone sales team dealing with small accounts.

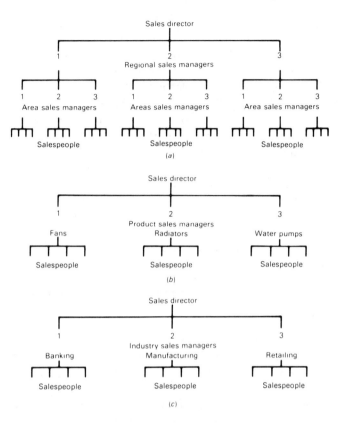

Fig 28   Organisation structures. (a) Geographical structure. The area sales
manager level is optional; where the number of salespeople (span
of control) under each regional manager exceeds eight, serious
consideration may be given to appointing area managers. (b)
Product specialisation structure. (c) Customer-based structure.

The term 'national account' is generally considered to refer to large and
important customers who may have centralised purchasing departments that
buy or co-ordinate buying for decentralised, geographically-dispersed business
units. Selling to such firms often involves:

(*i*) Obtaining acceptance of the company's products at the buyer's headquarters.
(*ii*) Negotiating long-term supply contracts.
(*iii*) Maintaining favourable buyer-seller relationships at various levels in the
buying organisation.
(*iv*) Establishing first-class customer service.

This depth of selling activity frequently calls for the expertise of a range of
personnel in the supplying company in addition to the salesperson. It is for this
reason that many companies serving national accounts employ *team selling*.

Team selling involves the combined efforts of such people as product specialists, engineers, sales managers and even directors if the buyer's decision-making unit includes personnel of equivalent rank. Team selling provides a method of responding to the various commercial, technical and psychological requirements of large buying organisations.

Lidstone and Melkman (1977) have noted that companies are increasingly structuring both external and internal sales staff on the basis of specific responsibility for accounts. Examples of such companies are those in the electronics industry, where internal desk staff are teamed up with outside staff around 'key' customers. These company sales forces are able, with reasonable accuracy, to forecast future sales levels at these key locations. Further, an in-depth understanding of the buyer's decision-making unit is developed by the salesperson being able to develop a relationship with a large number of individual decision-makers. In this way, marketing staff can be kept informed of customer requirements, enabling them to improve products and plan effective communications.

New/existing accoung structure

A further method of sales organisation is to create two teams of salespeople. The first team services existing accounts, while the second concentrates upon seeking new accounts. This structure recognises the following.

(*i*) Gaining new customers is a specialised activity demanding prospecting skills, patience, the ability to accept higher rejection rates than when calling upon existing customers, and the time to cultivate new relationships.

(*ii*) Placing this function in the hands of the regular sales force may result in its neglect since the salespeople may view it as time which could be better spent with existing customers.

(*iii*) Salespeople may prefer to call upon long-established customers whom they know rather than prospects where they might face rejection and unpleasantness.

Pioneer salespeople were used successfully by trading stamp companies to prospect new customers. Once an account was obtained it was handed over to a maintenance salesperson who serviced the account.

New account salespeople have been found to spend more time exploring the prospect's needs and provide more information to management regarding buyer behaviour and attitudes than salespeople working under a conventional system (Moss, 1979). The deployment of new account sales forces is feasible for large companies with many customers and where there is a continual turnover of key accounts which have to be replaced. The new account structure allows better planning of this vital function and eliminates competition between prospecting and servicing.

Functional specialisation

In industrial selling, companies sometimes separate their sales forces into development and maintenance sales teams. The development salespeople are highly trained in handling very technical new products. They will spend considerable time overcoming commercial, technical and installation problems for new customers.

A major reason why companies have moved to a development/maintenance structure is the belief that one of the causes of new product failure is the inadequacy of the sales force to introduce the product. Perhaps the cause of this failure is the psychological block each salesperson faces in terms of possible future problems with the buyer-seller relationship if the product does not meet expectations. Because of this, the salesperson is likely to doubt the wisdom of giving an unproven product his unqualified support. Employment of a development sales team can reduce this problem, although it is often only large companies who can afford such a team. Its use can provide other advantages, including clarity of purpose, effective presentation and reliable feedback from the market place.

This section has discussed the merits and weaknesses of the major sales organisational structures. In practice a combination may be used. For example, a company using a two-product group structure may, in order to minimise travelling expenses, divide the country into geographically-based territories with two salespeople operating within each one.

11.2 DETERMINING THE NUMBER OF SALESPEOPLE

11.2.1 THE WORKLOAD APPROACH

This method allows the number of salespeople needed to be calculated, given that the company knows the number of calls per year it wishes its salespeople to make on different classes of customer. Talley (1961) showed how the number of salespeople could be calculated by following a series of steps.

(i) Customers are grouped into categories according to the value of goods bought and potential for the future.

(ii) The call frequency (number of calls on an account per year) is assessed for each category of customer.

(iii) The total required workload per year is calculated by multiplying the call frequency and number of customers in each category and then summing for all categories.

(iv) The average number of calls per week per salesperson is estimated.

(v) The number of working weeks per year is calculated.

(*vi*) The average number of calls a salesperson can make per year is calculated by multiplying (*iv*) and (*v*).

(*vii*) The number of salespeople required is determined by dividing the total annual calls required by the average number of calls one salesperson can make per year.

Here is an example of such a calculation. The formula is:

$$\frac{\text{Number of}}{\text{salespeople}} = \frac{\text{Number of customers} \times \text{Call frequency}}{\text{Average weekly call rate} \times \text{Number of working weeks per year}}$$

Steps (*i*), (*ii*) and (*iii*) can be summarised in the following table.

Customer groups	No. of firms		Call frequencies per year		
A (Over £100,000 per year)	200	×	12	=	2,400
B (£50,000–£100,000 per year)	1,000	×	9	=	9,000
C (£15,000–£49,000 per year)	3,000	×	6	=	18,000
D (Less than £15,000)	6,000	×	3	=	18,000
Total annual workload				=	47,400

Step (*iv*) gives:
Average number of calls per week per salesperson   = 30
Step (*v*) gives:
Number of weeks   = 52
Less:

Holidays	4	
Illness	1	
Conferences/meetings	3	
Training	1	9
Number of working weeks		43

Step (*vi*) gives:
Average number of calls per salesperson per year   = 43 × 30
                                                                            = 1,290

Step (*vii*) gives:

$$\text{Sales force size} = \frac{47,400}{1,290} = 37 \text{ salesperson}$$

When prospecting forms an important part of the salesperson's job, potential customers can be included in the customer categories according to potential. Alternatively, separate categories can be formed, with their own call rates, to give an estimation of the workload required to cover prospecting. This is then added to the workload estimate derived from actual customers to produce a total workload figure.

The applicability of this method is largely dependent upon the ability of management to assess confidently the number of calls to be made on each category of customer. Where optimum call rates on customers within a particular category vary considerably, management may be reluctant to generalise. However, in a company quoted by Wilson (1983), although call rates varied between one and ten calls per day, for 80 per cent of the days seven or eight calls were made.

The method is of particular relevance to companies who are expanding into new geographical territories. For example, a company expanding its sphere of operation from England to Scotland could use a blend of past experience and judgment to assess feasible call frequencies in Scotland. Market research could be used to identify potential customers. The workload approach could then be used to estimate the number of salespeople needed.

11.2.2 THE PRODUCTIVITY APPROACH

This approach attempts to determine the optimum sales force size by calculating the likely effects on sales of adding (or subtracting) salespeople to an existing sales force. The optimum is reached when the costs of adding an additional salesperson equal the extra revenue gained. This method was developed by Semlow (1959), who showed that it was possible to estimate how much extra sales revenue could be expected to be generated by additional salespeople. By observing sales figures in different sized territories he found that, although salespeople in territories with higher potential achieved higher sales, the increase in sales was not proportional to the increase in potential. Thus a salesperson in a territory with twice the average potential would normally achieve higher than average sales, but not twice the average. One reason for this is that no matter how large a territory's potential, there is only so much work a salesperson can do in a given period.

The approach which will be discussed here is adapted from the work of Semlow. It involves two basic input figures:

(*i*) actual sales per salesperson (by value);
(*ii*) sales potential per territory (by value).

These figures are then plotted on a graph and a trend line drawn (see Fig. 29).

From this graph can be calculated total sales which may be expected for differing sizes of sales forces, i.e. average sales per salesperson multiplied by the number of salespeople. If the percentage gross margin is known, then the expected gross profits generated for each sales force size can be calculated. Gross profits (before salespeople's expenses) can be expected to increase at a decreasing rate. At some point the increase in gross profit will be completely offset by the additional cost of the extra salesperson. This, theoretically, is the optimum size of the sales force. In practice, such calculations provide guidelines as to the likely effects of expanding the sales force, but the exact scale of increase is likely to be tempered by managerial judgment and political and financial constraints.

For this method to have application, three conditions are necessary.

(*i*) It must be possible to make sensible estimates of territory potential.
(*ii*) The number of salespeople must be sufficient to provide adequate performance data and they must work in territories of varying potential so that the relationship between actual sales per salesperson and territory potential can be plotted.
(*iii*) An increase in the number of salespeople, and its consequent generation of higher sales revenue, will not bring about excessive retaliation by competition.

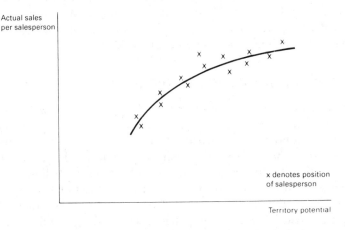

Fig 29   Graph of actual sales per salesperson against territory potential.

Semlow claims to have successfully used his method in furniture, mill supply, paper converting, stationery and other lines where the above conditions were found to apply. However he recognised that it would be difficult to apply 'where the direct selling activity is characterised by a few relatively large accounts and only a few salesmen'.

A further criticism of the approach is that it neglects other factors, for example, the geographical spread of customers, which may affect sales productivity.

11.2.3 THE 'VAGUELY RIGHT' APPROACH

This approach was developed by Lodish (1974), who used both hard and judgmental data to evaluate the optimum interrelationship of territory size, number of calls and sales force size. This is based on maximisation of contribution to fixed costs by equating territory and marginal profit values.

The approach is computer-based and is the basis of the CALLPLAN model. Lodish described the common approaches to sales force allocation, i.e. allocating calls in proportion to sales or potential, minimising travel time, defining territories by call frequencies and adding salespeople when they can be afforded,

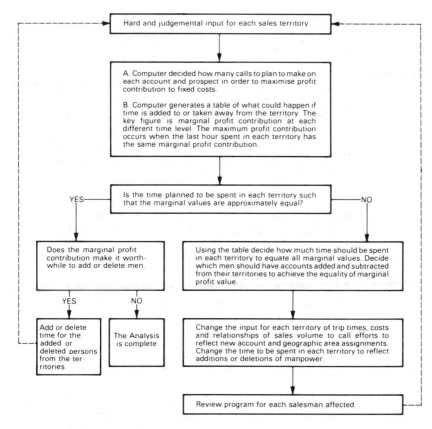

Fig 30   Lodish's 'vaguely right' approach

as 'precisely wrong', and consequently termed his approach as 'vaguely right'. The structure of the method can best be described by use of a schematic flowchart (see Fig. 30).

An advantage of the approach is that it is possible to update continuously from information supplied by the sales manager and his salespersons; it is thus adaptable. The model is written in a simple computer language, and results can be obtained within minutes.

Lodish points to the following major advantages of the approach.

(i) The problem of sales force size takes into account realistic goals of profitability in terms of sales volume and investment.

(ii) The objectives of the sales force are related to those of financial and productive capacity.

(iii) Management is provided with a structured framework with which to carry out its objectives.

(iv) Because of its simple and direct approach it should appeal to practical management in helping to apply judgment more soundly.

However, the approach is considered to have certain limitations (Meidan, 1982).

(*i*) Because of input data subjectivity, users must gain experience before it can be provided correctly.

(*ii*) Decisions as to whether any account can contribute to sales are subject to certain amounts of risk and uncertainty; with new accounts the uncertainty regarding potential is high.

(*iii*) The actual number of calls made may not be as originally intended, i.e. an account may decide to buy after the salesperson has called a certain number of times. There will be problems with computer programming if this certain number of times called is larger than the one initially estimated in the input information.

(*iv*) The methodology is not sophisticated enough to cope with consideration of a large number of different products or with situations where certain customers or accounts are only interested in a few products and not others.

By the middle 1970s five industrial and consumer product firms were using Lodish's approach to optimise the number of salespeople. These firms have indicated that deployment policies generated by the model have improved profitability by up to 50 per cent, with an average anticipated profit improvement of 9 per cent.

11.3 ESTABLISHING SALES TERRITORIES

There are two basic considerations which are used to allocate salespeople to territories. First, management may wish to balance workload between territories. Workload can be defined as:

$$W = n_i t_i + n t_k$$

where W = workload, n_i = number of calls to be made to customers in category i, t_i = average time required at call for each category i, n = total number of calls to be made and t_k = average time required to travel to each call. This equation is useful because it highlights the important factors which a sales manager must take into account when assessing workload. The number of calls to be made will be weighted by a time factor for each call. Major account calls are likely to be weighted higher than medium and small active accounts since, other things being equal, it makes sense to spend longer with customer who have higher potential. Also, calls on prospects may have a high weighting since the salesperson needs extra time to develop a new relationship and to sell himself, his company and its products. In addition, the time required to travel to each customer must be taken into account. Territories vary in their customer density, and so travel time must be allowed for in the calculation of workload.

The data will be determined partly by executive judgment, e.g. how long to spend with each customer type on average and, where a sales force already exists, by observation, e.g. how long it takes to travel between customers in different existing territories. These data can be obtained during field visits with salespeople, and estimates of current workloads calculated. For new sales teams the input into the formula will, of necessity, be more judgmental, but the equation does provide a conceptual framework for assessing territory workload.

The second consideration management may wish to use in working out territories is sales potential. Equalising workload may result in territories of widely differing potential. This may be accepted as a fact of life by some companies and dealt with by assigning their best salespeople to the territories of higher potential. Indeed, moving salespeople from lower potential territories to ones of higher potential could be used as a form of promotion. If company policy dictates that all salespeople should be treated equally, then a commission scheme based upon the attainment of sales quotas which vary according to territory potential should establish a sense of fairness. However if, after preliminary determination of territories by workload, sales potentials are widely disparate, it may be necessary to carry out some adjustment. It may be possible to modify adjacent territory boundaries so that a high potential territory surrenders a number of large accounts in return for gaining some smaller accounts from a neighbouring lower potential territory. In this way differences in sales potentials are reduced without altering workload dramatically. If this is not easily done it may be necessary to trade off workload for potential, making territories less similar in terms of workload but more balanced in terms of sales potential.

Designing territories calls for a blend of sound analysis and plain commonsense. For example, it would be crazy to design territories purely on the basis of equalising sales potential if the result produced strips of territory which failed to recognise the road system (especially motorways) as it exists in the country today.

11.4   COMPENSATION

11.4.1 COMPENSATION OBJECTIVES

Sales managers should consider carefully the type of compensation plan they wish to use. This is because there are a number of objectives which can be achieved through a compensation scheme. First, compensation can be used to motivate a sales force by linking achievement to monetary reward. Second, it can be used to attract and hold successful salespeople by providing a good standard of living for them, by rewarding outstanding performance and providing regularity of income. Third, it is possible to design compensation schemes which allow selling costs to fluctuate in line with changes in sales revenue. Thus, in poor years lower sales are offset to some extent by lower commission payments, and in good years increased sales costs are financed by higher sales revenue. Fourth, compensation plans can be formulated to direct the attention of sales personnel to specific company sales objectives. Higher commission can be paid on product lines the company particularly wants to move; special commission can be paid to salespeople who generate new active accounts if this is believed to be important to the company. Thus, compensation plans can be used to control activities.

11.4.2 TYPES OF COMPENSATION PLAN

There are, basically, three types of compensation plan:

(*i*)   fixed salary;
(*ii*) commission only;
(*iii*) salary plus commission.

Each will now be evaluated in terms of its benefits and drawbacks to management and salespeople.

Fixed salary

This method of payment encourages salespeople to consider all aspects of the selling function rather than just those which lead to a quick sales return. Salespeople who are paid on fixed salary are likely to be more willing to provide technical service, complete information feedback reports and carry out prospecting than if they were paid solely by commission. The system provides security to the salesperson who knows how much income he will receive each month and is relatively cheap to administer since calculation of commissions and bonuses is not required.

The system also overcomes the problem of deciding how much commission to give to each salesperson when a complex buying decision is made by a number of DMU members who have been influenced by different salespeople, perhaps in different parts of the country. Wilson (1983) cites the case of a sale of building materials to a local authority in Lancashire being the result of one salesperson influencing an architect in London, another calling on the contractor in Norwich and a third persuading the local authority itself.

However the method does have a number of drawbacks. First, no direct financial incentive is provided for increasing sales (or profits). Second, high-performing salespeople may not be attracted, and holding on to them may be difficult using fixed salary since they may perceive the system as being unfair and may be tempted to apply for jobs where financial rewards are high for outstanding performers. Third, selling costs remain static in the short term when sales decrease; thus the system does not provide the inbuilt flexibility provided by the other compensation systems.

Because of its inherent characteristics it is used primarily in industrial selling where technical service is an important element in the selling task and the time necessary to conclude a sale may be long. It is particularly appropriate when the salesperson sells very high-value products at very low volumes. Under these conditions a commission-based compensation scheme would lead to widely varying monthly income levels depending on when orders were placed. An Institute of Marketing study (PA Consultants, 1979) found that roughly one-third of salespeople are paid by this method in the UK.

Commission only

The commission-only system of payment provides an obvious incentive to sell. However, since income is dependent on sales results, salespeople will be reluctant to spend time on tasks which they do not perceive as being directly related to sales. The result is that sales personnel may pursue short-term goals, to the detriment of activities which may have an effect in the longer term; salespeople may be reluctant to write reports providing market information to management and spend time out of the field to attend sales training courses, for example.

The system provides little security for those whose earnings may suffer through no fault of their own, and the pressure to sell may damage customer-salesperson relationships. This is particularly relevant in industrial selling, where the decision-making process may be long and pressure applied by the salesperson to close the sale prematurely may be detrimental.

From management's perspective the system not only has the advantage of directly financing costs automatically, but also allows some control over sales activities through the use of higher commission rates on products and accounts in which management is particularly interested.

It is most often used in situations where there are a large number of potential customers, the buying process is relatively short and technical assistance and service is not required. Insurance selling is an example where commission-only payments are often used.

Salary plus commission

This system attempts to combine the benefits of both of the previous methods in order to provide financial incentives with a level of security. Since income is not solely dependent upon commission, management gains a greater degree of control over the salesperson's time than under the commission-only system, and sales costs are, to some extent, related to revenue generated. The method is attractive to ambitious salespeople who wish to combine security with the capability of earning more by greater effort and ability.

For these reasons it is the most commonly used method of compensating salespeople, although the method of calculating commission may vary. Extra payment may be linked to profits or sales generated, at a constant rate for all sales or only after a certain level of sales have been generated. Payment may be based upon a fixed percentage for all products and customers or at a variable rate.

11.5 CONCLUSIONS

Two management functions – organisation and compensation – have been discussed in this chapter. There are three methods of organising a sales force:

(*i*)   geographical;
(*ii*) product;
(*iii*) customer.

The customer-orientated approach has four variants:

(*i*)   market-centred;
(*ii*)   account-size;
(*iii*) new/existing accounts;
(*iv*)   functional.

Determining the number of salespeople needed may be accomplished by the workload or productivity approaches or by the 'vaguely right' approach which is computer-based.

Establishing sales territories will be determined by attempting to balance workload and sales potential.

Finally, the three major categories of compensation plan are examined. These are the fixed salary, commission-only and salary plus commission.

The next part of the text looks at the final area of sales management – sales control.

PRACTICAL EXERCISE – THE SILVERTON CONFECTIONERY COMPANY

Silverton Confectionery is a growing Berkshire-based company specialising in selling quality chocolates and sweets at higher-than-average prices through newsagents and confectioners.

At present their span of operation is limited to England and Wales, which is covered by a sales force organised along geographical lines. Each salesperson is responsible for sales of the entire product line in his territory and for seeking out new outlets in which to develop new business. The system works well with Silverton's salespeople, who are well known by their customers and, in most cases, well liked. The salesperson's responsibilities include both the selling and merchandising functions. They are paid on a salary plus commission system.

The success of this company, which has exploited a market niche neglected by the larger confectionery companies, has led Silverton management to expand into Scotland. You, as national sales manager, have been asked to recommend the appropriate number of salespeople required.

The coverage objective is to call upon all outlets with a turnover of over

£200,000 three times a year, those between £100,000 and £200,000 twice a year and those below £100,000 once a year. As a first step, you have commissioned a market research report to identify the number of outlets within each size category. The results are given below.

Category	No. of outlets
Under £100,000	2,950
£100,000–200,000	1,700
Over £200,000	380

A salesperson can be expected to call upon an average of sixty outlets a week and a working year, after holidays, sales meetings, training, etc., can be assumed to be forty-three weeks.

Discussion question

1 How many salespeople are required?

EXAMINATION QUESTIONS

1 The only sensible way to organise a sales force is by geographical region. All other methods are not cost efficient. Discuss.
2 How practical is the Semlow approach to sales force size determination?

PART FIVE
Sales Control

12 Sales Forecasting

12.1 PURPOSE

It is of the utmost importance that the sales manager has some idea of what will happen in the future in order that he or she can make plans in anticipation of that happening. There would otherwise be no point in planning and all that has been said in Chapter 11 would be negated. Many sales managers do not recognise that sales forecasting is one of their responsibilities, and leave such matters to accountants, who need the forecast in order that they can prepare budgets (dealt with in Chapter 13). Perhaps sales managers do not see the immediate need for forecasting and think that selling is a more urgent task. Indeed, the task of forecasting by the sales manager is often pushed to one side and hastily put together effort with no scientific base, little more than an educated guess, is the end result. The folly of such an attitude is examined during the course of this chapter.

When one is in a producer's market – similar to the situations in the immediate post-war years as was described in Chapter 1 – there is less of a need for forecasting as the market takes up all one's production; it is less a matter of selling and more a matter of allowing customers to purchase. However, in a buyer's market the situation is different, and the consequence of over-production is that one is left with unsold stock which is costly to finance in that such finance must come from working capital borrowings. The marginal money, i.e. the cost of borrowing the last pound of revenue, comes from the bank overdraft, which is at least base rate of borrowing plus 1 or 2 per cent. It can therefore be seen that over-production and stocking can be a costly business. Conversely, under-production can be a bad thing because sales opportunities might be missed due to long delivery times and the business might pass to a competitor who can offer quicker delivery.

Thus the purpose of the sales forecast is that it allows management to plan ahead and go about achieving the forecasted sales in what it considers to be the most effective manner. It is again emphasised that the sales manager is the person who should be responsible for this task. The accountant is not in a position to know whether the market is about to rise or fall; all that can be done to extrapolate from previous sales, estimate the general trend and make a forecast based on this. The sales manager is the person who should know which way the market is moving, and it is a negation of a major part of his or her duty if the task of sales forecasting is left to the accountant. In addition, the sales forecasting procedure must be taken seriously, because from it stems business planning; if the forecast is erroneous then such plans will also be incorrect.

12.2 PLANNING

It has been established that planning stems from the sales forecast and that the purpose of planning is to allocate company resources in such a manner as to achieve these anticipated sales.

A company can forecast its sales either by forecasting the market sales (called market forecasting) and then determining what share of this will accrue to the company or by forecasting the company's sales directly. Techniques for doing this are dealt with later in the chapter. The point is that planners are only interested in forecasts when the forecast comes down to individual products in the company.

We shall now examine the applicability and usefulness of the short-, medium- and long-term forecasts insofar as company planners are concerned and shall then look at each from individual company departmental viewpoints.

(i) SHORT-TERM FORECASTS. These are usually for periods up to three months ahead, and as such are really of use for tactical matters like production planning. The general trend of sales is less important here than short-term fluctuations.

(ii) MEDIUM-TERM FORECASTING. These have direct implications for planners. They are of most importance in the area of business budgeting, the starting point for which is the sales forecast. Thus if the sales forecast is incorrect, then the entire budget is incorrect. If the forecast is over-optimistic, then the company will have unsold stocks which must be financed out of working capital. If the forecast is pessimistic, then the firm may miss out on marketing opportunities because it is not geared up to produce the extra goods required by the market. More to the point is that when forecasting is left to accountants, they will tend to err on the conservative side and will produce a forecast that is less than actual sales, the implications of which have just been described. This serves to re-emphasise the point that sales forecasting is the responsibility of the sales manager. Such medium-term forecasts are normally for one year ahead.

(*iii*) LONG-TERM FORECASTS. These are usually for periods of five years and upwards. They are worked out from macro-environmental factors like government policy, economic trends, etc. Such forecasts are needed mainly by financial accountants for long-term resource implications, but such matters of course are board of directors' concerns. The board must decide what its policy is to be in establishing the levels of production needed to meet the forecasted demand; such decisions might mean the construction of a new factory and the training of a work force.

In addition to the functions already mentioned under each of the three types of forecast, other functions can be directly and indirectly affected in their planning considerations as a result of the sales forecast. Such functions include the following:

(*i*) It has already been mentioned that production need to know about sales forecasts so that they can arrange production planning. There will also need to be close and speedy liaison between production and the sales department to determine customer priorities in the short term. Production also needs long-term forecasts so that the capital plant decisions can be made in order to meet anticipated sales.

(*ii*) Purchasing usually receives its cue to purchase from the production department via purchase requisitions or bills of material. However in the case of strategic materials or long-delivery items it is useful for purchasing to have some advance warning of likely impending material or component purchases in order that they can better plan their purchases. Such advance warning will also enable purchasing to purchase more effectively from a price and delivery viewpoint.

(*iii*) Personnel is interested in the sales forecast from the manpower planning viewpoint.

(*iv*) It has already been mentioned that the financial and, more specifically, the costing function needs the medium-term forecast in order to budget. The next chapter details how use is made of the sales forecast through the sales budget and how such a function operates. The long-term forecast is of value to financial accountants in that they can provide for long-range profit plans and income flows. They will also need to make provision for capital items like plant and machinery needed in order to replace old plant and machinery and to meet anticipated sales in the longer term.

(*v*) Research and development will need forecasts, although their needs will be more concerned with technological matters and not with actual projected sales figures. They will want to know the expected life of existing products and what likely changes will have to be made to their function and design in order to keep them competitive. Market research reports will be of use to research and development in that they will be able to design and develop products suited to the market place; such a view reflects a marketing orientated approach to customer requirements. Here reports from salespeople in the field concerning the company's products and competitors' products will be useful in building up a general picture; such information will be collated and collected by the marketing research function.

(*vi*) Finally, marketing needs the sales forecast so that sales strategies and promotional plans can be formulated in order to achieve the forecasted sales. Such plans and strategies might include the recruitment of additional sales personnel, remuneration plans, promotional expenditures and other matters as detailed in Chapters 3 and 6.

It can thus be seen that an accurate forecast is important because all functions base their plans on such forecasts. The short-, medium- and long-term forecasts all have some relevance to some business function and, in the absence of reasonably accurate forecasting, where such plans are not based on a solid foundation, they will have to be modified later as sales turn out to be wide of those predicted in the sales forecast.

Now that the purpose of sales forecasting has been established, together with its role as a precursor to all planning activity, we can look at the different types of forecasting technique, bearing in mind that such forecasting is the responsibility of the sales function. Such techniques are logically split into two types, qualitative techniques and quantitative techniques, and each is dealt with in turn.

12.3 QUALITATIVE TECHNIQUES

These techniques are sometimes referred to as judgmental or subjective techniques because they rely more upon opinion and less upon mathematics in their formulation. They are often used in conjunction with quantitative techniques which are described in section 12.4.

12.3.1 CONSUMER/USER SURVEY METHOD

This method involves asking customers what their likely purchases are to be for the period it is wished to forecast; it is sometimes referred to as the market research method. For industrial products, where there are fewer customers, such research is often carried out by the sales force on a face-to-face basis. The only problem is that then you have to ascertain what proportion of their likely purchases will accrue to your company. Another problem is that customers (and salespeople) tend to be optimistic when making predictions for the future. Both of these problems can therefore lead to the possibility of multiplied inaccuracies.

For consumer products it is not possible to canvass customers through the sales force, and the best method is to interview them through a market research survey (probably coupled with other questions or through an omnibus survey where questions on a questionnaire are shared with other companies). Clearly, it will only be possible to interview a small sample of the total population and because of this the forecast will be less accurate. There is also a question of the type and number of questions one can ask on such a sample survey. It is better to canvass grades of opinion when embarking on such a study and these grades of opinion can reflect purchasing likelihoods. One can then go on to ask a question as to the likelihood of purchasing particular makes or brands which will, of course, include your own brand or model.

This method is of most value when there are a small number of users who are prepared to state their intentions with a reasonable degree of accuracy. It tends, therefore, to be limited to organisational buying. It is also a useful vehicle for collecting information of a technological nature which can be fed to one's own research and development function.

12.3.2 PANELS OF EXECUTIVE OPINION

This is sometimes called the jury method, where specialists or experts are counselled who have knowledge of the industry being examined. Such people can come from inside the company and can include marketing or financial personnel or indeed any others who have a detailed knowledge of the industry. More often, the experts will come from outside the company and can include management consultants who operate within the particular industry, usually working as economists. Sometimes external people can include personnel from customer organisations who are in a position to advise from a buying company's viewpoint. The panel thus normally comprises a mixture of internal and external personnel.

These experts come with a prepared forecast and must defend their stance in committee among the other experts. Their individual stances may be altered following such discussions. In the end, if disagreement results, mathematical aggregation may be necessary to arrive at a final compromise.

This type of forecasting method is termed a 'top down' method whereby a forecast is produced for the industry, and the company must then determine what its share will be of the overall forecast. Because the statistics have not been collected from basic market data (from the 'bottom up') there is difficulty in allocating the forecast out amongst individual products and sales territories, and any such allocation will probably be a very arbitrary matter. Thus the forecast represents aggregate opinion and is only useful when developing a general, rather than specific product-by-product, forecast.

A variation of this method is termed 'prudent manager forecasting' whereby company personnel are asked to assume the position of purchasers in customer companies. They must then look at company sales from a customer's viewpoint and 'prudently' evaluate these sales, taking into consideration such factors as external economic conditions, competitive offerings in terms of design, quality, delivery and price and whatever other factors are considered relevant to making an evaluation of the company's sales.

12.3.3 SALES FORCE COMPOSITE

This method involves each salesperson making a product-by-product forecast for his particular sales territory. Thus individual forecasts are built up to produce a company forecast; one can thus perhaps appreciate why it is sometimes termed the 'grass roots' approach. Each salesperson's forecast must be agreed with his or her area manager, and the divisional manager where appropriate, and eventually the sales manager agrees the final forecast.

Such a method is very much a 'bottom up' approach. Where remuneration is linked to projected sales (through quotas or targets) then there can be less cause for complaint because the forecast upon which such remuneration is based has stemmed from the sales force itself.

A variation of the above method is termed 'detecting differences in figures' and here each stage in the hierarchy produces a set of figures before meeting. The salesperson produces figures, broken down by product and by customer, and the area manager produces figures for the salesperson's territory. They then meet and must reconcile any differences in figures. The process goes on similarly with the area manager producing territory-by-territory figures and meeting with the regional manager who will have produced figures for his or her area, until it eventually reaches the sales manager and the entire forecast is ultimately agreed.

The immediate problem with the sales force composite method of sales forecasting is that when the forecast is used for future remuneration (through the establishment of sales quotas or targets) there will be a natural tendency for salespeople to produce a pessimistic forecast. This can be alleviated to a certain extent by linking sales expenses to the forecast as well as future remuneration. On the other hand, when remuneration is not linked to the sales forecast there is perhaps a temptation to produce an optimistic forecast in view of what was said earlier about customers and salespeople tending to overestimate. The consequence of the above is that a forecast might be produced that is biased either pessimistically or optimistically. As a corollary to the above it can also be argued that salespeople are too concerned with everyday events to enable them to produce objective forecasts and they are perhaps less aware of the wider or 'macro' factors affecting sales of their products. Thus their forecasts will tend to be subjective.

12.3.4 DELPHI METHOD

This method bears a resemblance to the 'panel of executive opinion' method and the forecasting team is chosen using a similar set of criteria. The main difference is that members do not meet in committee.

A project leader administers a questionnaire to each member of the team which asks questions, usually 'of a behavioural nature, e.g. 'Do you envisage new technology products supplanting our product lines in the next five years? If so, by what percentage market share?' The questioning then proceeds to a more detailed or pointed second stage which asks questions about the individual company, and the process can go on to further stages where appropriate. The ultimate objective is to translate opinion into some form of forecast. After each round of questionnaires the aggregate response from each round is circulated to members of the panel before they complete the questionnaire for the next round, so members are not completing their questionnaires in a void and they can moderate their response in the light of the averaged results.

The fact that members do not meet in committee means that they are not influenced by majority opinion and a more objective forecast might result. However, as a vehicle for producing a territory-by-territory or product-by-product forecast it has very limited value. It is of more use in providing general data about trends within the industry and is perhaps of greater value as a technological forecasting tool. It can also be useful for providing information about new products or processes which the company intends developing for ultimate manufacture and sale.

12.3.5 BAYESIAN DECISION THEORY

This technique has been placed under qualitative techniques, although it is really a mixture of subjective and objective techniques. It is not possible to describe the detailed workings of this method within the confines of this text; indeed it is possible to devote a whole text to the Bayesian technique alone!

The technique is similar to critical path analysis in that it uses a network diagram, and probabilities must be estimated for each event over the network. The basis of the technique can best be described by reference to a simple example. Owing to the fact that this chapter does not easily lend itself to the provision of a case study that can encompass most or all of the areas covered in the chapter, a detailed practical exercise, followed by appropriate questions covering the Bayesian decision theory technique, has been included at the end of the chapter, and this should give the reader an insight into its workings.

12.3.6 PRODUCT TESTING AND TEST MARKETING

This technique is of value for new or modified products for which no previous sales figures exist and for which it is difficult to estimate likely demand. It is therefore prudent to estimate likely demand for the product by testing it on a sample of the market beforehand.

Product testing involves placing the pre-production model(s) with a sample of potential users beforehand and noting their reactions to the product over a period of time by asking them to fill in a diary noting product deficiencies, how it was working, general reactions, etc. The type of products that can be tested in this fashion can range from household durables, e.g. vacuum cleaners, to canned foods, e.g. soups. However, there is a limit to the number of pre-production items that can be supplied (particularly for consumer durables) and the technique is really of value in deciding between a 'go' or 'no go' decision.

Test marketing is perhaps of more value for forecasting purposes. It simply involves the limited launch of a product in a closely defined geographical test area, e.g. a test town such as Bristol or a larger area such as the Tyne–Tees Television area. Thus a national launch is simulated in a small area, obviously at less expense. It is of particular value for branded foodstuffs, and the test market results can be grossed up to predict the national launch outcome. However, the estimate can only cover the launch and, over time, the novelty factor of a new product might wear off. In addition, it gives competitors an advantage because they can observe the product being test marketed and any potential surprise advantage will be lost. It has also been known for competitors to deliberately attempt to foul up a test marketing campaign by increasing their promotional activity in the area over the period of the test market.

12.4 QUANTITATIVE TECHNIQUES

Quantitative forecasting techniques are sometimes termed objective or mathematical techniques in that they rely more upon mathematics and less upon judgment in their computation. These techniques are becoming very popular with the onset of sophisticated computer packages, some tailor-made for the company needing the forecast.

It is not proposed to go into the detailed working of such techniques because they require specialist skills in their own right; indeed it would be possible to devote a textbook to one technique alone! Some quantitative techniques are very simple whilst others are extremely complex. The remainder of this chapter attempts to explain such techniques so that the reader will at least have an appreciation of their usefulness and applicability to his or her individual forecasting problems. If the problem calls for one of the specialist mathematical techniques then the answer must be to consult a specialist and not attempt it on the basis of the incomplete information given here.

Quantitative techniques can be divided into two types:

(i) TIME SERIES ANALYSIS. The only variable that the forecaster considers is time. These techniques are relatively simple to apply, but the danger is that too much emphasis might be placed upon past events to predict the future. The techniques are useful in predicting sales in markets that are relatively stable and not susceptible to sudden irrational changes in demand. In other words it is not possible to predict downturns or upturns in the market, unless the forecaster deliberately manipulates the forecast to incorporate such a downturn or upturn.

(ii) CAUSAL TECHNIQUES. It is assumed that there is a relationship between the measurable independent variable and the forecasted dependent variable. The forecast is produced by putting the value of the independent variable into the calculation. One must choose a suitable independent variable and the period of the forecast to be produced must be considered most carefully.

The techniques are thus concerned with cause and effect. The problem arises when one attempts to establish reasons behind these cause and effect relationships; in many cases there is no logical explanation. Indeed, there is quite often nothing to suppose that the relationship should hold good in the future. This reasoning behind causal relationships may not be too clear at this stage, but once the techniques are examined later in the chapter it should become self-evident.

The first set of techniques that are examined are those concerned with time series analysis.

12.4.1 QUANTITATIVE TECHNIQUES (TIME SERIES)

Moving averages

This method averages out and smooths data in a time series. The longer the time series, the greater will be the smoothing. The principle is that one subtracts the earliest sales figure and adds the latest sales figure. The technique is best explained through the following simple example; it can be seen that using a longer moving average produced a smoother trend line than using a shorter moving average.

Table 7. Office Goods Supplies Ltd, annual sales of briefcases, moving average

Year	Number	Three year Total	Three year Average	Five year Total	Five year Average
1975	1,446	–	–	–	–
1976	1,324	4,179	1,393	–	–
1977	1,409	3,951	1,317	6,543	1,309
1978	1,218	3,773	1,258	6,032	1,206
1979	1,146	3,299	1,100	5,855	1,171
1980	935	3,228	1,076	5,391	1,078
1981	1,147	3,027	1,009	4,953	991
1982	945	2,872	957	4,810	962
1983	780	2,728	927	5,049	1,008
1984	1,003	2,957	986	4,706	941
1985	1,174	2,981	994	4,805	961
1986	804	3,022	1,007	5,186	1,037
1987	1,044	3,009	1,003	5,470	1,094
1988	1,161	3,492	1,164	–	–
1989	1,287	–	–	–	–

These data are reproduced graphically (see Fig. 31) and it can be seen that averaging smooths out the annual sales figures. The five-year averaging produces a smoother line than the three-year averaging. One can then produce a forecast by extending the trend line, and it is up to the individual forecaster to decide whether three-year or a five-year averaging is better. Indeed, it is sometimes unnecessary to smooth the data (in the case of a steady trend) and in such a case the technique is termed trend projection. Generally speaking, the more the data fluctuates, the more expedient it is to have a longer averaging period.

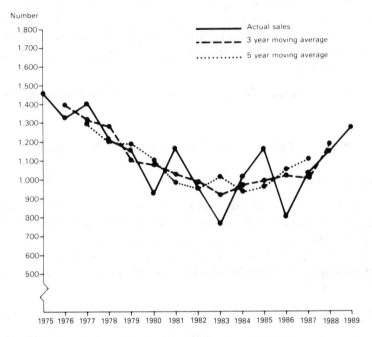

Fig 31   Office Goods Supplies Ltd, annual sales of briefcases, moving average.

Exponential smoothing

This is a technique that apportions varying weightings to different parts of the data from which the forecast is to be calculated. The problem with moving averages and straightforward trend projection is that it is unable to predict a downturn or upturn in the market (unless the forecaster deliberately places a downturn or upturn in the data). In this technique the forecaster apportions appropriate degrees of 'typicality' to different parts of the time series.

It is not proposed to explain the detailed mathematics behind the technique, because this is not a sales forecasting textbook. Instead, the statistics used in the previous example have been taken and, from this, weightings have been applied to earlier parts of the series. These weightings are applied by the forecaster according to his or her own judgment as to how 'typical' earlier parts of the data are in the production of a forecast (although there is a mathematical technique for deciding this if necessary).

In the moving averages technique the forecast will take some time to respond to a downturn or upturn, whereas with the exponential smoothing method the response can be immediate. In this example the forecaster has apportioned greater weightings to downturn periods of trade than to upturn periods, and the forecast will thus reflect another downturn period for 1990. Had a moving averages forecast been used, this would have produced a less steep continuum of the 1986–9 upturn trend.

In practice the technique is simple to operate, but it is essentially a computer technique. The forecaster can very simply alter the smoothing constant for different periods to produce a number of alternative forecasts; the skill lies in determining the degree of weightings for earlier and later parts of the time series.

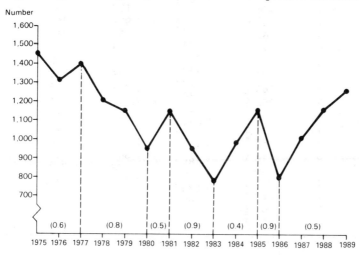

Fig 32 Office Goods Supplies Ltd, annual sales of briefcases, exponential smoothing (weighting shown in brackets).

Time series analysis

This technique is useful when seasonality occurs in a data pattern. It is of particular use for fashion products and for products that respond to seasonal changes throughout the year. It can be used for cyclical changes in the longer term (like patterns of trade) but there are better techniques available for dealing with such longer-term trends. Thus its best application is where the seasonal pattern is repeated on a fairly regular annual basis. These seasonal movements are measured in terms of their deviation from the aggregate trend.

The technique is best explained graphically by using data from the previous example. The quarterly sales of briefcases have been taken for Office Goods Supplies Ltd for the years 1985–9, and it can be seen that sales exhibit a seasonal pattern, with a peak of sales in the final quarter of each year.

When the sums of quarterly deviations from the trend are added, the resultant sum is +40 in this particular case. The total sum must equal zero, otherwise it would mean that a positive bias would be built into the forecast. However, this correction must come from all figures equally, and is calculated as:

$$40/4 = +10$$

Table 8. *Office Goods Supplies Ltd, quarterly sales of briefcases*

Year	Quarter	Unit sales	Quarterly moving total	Sum of pairs	Divided by 8 to find trend	Deviations from trend
1985	1	207				
	2	268	= 1,174	= 2,295	287	− 64
	3	223	1,121	2,136	267	+209
	4	476	1,015	= 1,934	242	− 88
1986	1	154	919	1,723	215	− 53
	2	162	= 804	= 1,643	205	− 78
	3	127	839	1,779	222	+139
	4	361	940	= 1,935	242	− 53
1987	1	189	995	2,039	255	+ 8
	2	263	= 1,044	= 2,110	264	− 82
	3	182	1,066	2,156	269	+141
	4	410	1,090	= 2,197	275	− 64
1988	1	211	1,107	2,268	284	+ 3
	2	287	= 1,161	= 2,346	293	− 94
	3	199	1,185	2,433	304	+160
	4	464	1,248	= 2,497	312	− 77
1989	1	235	1,249	2,536	317	+ 33
	2	350	= 1,287			
	3	200				
	4	502				

Table 9. *Office Goods Supplies Ltd, sum of quarterly deviations from trend*

Quarter	1	2	3	4	
Year					
1985	−	−	− 64	+209	
1986	− 88	−53	− 78	+139	
1987	− 53	+ 8	− 82	+141	
1988	− 64	+ 3	− 94	+160	
1989	− 77	+33	−	−	
Sum	− 282	− 9	− 318	+649	= +40

Therefore + 10 must be subtracted from each quarter's figures. The corrected figures are then:

Quarter	1	2	3	4	
Corrected deviations	− 292	− 19	− 328	+ 639	= 0

In this particular example these figures must now be divided by 4 to produce a yearly aggregate (because four years' data has been used in their compilation) and the figures from which the forecast will be derived are as follows:

Quarter	1	2	3	4	
Deviations	− 73	− 5	− 82	+ 160	= 0

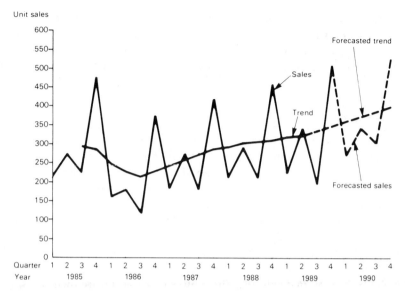

Fig 33   Office Goods Supplies Ltd, quarterly sales of briefcases and one year forecast.

Table 10. *Office Goods Supplies Ltd, forecasted trend figures and deviations from trend that have been applied*

Year	Period	Trend	Deviation	Forecast
1989	3	326	− 82	244
	4	334	+ 160	494
1990	1	343	− 73	270
	2	352	− 5	347
	3	360	− 82	278
	4	369	+ 160	529

The figures in the table were derived as follows. Unit sales are added to provide a one year total. This total then summates the one year moving sales by taking off the old quarter and adding on the new quarter. The quarterly moving totals are then paired in the next column (to provide greater smoothing) and this sum is then divided by 8 to ascertain the quarterly trend. Finally, the deviations from trend are calculated by taking the actual figure (in unit sales) from the trend, and these are represented in the final column as deviations from the trend.

The statistics are then incorporated into a graph and the unit sales and trend are drawn in. The trend line is extended by sight (and it is here that the forecaster's skill and intuition must come in). The deviations from trend are then applied to the trend line, and this provides the sales forecast.

In this particular example it can be seen that the trend line has been extended on a slow upwards trend similar to previous years. The first two figures for periods 3 and 4 of 1989 are provided as a forecast, but these quarters have, of course, passed and the figures are disregarded. The four quarters of 1990 have been forecasted, and these are included in the graph.

The technique, like many similar techniques, suffers from the fact that downturns and upturns cannot be predicted, and such data must be subjectively entered by the forecaster through manipulation of the extension to the trend line.

Z (or Zee) charts

This technique is merely a furtherance of the moving averages technique. In addition to providing the moving annual total, it also shows the monthly sales and the cumulative sales; an illustration of the technique shows why it is termed Z chart. Each Z chart represents one year's data and it is best applied using monthly sales data. As a vehicle for forecasting it provides a useful medium where sales for one year can be compared with previous years using three criteria (monthly, cumulative and moving annual).

The sales of briefcases for Office Goods Supplies Ltd have been provided for each month of 1988 and 1989 and this is sufficient to provide data for the Z chart as can be seen in Table 11. The figures in Table 11 are then transposed graphically in Fig. 34.

Table 11. *Office Goods Supplies Ltd, monthly sales of briefcases 1988/9*

| Month | Unit sales | | Cumulative | Moving annual |
	1988	1989	sales 1989	total
Jan	58	66	66	1,169
Feb	67	70	136	1,172
Mar	86	99	235	1,185
Apr	89	102	337	1,198
May	94	121	458	1,225
Jun	104	127	585	1,248
Jul	59	58	643	1,247
Aug	62	69	712	1,254
Sep	78	73	785	1,249
Oct	94	118	903	1,273
Nov	178	184	1,087	1,279
Dec	192	200	1,287	1,287

Moving annual sales are obtained by adding on the new month's figure and taking off the old month's figure, twelve months previously. The cumulative sales are obtained by adding each month to the next month, and the bottom line of the Z is the monthly sales.

The method is very much a comparison by sight method and in this case would be used for the medium-term (one year) sales forecast. However, as a serious method for prediction its uses are limited; its main use is for comparison.

Miscellaneous

This final section very briefly describes two techniques that are very much computer techniques; to describe their workings in detail would take a disproportionate amount of space together with a detailed knowledge of mathematics. They rely in their application upon sophisticated computer packages, and if the reader wishes to pursue the techniques further then the advice would be to go to a software specialist who can advise as to their

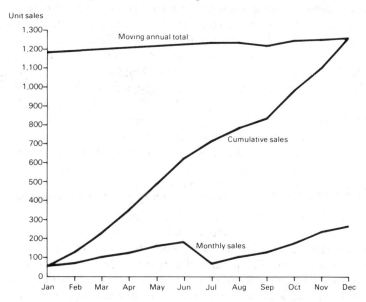

Fig 34   Office Goods Supplies Ltd, monthly sales of briefcases, Z-chart for 1989.

applicability and to their degree of accuracy for the desired intention. This is not to say that the forecaster (say the sales manager) should necessarily need to have a detailed knowledge of the technique that is being applied; all he needs to know is what the forecast will do and its degree of likely correctness.

The first of these techniques is Box–Jenkins, named after the people who developed it. It is a sophistication of the exponential smoothing technique which applies different weightings to different parts of the time series. In the case of this technique, the computer package takes earlier parts of the time series and manipulates and weights parts of this against known sales from later parts of the time series. The weighting that provides the best fit is finally deduced and this can then be used for the forecast. It is reasonably accurate for short- and medium-term forecasting, and it is predicted that its application will increase as more powerful personal computers are developed.

The other technique is termed X-11 and was developed by an American called Julius Shiskin. It is what is termed a decomposition technique and it breaks a time series down into trend cycles, seasonal cycles and irregular elements. It is an effective technique for medium-term forecasting and it incorporates a number of analytical methods into its computation.

12.4.2 QUANTITATIVE TECHNIQUES (CAUSAL)

Leading indicators

This forecasting method seeks to define and establish a linear regression relationship between some measurable phenomenon and whatever is to be forecasted. It is not appropriate to enter into a discussion of the technique of linear regression within the confines of this text; should the reader wish to pursue the technique further, most reasonably advanced statistical texts will explain the method adequately and explain its applicability.

The best way to explain the technique is to consider the following simple example. The sale of children's bicycles depends upon the child population, so a sensible leading indicator for a bicycle manufacturer would be birth statistics. The bicycle manufacturer will therefore seek to establish a relationship between the two and, if the manufacturer is considering children's first two-wheeler bicycles (say at age 3 years old on average), then births will precede first bicycles by three years. In other words first bicycles will lag births by three years.

The example is obviously an over-simplification, and there are forecasting packages available that permute a number of leading indicators, i.e. they are indicators that are ahead of actual sales, and it is possible to provide the permutation that best fits known sales, where the sales are lagged in time and the indicator is leading. The permutation that best fits the known sales to the indicator (or permutation of indicators) is the one to use in the forecast. Thus the permutation is constantly under review as time goes on. As forecasts pass into actual sales, so the forecasting permutation is modified to take account of the most recent sales.

This more sophisticated type of forecasting just described uses what is known as correlation analysis to establish the relationship, and again the reader is directed to any reasonably advanced statistics textbook for a fuller explanation of its workings and its implications.

Simulation

This forecasting methodology has only become possible with the widespread use of the digital computer. Leading indicator forecasting establishes relationships between some measurable phenomenon and whatever is to be forecasted, whilst simulation uses a process of iteration, or trial and error, to arrive at the forecasting relationship. In a reasonably complicated forecasting problem (of which most are that utilise this technique) the number of alternative possibilities and outcomes is vast. When probabilities of various outcomes are known, the technique is known as Monte Carlo simulation and it depends upon a predetermined chance of a particular event occurring (it is no coincidence that the technique derives from probabilities worked out for gambling games).

It is difficult to explain the technique further without entering into complex mathematical discussions and explanations. Insofar as this text is concerned, it is sufficient that the reader is aware of such a technique; if further information is to be sought, a professional forecaster must be consulted. It is essentially a digital computer technique, and to apply it successfully requires the help of an expert.

Diffusion models

Most of the techniques that have been discussed so far have depended upon a series of past sales for the company and the industry to be available before a forecast can be calculated. However, when new products are introduced to the market, and the products are not simply extensions or re-designs of old products, then the technique for estimating sales comes from a body of theory called the diffusion of innovations. One of the authors has already made a study of the subject and has produced a forecast for video recorders which utilised the Bass diffusion model (Lancaster and Wright, 1983).

Again, as with most of these causal techniques, the mathematics are complicated and the best advice for the sales manager seeking to apply such a technique to a new product would be to seek the advice of a specialist. This is essentially a digital computer technique and it is complicated in its computation.

Basically, diffusion theory assumes that the new product has four basic units:

(*i*) the innovation;
(*ii*) the communicaton of the innovation among individuals;
(*iii*) the social system;
(*iv*) time.

The theory goes on to say that the innovation can be categorised into one of the following groupings.

(*i*) Continuous.
(*ii*) Dynamically continuous.
(*iii*) Discontinuous.

This latter is a hierarchical listing, with the innovations being more widely removed from previous technology as one moves further down the list. This means that the further down the hierarchy the innovation is placed, the lower will be the degree of likely acceptance. In the early days of a product innovation, knowledge must be communicated to as many individuals as possible, especially those who are likely to be influential in gaining wider appeal for the innovation. This communication process is broken down into formal and informal communication. It is these two elements that are fed into the forecasting model and as such the model can be applied without large amounts of past sales data. The formal communication is controlled by the company and includes such data as advertising expenditure and sales support for the launch and the informal element relates to such matters as family and reference group influences.

Once the innovation has been launched, a measure of the rate of adoption is needed in order to produce a useful forecast. Products are born, they mature and eventually die, and it is important to the forecaster using this technique that the first few points of the launch sales are known in order to be able to determine the rate of adoption. Thus a forecast can be made using only a small amount of data covering the early launch period. An assumption is therefore made that the product being considered has a life cycle curve and that new product acceptance is through a process of imitation, i.e. later purchasers will follow the innovators.

The use of computer software in sales forecasting

Since the first edition was written, many developments have taken place in the field of software with much designed specifically for sales forecasting purposes. This section basically attempts to present a 'state of the art' critical review of such software available at the time of writing. The information for this section has been provided by the Economic and Social Research Council funded Centre in Economic Computing at the London School of Economics and Political Science.

AUTOREG from LSE Computer Centre. Designed for the estimation, testing and analysis of empirical models and for Monte Carlo investigations of finite sample distributions.

DATAFIT from Oxford Electronic Publishing. Provides various estimation methods and many diagnostic tests through the medium of graphics.

EPS from DRI Europe Ltd. An integrational device that is used for financial, econometric and statistical analysis. It has capabilities of modelling, regression analysis, data management, manipulation and transformation.

EXEC*U*STAT from Mercia Software Ltd. Combines business statistics with high quality graphical output. It provides for quick analysis of data.

FOCA from Timberlake Clark Ltd. Offers modern quantitative forecasting of time series using exponential smoothing, spectral analysis, Box–Jenkins and adaptive filtering.

FORECAST PLUS from Molimerx Ltd. Includes a tutorial that teaches the basis of forecasting and is useful for those with limited knowledge of computer-based forecasting. It has trading day adjustments and an exploratory package that helps the forecaster decide which technique is best for the data.

MINITAB from CLE. COM Ltd. A general purpose data analysis system that is easy to use. Its features include descriptive statistics, regression analysis with diagnostics, residual analysis and step-wise procedures, time series analysis including robust smoothers and Box–Jenkins operations.

MODLER from Alphametrics Ltd. A fully integrated system which incorporates a full range of facilities for data analysis including: managing large amounts of data of different kinds and frequencies in readily accessible databanks; transforming data instantly in a variety of statistical ways; automatic frequency conversion; making tables and graphics; performing regressions;

direct transfer of estimation results into a model with automatic normalisation; the building, solution and editing of small and large-scale models; comparative solution displays; alignment of model to a base solution.

MREG from Cambridge Econometrics Ltd. An integrated system for data handling and estimation which includes facilities for simulating simple models.

PC-GIVE from The Institute of Economics & Statistics, Oxford University. Menu-driven with embodied up-to-date econometric methodology comprising a large range of econometric tests that are not found in other packages. It is fast and easy to use.

PREDICT! from Risk Decisions. A business modelling tool that uses a spreadsheet layout and estimates by the Box–Jenkins method.

RAL from Burroughs Marketing Ltd has a library of statistical and econometric capabilities which enables users with little programming experience to add new routines and subroutines for personal diagnostics.

RATS from Timberlake Clark Ltd. An econometric package that performs time series and cross sectional regression. It is designed for forecasting of time series, although small cross-sectional and panel data may also be used.

SAS/ETS from SAS Software Ltd. An econometrics and time series library which provides forecasting, planning and financial reporting. It contains procedures for time series analysis, linear and non-linear systems simulation, seasonal adjustments and its applications include econometric modelling, cash-flow planning as well as sales forecasting.

SORITEC from Timberlake Clark Ltd. Includes non-linear and simultaneous estimation techniques, simultaneous non-linear simulation and solution, a full matrix processing language and transfer function estimation.

SPSS-PC+ from SPSS (UK) Ltd. A fully interactive data analysis package with full screen editing facilities, data entry and validation and a range of analytical and reporting procedures.

SPSS-X from SPSS (UK) Ltd. A simple statistical and reporting package. It provides a wide range of facilities from data validation to sophisticated tables, graphics and mapping.

STATGRAPHICS from Cocking & Drury Ltd. A statistical and graphics package that includes plotting functions (2D and 3D), descriptive methods, estimation and testing, distribution fitting, exploratory data analysis, analysis and variance, regression analysis, time series analysis including Box–Jenkins ARIMA modelling, multivariate and non-parametric methods and experimental design.

STATPAC GOLD from Molimerx Ltd with batch and interactive processing and good graphics which requires less memory than most other packages.

TSA from Numerical Algorithms Group. Allows interactive analysis of one or two time series using Box–Jenkins, ARIMA models and/or frequency domain analysis supported by graphical output.

TSP from the Universities of Edinburgh and Aberdeen. A user-friendly language for econometrics. Data and commands are entered in free format, data transformation is operated with algebraic statements and output from one procedure is easily used as input data to another.

XYZ: MODEL from 4-5-6 World Ltd. Translates Lotus 1-2-3 or Symphony worksheets into a modelling language and back again. The program deduces the underlying model structure inherent in existing operational spreadsheets and displays them in a clear manner.

This listing can never be completely up-to-date, but it is the best available at the time of writing. It only lists those packages that are available in the United Kingdom, although many more are available in the USA.

12.5   CONCLUSIONS

The purpose of sales forecasting has been explained and it has been emphasised that this function rests with sales management. Its importance to the planning process has been established; without reasonably accurate forecasting, planning will be in vain. The purpose of forecasting has been considered in the short-, medium- and long-term, and the usefulness of each has been established within the major functions of any manufacturing or service concern.

Forecasting has been considered under the headings of qualitative and quantitative techniques, with the latter being split into time series methods and causal methods. Qualitative techniques and time series methods have been explained in the amount of detail required to give the reader a working knowledge of their application. However, causal methods depend largely upon the use of the digital computer, and their computation relies to a great extent upon advanced mathematics. As such, the techniques have been described but not explained in workable detail.

The next chapter is concerned with sales budgets, taking the sales forecasting procedure to its next logical step.

PRACTICAL EXERCISE – CLASSICAL REPRODUCTIONS LTD

Background to the application of Bayesian decision theory

It has been pointed out throughout the chapter that since the 1960s we have seen the development of sophisticated statistical techniques for problem solving where information is incomplete or uncertain. The new area of statistics has a variety of names – statistical decision theory, simple decision theory and Bayesian decision theory (after the Reverend Thomas Bayes 1702–61). These names can be used interchangeably, but for the purposes of this case we shall use the term Bayesian decision theory.

Bayesian decision theory is a relatively new, and somewhat controversial, method for dealing with future uncertainties. Applied to forecasting, the technique incorporates the firm's own guesses as data inputs into the calculation of a sales forecast. There are essentially two ways of conceiving probability:

(*i*) as a physical property, inherent to a physical system;
(*ii*) as a measure of belief in the truth of some statement.

Until the late 1950s most statisticians held the first view of probability, with the probability of an event being the relative frequency with which the event might occur. Since this period there has been a rethink on the meaning of probability, and it is now regarded more as a measure of belief. This latter approach is termed Bayesian statistics. The Bayesian view is that probability is a measure of our belief, and we can always express our degree of belief in terms of probability.

To use the Bayesian approach, the decision-maker must be able to assign a probability to each specified event or state of nature. The sum of these probabilities must add to one. These probabilities represent the strength of the decision-maker's feeling regarding the likelihood of the occurrence of the various elements of the overall problem. It is because of the subjective nature of the process in generating these probabilities that Bayesian decision-making is so useful in solving business problems for which probabilities are often unknown. It is also the reason why many practitioners often reject the Bayesian approach; in fact some of the more conservative statisticians have termed it 'the quantification of error'!

In practical business problems, decisions are often delegated to persons whose levels of expertise should be such as to enable them to assign valid probabilities to the occurrences of various events. These probabilities will be subjective evaluations based on experience, intuition and other factors like available published data, all of which are acquired prior to the time that the decision is made. For this reason such subjective probability estimates are referred to as the prior probability of an event.

In business decision-making we must decide between alternatives by taking into account the monetary repercussions or expected value of our actions. A manager who must select from a number of available investments should consider the profit and loss that might result from each option. Applying Bayesian decision theory involves selecting an option and having a reasonable idea of the economic consequences of choosing that action.

Once the relevant future events have been identified and the respective subjective prior probabilities have been assigned, the decision-maker computes the expected payoff for each act and chooses the act with the most attractive expected payoff. If payoffs represent income or profit, the decision-maker chooses the act with the highest expected payoff.

The Bayesian technique can be used to solve quite complex problems, but in this example we use a relatively simple problem by way of illustration and explanation. However, the principles are similar for simple or difficult problems.

Bayesian decision theory applied to Classical Reproductions Ltd

This UK manufacturer of fine reproduction English furniture is considering venturing into the United States market. The company is to appoint an agent who will hold stock and sell the furniture to quality retail stores.

In order for the firm to gain economies in freight charges, consignments need to be fairly large, and it is planned that the first consignment will be £2 million worth of furniture.

This type of furniture is particularly fashionable in the USA at present and commands high prices. Classical Reproductions' management expect that this furniture will remain heavily in demand so long as the economic conditions in the USA remain buoyant. If economic conditions take a turn for the worse, then demand and prices will fall dramatically, because such products are a deferrable purchase.

To finance the manufacture, shipping, warehousing and other costs associated with the venture, the company is raising capital from a bank. Although the venture looks sound there is uncertainty as to the future direction of the USA economy over the next twelve months. The decision facing management is whether to risk going ahead with the venture now, when demand for their products is going to be high, but with the possibility of the economy deteriorating, or to postpone the venture until the economic outlook in the USA is more certain, but during which time tastes might change.

Let us assume that the management feel that the direction of the United States economy could go in one of three ways in the next twelve months:

(*i*)   continue to be buoyant;
(*ii*) a moderate downturn;
(*iii*) a serious recession.

The direction of the economy is an event (E) or a state of nature that is completely outside the control of the company.

Let us also assume that management has decided on three possible courses of action (A):

(*i*)   export now while demand is high;
(*ii*) delay the venture by 1 year;
(*iii*) delay the venture by 2 years.

Management has made a forecast of the likely expected profit for each of the possible courses of action for each of the three possible events, and this information is shown in the table below.

Events (E)	Actions (A)	Export now (£)	Delay 1 year (£)	Delay 2 years (£)
Economic conditions remain good		800,000	600,000	500,000
Moderate downturn in economy		450,000	370,000	200,000
Economic recession		− 324,000	50,000	80,000

Management wishes to make the decision that will maximise the firm's expected profit. They assign subjective prior probabilities to each of the possible events:

Event	Probability
Economic conditions remain good (A)	0.4
Moderate downturn in economy (B)	0.3
Economic recession (C)	0.3
	1.0

These prior probabilities are now incorporated into a decision tree (see Fig. 35) which is made up of a series of nodes and branches. The decision points are denoted by a square and chance events by circles. The node on the left (square) denotes the decision the firm has to make. Each branch represents an alternative course of action or decision. Each branch leads to a further node (circle) and from this, further branches denote the chance events.

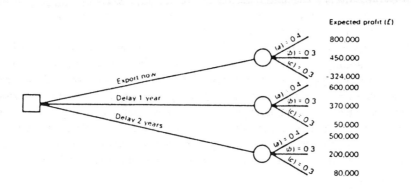

Fig 35   Decision tree for Classical Reproductions Ltd. (a) Economy remains buoyant. (b) Moderate downturn. (c) Recession.

The expected value (EV) should now be calculated for each forecast and then totalled for each alternative course of action. This is done in the 'payoff table' below by multiplying the expected profit for each event by their assigned probabilities and summing these products.

(*i*) Action 1 – export now:

Event (E)	Probability	Expected Profit (£)	Expected value (£)
A	0.4	800,000 .	320,000
B	0.3	450,000	135,000
C	0.3	– 324,000	– 97,200
Total EV for this alternative			£357,800

(*ii*) Action 2 – delay 1 year:

Event (E)	Probability	Expected Profit (£)	Expected value (£)
A	0.4	600,000	240,000
B	0.3	370,000	111,000
C	0.3	50,000	15,000
Total EV for this alternative			£366,000

(*iii*) Action 3 – delay 2 years:

Event (E)	Probability	Expected Profit (£)	Expected value (£)
A	0.4	500,000	200,000
B	0.3	200,000	60,000
C	0.3	80,000	24,000
Total EV for this alternative			£284,000

The firm decides to delay the venture by one year because the maximum expected payoff is associated with this. Since the act is selected under conditions of uncertainty, the EV of £366,000 is referred to as the EV under uncertainty and the act is referred to as the optimal act.

In this example the probabilities that have been assigned to events have been prior probabilities, so called because they have been arrived at prior to the acquisition of sampling or experimental information. As a rule, these prior probabilities are subjective, representing the decision-maker's belief that various events will happen. The analysis which is carried out using these prior probabilities is called prior analysis. Following prior analysis, the decision-maker must decide whether to go ahead with the optimal act indicated by prior analysis, or to obtain further information in the hope of making a better and more certain decision.

Additional information may be obtained by conducting a survey, by carrying out an experiment or by some other means. If this additional information is acted upon, the decision-maker will have to substitute new probabilities for the prior probabilities. Another analysis will then have to be undertaken using this new information. These new probabilities are called posterior probabilities.

Naturally, generating further information can be costly and the decision-maker must decide if the potential result is worth the cost. To extend this final point, let us find the expected value with perfect information when the prior probabilities are as follows:

(A)	Economic conditions remain buoyant	= 0.4
(B)	Relative economic decline	= 0.3
(C)	Recession	= 0.3

If economic conditions remain buoyant, the optimum choice would be to export now. If there is a moderate downturn in the economy, the optimum choice would still be to export now. If there is a recession, the optimal choice will be to delay for two years.

Calculation of expected profit with perfect information

Event	Profit for optimal act	Probability	Expected value (£)
A	800,000	0.4	320,000
B	450,000	0.3	135,000
C	80,000	0.3	24,000
			£479,000

Thus we find the expected value of perfect information (EVPI):

£479,000 – £366,000 = £113,000

This value of £113,000 can be interpreted as the expected opportunity loss for the optimal act under uncertainty and is the cost of uncertainty. The decision-maker can do no better than obtain perfect information, so this figure is the maximum he would be willing to pay for additional information that he knows will be less than perfect.

Practical questions

1   Carry out a full decision analysis for Classical Reproductions Ltd, using the following information.

Events (E)	Actions (A)	Export now (£)	Delay 1 year (£)	Delay 2 years (£)
Economic conditions remain good	(A)	700,000	560,000	410,000
Moderate downturn in economy	(B)	520,000	400,000	300,000
Economic recession	(C)	– 296,000	26,000	29,000

Prior probabilities for the various events for the next twelve months are:

(A) = 0.3
(B) = 0.4
(C) = 0.3

2   Carry out a pre-posterior analysis and find the expected value of perfect information (EVPI).
3   Having applied Bayesian decision theory to this example, what do you consider are its advantages and disadvantages?

EXAMINATION QUESTIONS

1   What is the place of sales forecasting in the company planning process?
2   Distinguish between qualitative and quantitative forecasting techniques. What are the advantages and disadvantages associated with each approach?

13 Budgeting and Evaluation

13.1 PURPOSE OF BUDGETING

An organisation needs to budget in order to ensure that its expenditure does not exceed its planned income. It has already been shown that the sales forecast is the starting point for business planning activities. The company costing department takes the medium-term sales forecast as its starting point, and from this budgets are then apportioned to departments (or cost centres in accounting parlance). Budgets state limits of spending; they are thus a means of control. The company can plan its profits based upon anticipated sales, minus the cost of achieving those sales (which is represented in the total budget for the organisation).

The consequence of an incorrect medium-term forecast can be immediately seen because then the whole company profit plan will be incorrect. It has already been mentioned, but it is re-emphasised here, that if the forecast is pessimistic and the company achieves more sales than those forecast, then potential sales might be lost owing to unpreparedness and insufficient working finance and facilities being available to achieve those sales. On the other hand, if the sales forecast is optimistic and sales revenue does not match anticipated sales, then revenue problems will arise, with the company having to approach a lending institution – most probably a bank – to fund its short-term working capital requirements (which can be very expensive when interest rates are high). This latter factor is a prime cause of many business failures, not necessarily because of bad products or a bad sales force, but through insufficient money being available to meet working capital requirements. These problems all stem from incorrect medium-term forecasting in the first place.

13.2 BUDGET DETERMINATION

Departmental budgets are not prepared by cost accountants. Cost accountants, in conjunction with general management, apportion overall budgets for individual departments. It is the departmental manager who determines how overall departmental budget will be utilised in achieving the planned-for sales (and production). For instance, a marketing manager might decide that more needs to be apportioned to advertising and less to the physical effort of selling in order to achieve the forecasted sales. He or she will therefore apportion the budget accordingly and may concentrate upon image rather than product promotion; it is a matter of deciding beforehand where the priority must lie when planning for marketing.

Thus, the overall sales forecast is the basis for company plans and the sales department budget (other names include sales and marketing department budget and marketing department budget) is the basis for marketing plans in achieving those forecasted sales. The sales department budget is consequently a reflection of marketing's forthcoming expenditure in achieving those forecasted sales.

At this juncture it is useful to make a distinction between the sales department budget and the sales budget. The sales department budget is merely the budget for running the marketing function for the budget period ahead. Cost accountants split this budget into three elements of cost.

(*i*) The selling expense budget includes those costs directly attributable to the selling process, e.g. sales personnel salaries and commission, sales expenses and training.

(*ii*) The advertising budget includes those expenses directly attributable to above-the-line promotion, e.g. television advertising, and below-the-line promotion, e.g. a coupon redemption scheme. Methods of ascertaining the level of such a budget are as follows:
   - A percentage of last year's sales.
   - Parity with competitors, whereby smaller manufacturers take their cue from a larger manufacturer and adjust their advertising budget in line with the market leader.
   - The affordable method, where expenditure is allocated to advertising after other cost centres have received their budgets. In other words, if there is anything left over it goes to advertising.
   - The objective and task method calls for an ascertainment of the advertising expenditure needed to reach marketing objectives that have been laid down in the marketing plan.
   - The return on investment method assumes that advertising is a tangible item that extends beyond the budget period. It looks at advertising expenditures as longer-term investments and attempts to ascertain the return on such expenditures.
   - The incremental method is similar to the previous method; it assumes that the last unit of money spent on advertising should bring in an equal unit of revenue.

The first method assumes that increasing sales will generate increasing promotion and vice versa, whereas the converse might be the remedy, i.e.

a cure for falling sales might be to increase the advertising spend. The second method assumes status quo within the market place. The third method does not really commend itself because the assumption is that advertising is a necessary evil and should only be entered into when other expenditures have been met. It quite often happens in times of company squeezes that advertising is the first item to be cut because of its intangibility. The cure for the company ailment might rest in increased promotional awareness. The fourth method seems to make sense, but accountants contend that marketing personnel will state marketing objectives without due regard to their value, and such objectives may not sometimes be related to profits. The fifth and sixth methods seem to make sense, but the main difficulties are in measuring likely benefits like increased brand loyalty resulting from such advertising expenditures, and determining when marginal revenue equals marginal expenditure. In practice, firms often use a combination of methods, e.g. the fourth and fifth methods, when deciding their advertising budget.

(*iii*) The administrative budget represents the expenditure to be incurred in running the sales office. Such expenses cover the costs of marketing research, sales administration and support staff.

The marketing manager (or whoever is responsible for the overall marketing and selling function) must then determine, based upon the marketing plan for the year ahead, what portion of the sales department budget must be allocated to each of the three parts of the budget described above. Such expenditure should of course ensure that the forecasted sales will be met as the forecasting period progresses.

What has been stated so far relates to the sales department budget; the sales budget itself has not been dealt with. The sales budget has far more implications for the company and this merits a separate section by way of explanation.

13.3 THE SALES BUDGET

The sales budget may be said to be the total revenue expected from all products that are sold, and as such this affects all other aspects of the business. Thus, the sales budget comes directly after the sales forecast.

It can therefore be said that the sales budget is the starting point of the company budgeting procedure because all other company activities are dependent upon sales and the total revenue anticipated from the various products that the company sells. This budget affects other functional areas of the business, namely finance and production, because these two functions are directly dependent upon sales. Figure 36 best explains the sales budgeting procedure.

Figure 36 represents the way cost accountants view the budgeting procedure. From the sales budget comes the sales department budget (or the total costs

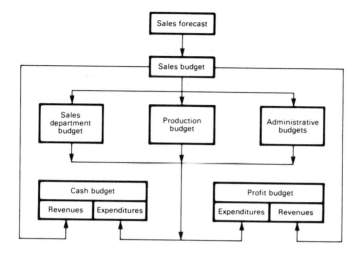

Fig 36   The budgetary process.

in administering the marketing function, which has been dealt with earlier in the chapter); the production budget covers all the costs involved in actually producing the products; and the administrative budget covers all other costs like personnel, finance, etc., and costs not directly attributable to the production and selling processes.

The sales budget thus is the revenue earner for the company and the other budgets represent expenditures incurred in achieving the sales. Cost accountants also have cash budgets and profit budgets, each with revenue provided from company sales. It is not proposed to go into why they split into cash and profit budgets; if the reader wishes to know more about the mechanism and thinking involved here, then any simple text on cost accountancy should provide an adequate explanation.

13.4 BUDGET ALLOCATION

The sales budget itself is a statement of projected sales by individual salespeople. The figure that reaches the individual salesperson is sometimes called the sales quota or sales target and this is the amount that must be sold in order to achieve the forecasted sales. Such quotas or targets are therefore performance targets that must be reached, and quite often incentives are linked to salespeople reaching (and surpassing) such quotas or targets. Such incentives have already been dealt with in Chapters 10 and 11.

Each salesperson knows the individual amount he or she must sell in order to achieve their quota, and such quotas are in effect performance targets. Quotas need not necessarily be individually based, but can be group based – say, collectively throughout a region – with everybody from the regional or area manager downwards equally sharing the sales commission. Quotas may also be for much shorter periods than the one year. The entire year's budget may be broken down in the same manner, say, month by month; when administered in this way the time horizon is more realistic and immediate than one year. Thus there is more of an incentive for a salesperson to achieve the quota or target.

For established firms the most common practice of budget allocation is simply to increase (or decrease) last year's individual budgets or quotas by the appropriate percentage, depending on the change in the overall sales budget. However, periodically it is sensible to review individual sales quotas in order to establish if they are reasonable given current market conditions.

The first step in this procedure is to attempt to determine the sales potential of territories. Usually surrogate measures will be employed to give at least relative measures of potential. For consumer products, disposable incomes and number of people in the target market may be used to assess relative potential. For industrial products, the number and size of potential customers may be used. Another factor to be taken into account is workload. Obviously two territories of equal potential may justify different quotas if one is compact while the other is more widespread. By assessing sales potential for territories and allowing for workload, the overall sales budget can be allocated in as fair a manner as possible between salespeople.

Not only does the sales quota act as an incentive to the sales force; it also acts as a prime measure of performance. The following sections of this chapter look at the whole area of evaluation of sales personnel.

13.5 THE PURPOSE OF EVALUATION

The prime reason for evaluation is to attempt to attain company objectives. By measuring actual performance against objectives, shortfalls can be identified and appropriate action taken to improve performance. However, evaluation has other benefits. Evaluation can help improve an individual's motivation and skills. Motivation is affected since an evaluation programme will identify what is expected of him or her, and what is considered good performance. Second, it provides the opportunity for the recognition of above average standards of work performance, which improves confidence and motivation. Skills are affected since carefully constructed evaluation allows areas of weakness to be identified, and effort to be directed to the improvement of skills in those areas.

Thus, evaluation is an important ingredient in an effective training programme. Further, evaluation may show weaknesses, perhaps in not devoting enough attention to selling certain product lines, which span most or all of the sales team. This information may lead to the development of a compensation plan designed to encourage salespeople to sell those products by means of higher commission rates.

Evaluation provides information which affects key decision areas within the sales management function. Training, compensation, motivation and objective setting are dependent on the information derived from evaluation. It is important, then, that sales management develop a system of information collection which allows fair and accurate evaluation to occur.

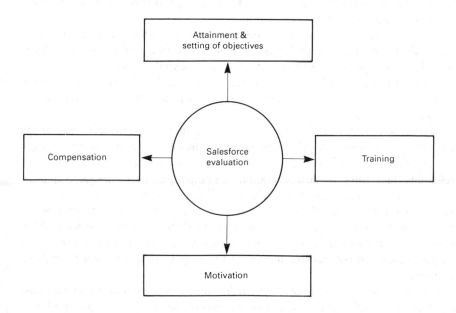

Fig 37   The central role of evaluation in sales management.

13.6 SETTING STANDARDS OF PERFORMANCE

Evaluation implies the setting of standards of performance along certain lines which are believed to be important for sales success. The control process is based upon the collection of information on performance so that actual results can be compared against those standards. For the sales team as a whole the sales budget will be the standard against which actual performance will be evaluated. This measure will be used to evaluate sales management as well as individual salespeople. For each salesperson, his or her sales quota will be a prime standard of sales success.

Standards provide a method of fairly assessing and comparing individual salespeople. Simply comparing levels of sales achieved by individual salespeople is unlikely to be fair since territories often have differing levels of sales potential and varying degrees of workload.

13.7 GATHERING INFORMATION

The individual salesperson will provide much of the information upon which evaluation will take place. He or she will provide head office with data relating to sales achieved by product/brand and customer, a daily or weekly report of the names of customers he has called on, and problems and opportunities revealed, together with expense claims.

Such information will be supplemented by sales management during field visits. These are important in providing more qualitative information on how the salesperson performs in front of customers as well as giving indications of general attitudes, work habits and degree of organisational ability, all of which supplement the more quantitative information provided by the salesperson himself.

Market research projects can also provide information on the sales team from customers themselves. A specific project, or a more general one which focuses on the full range of customer–seller relationships, e.g. delivery, product reliability, etc., can provide information on salespeople's performance. A market research study commissioned by Perkins Engines (Reed, 1983) found that salespeople with technical backgrounds were basing their sales presentation on features which were not properly understood by their audience. This led Perkins Engines to retrain their sales force so that their sales presentation focused upon simple presentation of features and the customer benefits which arose from these features.

Finally, company records provide a rich source of information for evaluation. Records of past sales levels, calls achieved, expense levels, etc., can provide bases for comparison and indications of trends which can be used both for evaluation and objective setting.

13.8 MEASURES OF PERFORMANCE

13.8.1 QUANTITATIVE MEASURES OF PERFORMANCE

There are two fundamental groups of performance measure. For both groups, management may wish to set targets for their sales team. One group is a set of input measures which are essentially diagnostic in nature – they help to provide indications of why performance is below standard. Key output measures relate to sales and profit performance. Specific output measures for individual salespeople include:

(*i*)   sales revenue achieved;
(*ii*)   profits generated;
(*iii*)   percentage gross profit margin achieved;
(*iv*)   sales per potential account;

(*v*)   sales per active account;
(*vi*)   sales revenue as a percentage of sales potential;
(*vii*) number of orders;
(*viii*) sales to new customers;
(*ix*)   number of new customers.

All of these measures relate to output.
   The second group of measures relates to input and include:

(*i*)   number of calls made;
(*ii*)   calls per potential account;
(*iii*) calls per active account;
(*iv*)   number of quotations (in part, an output measure also);
(*v*)   number of calls on prospects.

By combining output and input measures a number of hybrid ratios can be determined. For example:

(*i*)   Strike rate $= \dfrac{\text{Number of orders}}{\text{Number of quotations}}$

(*ii*)   sales revenue per call ratio
(*iii*) profit per call ratio   } call effectiveness
(*iv*)   order per call ratio

(*v*)   average order value $= \dfrac{\text{Sales revenue}}{\text{Number of orders}}$

(*vi*)   Prospecting success ratio $= \dfrac{\text{Number of new customers}}{\text{Number of prospects visited}}$

(*vii*) Average profit contribution per order $= \dfrac{\text{Profits generated}}{\text{Number of orders}}$

All of these ratios can be applied to individual product and customer types.
   These ratios help to answer the following questions.

(*i*)   Is the salesperson achieving a satisfactory level of sales?
(*ii*)   Is sales success reflected in profit achievement?
(*iii*) Is the salesperson 'buying' sales by giving excessive discounts?
(*iv*)   Is the salesperson devoting sufficient time to prospecting?
(*v*)   Is time spent prospecting being rewarded by orders?
(*vi*)   Does the salesperson appear to be making a satisfactory number of calls per week?
(*vii*) Is he or she making enough repeat calls on different customer categories? Is he making too many calls on low potential customers?
(*viii*) Are calls being reflected in sales success?
(*ix*)   Are the number of quotations being made reflected in orders taken?
(*x*)   How are sales being achieved – a large number of small orders or a few large orders?
(*xi*)   Are the profits generated per order sufficient to justify calling upon the account?

Many of these measures are clearly diagnostic. They provide pointers to possible reasons why a salesperson may not be reaching his sales quota. Perhaps he or she is lazy – not making enough calls. Perhaps call rate is satisfactory but call effectiveness, e.g. sales per call, is low, indicating a lack of sales skill. Maybe the salesperson is calling on too many established accounts and not enough new prospects.

Ratios also provide clues to problem areas which require further investigation. A low strike rate (order to quotations) suggests the need for an analysis of why orders are not following quotations. Poor call effectiveness suggests a close examination of sales technique to identify specific areas of weakness so that training can be applied most effectively.

A further group of quantitative measures will explore the remuneration which each salesperson receives. The focus will be on expenses and compensation. With respect to expenses, comparisons will be made between salespeople, and between current year and last year. Ratios which may be used include:

(*i*)   expenses/sales revenue generated;
(*ii*) expenses/profit generated;
(*iii*) expenses per call;
(*iv*) expenses per square mile of territory.

Such measures should give an indication of when the level of expenses is becoming excessive.

Compensation analysis is particularly valuable when:

(*i*) a large part of salary is fixed;
(*ii*) salespeople are on different levels of fixed salary.

The latter situation will be found in companies which pay according to the number of years at the firm or according to age. Unfairness, in terms of sales results, can be exposed by calculating for each salesperson the following two ratios:

(*i*) total salary (including commission)/sales revenue;
(*ii*) total salary (including commission)/profits.

These ratios will reveal when a compensation plan has gone out of control, and will allow changes to be made before lower-paid higher-achievers leave for jobs which more closely relate pay to sales success.

A study by Jobber, Hooley and Shipley (1989) surveyed a sample of 450 industrial products organisations (that is firms manufacturing and selling repeat industrial goods such as components, and capital goods such as machinery). The objective was to discover the extent of usage of sales evaluation criteria among small (less than £3 million sales turnover) and large (greater than £3 million sales turnover) firms. Table 12 shows that there is a wide variation in the usage of output criteria among the sample of firms, and that large firms tend to use more output criteria than small organisations.

Table 12. *A comparison of the usage of salesforce evaluation output criteria between small and large organisations*

Evaluative criteria	Small firms %	Large firms %	Statistically significant difference[1]
Sales			
Sales volume	87.2	93.1	
Sales volume by product or product line	61.2	80.3	*
Sales volume by customer or customer type	48.2	59.5	
Sales volume per order	22.4	26.7	
Sales volume by outlet or outlet type	22.4	38.9	*
Sales volume per call	12.9	24.4	*
Market share	32.9	57.3	*
Accounts			
Number of new accounts gained	58.8	55.7	
Number of accounts lost	44.7	42.7	
Amount of new account sales	57.6	54.2	
Number of accounts on which payment overdue	41.2	38.2	
Proportion/number of accounts buying full product line	14.1	16.0	
Profit			
Gross profit generated	58.8	48.9	
Net profit generated	38.8	42.7	
Gross profit as a percentage of sales volume	47.1	45.0	
Net profit as a percentage of sales volume	38.8	34.4	
Return on investment	28.2	26.7	
Profit per call ratio	12.9	12.2	
Orders			
Number of orders taken	48.2	38.2	
Number of orders cancelled	14.1	13.7	
Order per call ratio	25.9	29.0	
Strike rate $\left(\dfrac{\text{Number of orders}}{\text{Number of quotations}}\right)$	37.9	40.5	
Average order value	28.2	26.0	
Average profit contribution per order	21.2	16.8	
Value or orders to value of quotations ratio	29.4	21.4	
Other output criteria			
Number of customer complaints	23.5	22.3	

Note: [1] * indicates significant at $p<0.05$

Table 13 shows that the usage of input criteria is also quite variable with statistics relating to calls the most frequently used by both large and small firms. Again, there is a tendency for large firms to use more input criteria when evaluating their salesforces.

Table 13. *A comparison of the usage of salesforce evaluation input criteria between small and large organisations*

Evaluative criteria	Small firms %	Large firms %	Statistically significant difference[1]
Calls			
Number of calls per period	49.4	69.7	*
Number of calls per customer or customer type	15.3	37.4	*
Calls on potential new accounts	56.5	53.8	
Calls on existing accounts	55.3	61.8	
Prospecting success ratio: (Number of new customers) / (Number of potential new customers visited)	28.2	32.8	
Expenses			
Ratio of sales expense to sales volume	38.8	45.4	
Average cost per call	21.2	30.8	
Other input criteria			
Number of required reports sent in	42.0	42.0	
Number of demonstrations conducted	23.5	22.3	
Number of service calls made	21.2	23.1	
Number of letters/telephone calls to prospects	14.1	7.7	

Note: [1] * indicates significant at $p < 0.05$

These quantitative measures cannot solely produce a complete evaluation of salespeople. In order to provide a wider perspective, qualitative measures will also be employed.

13.8.2 QUALITATIVE MEASURES OF PERFORMANCE

Assessment along qualitative lines will necessarily be more subjective and will take place, in the main, during field visits. The usual dimensions which are used are given below.

(*i*) SALES SKILLS. These may be rated using a number of sub-factors.
- Handling the opening and developing rapport.
- Identification of customer needs, questioning ability.
- Quality of sales presentation.
- Use of visual aids.
- Ability to overcome objections.
- Ability to close the sale.

(*ii*) CUSTOMER RELATIONSHIPS.
- How well received is the salesperson?
- Are customers well satisfied with the service, advice, reliability of the salesperson, or are there frequent grumbles and complaints?

(*iii*) SELF ORGANISATION. How well does the salesperson carry out the following?

- Prepare calls.
- Organise routing to minimise unproductive travelling.
- Keep customer records up to date.
- Provide market information to headquarters.
- Conduct self-analysis of performance in order to improve weaknesses.

(iv) PRODUCT KNOWLEDGE. How well informed is the salesperson regarding the following?
- His or her own products and their customer benefits and applications.
- Competitive products and their benefits and applications.
- Relative strengths and weaknesses between his own and competitive offerings.

(v) COOPERATION AND ATTITUDES. To what extent will the salesperson:
- respond to the objectives determined by management in order to improve performance, e.g. increase prospecting rate;
- cooperate with suggestions made during field training for improved sales technique;
- use his or her own initiative;

and what are his or her attitudes towards:
- the company and its products;
- hard work.

Table 14. A comparison of the usage of qualitative salesforce evaluation criteria between small and large organisations

Evaluative criteria	Small firms %	Large firms %	Statistically significant difference[1]
Skills			
Selling skills	81.9	86.9	
Communication skills	77.1	85.4	
Knowledge			
Product knowledge	94.0	90.8	
Knowledge of competition	80.7	83.1	
Knowledge of company policies	56.6	68.5	
Self management			
Planning ability	77.1	76.2	
Time management	54.2	61.5	
Judgment/decision-making ability	74.7	68.5	
Report preparation and submission	63.9	77.7	*
Personal characteristics			
Attitudes	91.6	88.5	
Initiative	92.8	83.1	
Appearance and manner	90.4	86.9	
Aggressiveness	45.8	50.8	
Creativity	49.4	56.9	

Note: [1] indicates significant at $p < 0.05$.

The study by Jobber, Hooley and Shipley (1989) referred to earlier also investigated the use of qualitative evaluative measures by industrial goods companies. Table 14 shows the results with most criteria being used by the majority of the sales managers in the sample. Although differences between small and large firms were not so distinct as for quantitative measures, more detailed analysis of the results showed that managers of small firms tended to hold qualitative opinions 'in the head', whereas managers of large firms tended to produce more formal assessments, for example in an evaluation report.

As mentioned earlier, the use of quantitative and qualitative measures is interrelated. A poor sales per call ratio will inevitably result in close scrutiny of sales skills, customer relationships and degree of product knowledge in order to discover why performance is poor.

For an evaluation and control system to work efficiently, it is important for the sales team to understand its purpose. For them to view it simply as a means for management to catch them out and criticise performance is likely to breed resentment. It should be used, and be perceived, as a means of assisting salespeople in improving performance. Indeed, the quantitative output measures themselves can be used as a basis for rewarding performance when targets are met. In essence, controls should be viewed in a positive manner, not a negative one.

13.9 CONCLUSIONS

This chapter has shown the importance of the sales budget in motivating and controlling the sales force. The sales budget, which itself is determined by the sales forecast, is broken down into sales quotas or targets for individual salespeople and regions. Monetary incentives may be linked to the attainment of quotas and they may be used as one yardstick of achievement.

A more detailed look at the kinds of measures used to evaluate salespeople is then taken. Two broad measures are used – quantitative and qualitative indicators. Such measures can be used to evaluate, control and motivate salespeople towards better performance.

PRACTICAL EXERCISE – MACLAREN TYRES LTD

MacLaren Tyres is a company involved in the import and marketing of car tyres manufactured in the Far East. David MacLaren established the business in 1978 when a friend living in Singapore told him of the supply of tyres from that area which substantially undercut European prices. Although Far-Eastern tyres were not as long lasting as European (average 18,000 miles compared with 25,000), they were produced to a high standard which meant that problems like weak spots, cracks and leaks were no more serious than with European tyres.

MacLaren believed that a viable target market existed for the sale of these tyres in the UK. He was of the opinion that a substantial number of people were interested primarily in the purchase price of tyres. This price-sensitive target market could roughly be described as the mid-lower income, working-class family man who owned a secondhand car which was over three years old.

He decided to buy a consignment of tyres and visited tyre centres to sell them. Initially business was slow but gradually, as distributors began to believe in the quality of the tyres, sales grew.

By 1985 MacLaren had taken on the role of general manager and had recruited five salespeople to handle the sales function. A brief personal profile produced by MacLaren of each of his salespeople is given below.

Profiles of MacLaren salesmen

Peter Killick

Joined the company in 1980. Has an HND (business studies) and previously worked as an insurance salesman for two years. Aged 27. Handles the Tyneside area. Gregarious and extrovert.

Gary Olford

Joined the company in 1981. No formal qualitifactions but sound track record as a car salesman and, later, as a toy salesman. Aged 35. Handles the Manchester/Liverpool area. Appears to be hard-working but lacks initiative.

Barrie Wilson

Joined the company at the same time as Olford. Has an HNC (mechanical engineering). Was a technical representative for an engineering firm. Aged 28. Handles the London area. Appears to enjoy his work but lacks the necessary 'push' to be really successful in selling.

Ron Haynes

Joined the company in 1982. Has a degree in industrial technology. Previous experience includes selling bathroom suites and textile fabrics. Aged 29. Covers the Birmingham area. Appears to lack enthusiasm but sales record is about average.

Kevin Harris

Joined MacLaren Ltd in 1984. Has a degree in business studies. Only previous experience was as a marketing assistant during the industrial training period of his degree. Aged 23. Handles the Bristol area. Keen but still very raw.

Sales force data

MacLaren decided that the time had come to look in detail at the sales records of his men. His plan was to complete a series of statistics which would be useful in evaluating their performance. Basic data for the year 1984/4 relevant to each man is contained below.

	Sales (£000s)	Gross margin (£000s)	Live accounts (1984/5)	Calls made	Number of different customers called upon
Killick	298	101	222	1,472	441
Olford	589	191	333	1,463	432
Wilson	391	121	235	1,321	402
Haynes	440	132	181	1,152	211
Harris	240	65	296	1,396	421

Market data

From trade sources, and from knowledge of the working boundaries each man operated in, MacLaren was able to produce estimates of the number of potential accounts and territory potential for each area.

	No. of potential accounts	Territory potential (£000s)
Killick (Tyneside)	503	34,620
Olford (Lancashire)	524	36,360
Wilson (London)	711	62,100
Haynes (Birmingham)	483	43,800
Harris (Bristol)	462	38,620

Discussion questions

1 Evaluate the performance of each of MacLaren's salespeople.
2 What further information is needed to produce a more complete appraisal?
3 What action would you take?

EXAMINATION QUESTIONS

1 What is a sales budget? Discuss the importance of the sales budget in the corporate budgetary process.
2 Quantitative measures of the performance of sales representatives are more likely to mislead than guide evaluation. Do you agree?

APPENDIX 1 Examination Technique

INTRODUCTION

Many able and talented students fail to do justice to themselves in examinations. This section of the book is designed to help remedy the problem of under-achievement by providing some guidelines on effective ways of preparing for examinations. However, before dealing with specific points of detail, the importance of positive thinking needs to be emphasised; intending examinees must have confidence in their own potential. Such confidence can be developed by giving yourself adequate time to prepare for examinations and by paying attention to the following points on examination technique.

PLANNING AND SETTING OBJECTIVES

Only the very talented or very lucky candidates can sit down and do all their revision the night before the examination. The vast majority of individuals need to plan their work and set themselves objectives. By doing this, substantial improvements in examination performance can be achieved.

The need to plan and organise work prior to an examination sounds self-evident but in practice substantial numbers of examinees pay insufficient attention to this aspect of their preparation. A first stage in planning is to obtain a good idea of what is expected of you by examining a copy of the relevant syllabus. This will state the general objectives of the course and will detail the topics to be covered. If you are studying for an examination which will be set and marked by the college you are attending, obtaining a syllabus should be a simple matter of requesting it from your tutor, assuming that you have not been given one at the outset of the course. Candidates for examinations set by an external body can obtain a syllabus from the examining authority. Usually this will be quite detailed and will give a precise indication of the relative importance of topics. Once you have obtained a syllabus check it carefully against your course notes to ensure that they provide a complete coverage of topics.

The next stage in planning involves finding out about the requirements for the examinations by obtaining copies of past papers and checking that there have not been any changes in the examination regulations since the previous paper. Amongst the most important pieces of information you will derive from the exmaination papers is the amount of time available to answer each question. As part of your revision programme you should practise completing answers to questions within the time limit. This point cannot be stressed too strongly; to use a sporting analogy, it is clear that many students prepare for an exam. as if for a marathon, by practising writing long essays, and during the examination find for the first time that they have to take part in an 800 metres event! The specimen examination answers which are frequently available for professional examinations provide a very useful aid when trying to establish the type and length of answers required.

Finding out the date and time of your examination is obviously important and allows you to draw up a revision timetable. For most people 'little and often' is a more effective and less painful way of revising than intensive and lengthy periods over a short period of time. However, it must be admitted that circumstances and individual preferences do not always permit or require this general rule to be followed. A revision timetable will therefore reflect your own particular needs, but should attempt to be as specific as possible about time allocations and the topics to be covered.

Once you have drawn up a timetable check the topics covered against those indicated on the syllabus to ensure a match between the two. If at all possible set objectives for each topic on the timetable and check progress against these. Few people will be able to work precisely according to every aspect of their timetable, because of unforeseen circumstances, but do attempt to catch up on the schedule as soon as possible, even if it requires extra work. However, do not study very late at night, particularly immediately prior to the examination; this might actually impair your performance and, even worse, your health.

REVISION

It is impossible to give hard and fast rules about when to start revising, but about eight weeks before the examination is a reasonable guideline. It is possible to start earlier than this but most students will not have finished their course of study before this time. Many students leave much less than eight weeks for revision, but this may result in limited or superficial coverage of the syllabus and over-heavy reliance on 'question spotting'.

The importance of active learning cannot be over-emphasised when revising. Innumerable candidates for examinations have spent hours and hours reading as part of their revision programme without actually remembering or understanding anything but a fraction of their work. One very effective way of promoting active learning is to take brief notes on the topic being revised. These brief notes should incorporate all the sources of information relevant to the topic such as lecture notes, textbooks, examples, your own ideas and so on. When making notes try to write down the key points and space the notes out so that you can find topics quickly at a later date. Diagrams and illustrations can be used, as these often serve as useful aids to one's memory.

Some students find it useful to condense their notes with each successive revision session. Thus what start out as reasonably detailed notes on a particular topic are eventually reduced to a few basic statements and key words which provide leads into the main aspects of the problem.

Another useful way to promote active learning is to set tests every few days on the areas you have revised. Many students do not find it easy to set such tests. It may be possible to obtain the cooperation of a tutor to set the tests, but in any event past examination questions and discussion questions from textbooks should provide help when setting these self-evaluation tests. Of course it is important that the time allocated to the test is closely related to the time available during the examination. When the test has been completed, evaluation of performance is important and, although self-evaluation is fundamental, the views of fellow students, tutors or other hopefully knowledgeable third-parties can be invaluable.

A revision aid which is much under-utilised is that of studying with groups of other students who are revising for the same examination. This form of group work provides a forum for pooling information, questioning ideas and evaluating performance. The organisation of such groups can take many forms including brainstorming sessions, individual presentations on selected topics, informal discussions of questions and so on. One of the main benefits of this type of approach to revision is that it encourages brevity and a full understanding of subjects which have to be discussed with fellow students. It is, of course, vital that the discussions do concentrate on the work for the examination and are not sidetracked onto other perhaps more immediately pleasant topics.

READING AND REMEMBERING

It has already been pointed out that long hours spent reading do not necessarily result in the effective acquisition of knowledge and that note taking is one way of improving learning whilst reading. However, the process of reading about a subject also involves skills which can be improved. The most obvious point about different individuals' reading skills is the speed at which they read. Some people read very much more quickly than others and, if this can be combined with good understanding, it is obviously an advantage when revising. At the same time fast reading speeds for their own sake are not necessarily advantageous; understanding and remembering are the ultimate objectives.

Quick and efficient reading can be developed by paying attention to a number of points. First of all it is helpful to adopt a comfortable, but not soporific, position in good light and to approach the reading in a positive manner rather than viewing it as an unpleasant task. Then it is wise to develop the habit of reading in sections, i.e. looking at the meaning of sentences as a whole rather than concentrating on each word in isolation. This practice of reading in sections is not easy to describe but the more you read with this principle in mind the more your reading skills are likely to improve. A further point to bear in mind when developing an approach to quick and efficient reading is not to read for too long. Although there are individual differences in this respect, approximately thirty to forty minutes at a time is usually the maximum time span before a break of several minutes should be taken.

Finally it is important to re-emphasise the importance of making brief notes on the material being read. These should include details of points not fully understood so that you can pursue them with your tutor or study group.

A valuable spin-off of reading widely is that it can help to improve your vocabulary. A good vocabulary is undoubtedly an invaluable asset when it comes to interpreting and answering examination questions. Unless you are quite clear about what particular words in an examination question mean, you are going to waste time thinking about them and ultimately may completely misinterpret the question. To avoid this pitfall it is good practice to make a list of words encountered in your reading which cause difficulty, along with their dictionary definition. This list should be committed to memory and the words should be used where appropriate in self-evaluation tests.

The role of good note-taking and self-evaluation tests in promoting effective learning have already been stressed. One other way to remember information is by using word association. Perhaps the most common way of using this technique is to take the first letter of each of the words to be remembered and to make them into another word. For example, AIDA can be used to remember the key factors in selling and for advertising, namely, attention, interest, desire and action. Other word association techniques might involve making up simple stories or rhymes. The objective of all of these aids to remembering is to increase your familiarity with, and ease of recall of, the subject matter being revised.

REMEMBERING AND APPLYING KNOWLEDGE

The main objective when revising is to collect together all relevant information and attempt to remember it in context. However, this is not an end in itself since it is necessary to be able to use this information to answer the examination questions. Practice in applying knowledge to questions before the examination is as important as remembering it. Probably the most common cause of students under-achieving in examinations is that they do not answer the question! Instead they just write down an expanded version of their notes on the topic, which are unlikely to address themselves to the particular issues raised in the question.

The problem of applying knowledge is relatively simple if the examination questions are predominantly descriptive. This type of question merely requires you to demonstrate your knowledge about a particular topic without having to demonstrate higher level skills of analysis. Such questions will typically start with words such as 'Describe', 'State', 'Outline', 'Explain' and 'Define'. When answering descriptive questions include relevant definitions and explanations of all the points required by the question. Good answers will probably also include examples and/or empirical evidence to illustrate the points covered.

Analytical questions pose much greater difficulties in terms of using knowledge to answer a question. The hierarchy of skills illustrated in the diagram indicates the broad difference between descriptive and analytical questions.

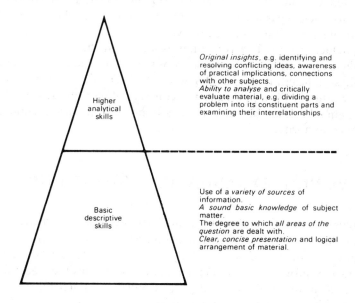

Fig A1   Hierarchy of skills.

Questions which are analytical in nature will start with words such as 'Discuss', 'Evaluate', 'Assess', 'Criticise', and 'Analyse'. This type of question requires the examinee to show early in the answer that the question is understood and to set up a framework for the remainder of the answer. It is then important to present the relevant points of view, support them with examples and show awareness of the criticisms which can be levelled at particular points of view.

An answer to an analytical question should end with a conclusion which summarises very briefly the key issues and presents the student's own considered judgment on the topic.

Some questions will have a clear descriptive component and an analytical component as in the following example. 'Identify the main elements of the marketing mix and assess their relative importance for marketing consumer durables.' In such cases it is reasonable to assume that the descriptive part will be allocated a lower proportion of the total marks than the analytical component. This should be reflected in the amount of time spent in answering the two parts of the question.

EXAMINATION NERVES

Careful revision and preparation should help to minimise the problem of examination nerves. Last minute panic could mean not obtaining the mark one's preparation warrants. It is important to keep calm and believe in yourself. Those individuals who are particularly prone to stress should talk about it with friends, family or welfare counsellors, as the very act of discussing the problem may help to reduce anxiety. Everyone finds examinations stressful to some extent, but if the exams are approached in a positive manner and by a candidate in good physical health this stress should not be harmful. Of course if there are health or other medical problems a doctor should be approached well before the examination and the relevant details brought to the attention of the examining authority.

ANSWERING EXAMINATION QUESTIONS

Once under examination conditions, and when the examination questions have been distributed, it is vital that time is taken to read all the instructions and questions carefully. If questions are then rated in terms of whether they can be adequately answered, it should finally be possible to list the required number of questions in the order they will be attempted. As a general rule it is wise to begin with a question where the subject matter is well known. This helps to build up confidence and means the more difficult ones can be left until later.

The next step is to make an essay plan after thinking about the question for a few minutes. This plan will consist of brief notes made on the answer paper in which the main points and structure of the essay will be outlined. Writing an essay plan helps to give direction to an answer and enables the scope of the answer to be gauged. Gauging the scope of an answer is an important prerequisite to deciding how much time can be devoted to its component parts. It is good practice to start your actual answer on a new page and when it is finished to lightly cross out the essay plan. The plan should, however, be handed in at the end of the examination.

When writing an essay under examination conditions students should attempt to make their writing as legible as possible as this will avoid trying the patience of the examiner who ultimately marks the paper. Other simple but important points to remember include numbering the answers correctly, and making sure that any additional papers have your name on and are attached to the answer book in the correct order.

One of the keys to success during an examination is correct pacing, so that an equal amount of time is spent on each answer. This skill should have been developed during revision and cause few difficulties during the real examination. If a question has not been finished during its allocated time it should be brought to a swift conclusion and the next one commenced. The value of completing all of the required number of questions cannot be over-emphasised. It is very difficult to get a good overall mark if the final question is not attempted or only just started when time expires. Allow time for planning before each question.

Answers should be written in a clear and logical manner with as good a style as the conditions permit. As time is at a premium, avoid waffle, do not keep repeating certain words. It is not usually necessary to rewrite the question before starting – this wastes valuable time. Refer to the question on the examination paper and circle key words as appropriate. The length of an answer is obviously dependent on size of handwriting, time available and knowledge of the subject, but as a general rule at least two or three sides of A4 paper are needed to write an adequate answer.

The style in which an examination answer is written depends on the nature of the examination and the particular question asked; some papers require answer in essay form, others require reports and in some instances the examinee must present an analysis of a case study. It is important to research the issue of the required style of answers and to practise preparing them before the examination.

Essay-type answers can take many forms but will usually have:

(*i*) an opening paragraph which goes to the heart of the question and gives an indication of how the problem will be approached;
(*ii*) the main body of the answer in which the examinee puts forward a reasoned case supported by appropriate facts and empirical evidence; and
(*iii*) a conclusion which draws together the strands of the argument and relates them back to the question.

There is no doubt that some students find writing essays under examination conditions difficult. In such cases it may be possible to introduce some greater degree of structure by using numbered headings and sub-headings within the answer. However, these should not degenerate into notes; on the whole this style is more appropriate to descriptive rather than analytical answers.

Case studies are an increasingly common feature of many examinations and may require answers to be presented in report form. Any question which does specifically ask for a report will almost certainly involve a proportion of total marks being awarded for the layout and presentation of the answer. In these circumstances examinees must take care over the form of their answer by paying attention to correct report format, although allowances will be made by the examiner for the fact that it has been prepared under examination conditions.

CONCLUSION

Passing examinations is not an end in itself. A course of study should be seen as a vehicle for personal development and improved understanding. It may also help individuals to obtain a new or better job. Those students who select their course of study carefully, apply themselves diligently and revise in a systematic manner should be able to cope with the final hurdle of an examination without too much difficulty. Obviously, things do go wrong on occasion and most people do fail a few examinations during their education but this should not be seen as the end of the world. Opportunities for retaking the examination or other courses of study are usually available if mishaps do occur.

APPENDIX 2 Customer Brief for Practical Exercise, Chapter 10

You are 42 years old with two children (girl 13, boy 10). You want the pen for your daughter. She has been using a ball-point up to now but as she will be starting her GCSE course soon you want her to use an ink pen.

APPENDIX 3 Leading Professional Bodies in the UK and Ireland

ASSOCIATION OF EXHIBITION ORGANISERS, 10 Manchester Square, London W1M 5AB. Tel: (071) 486 1951.

ASSOCIATION OF MARKET SURVEY ORGANISATIONS LTD, c/o Marplan Ltd, 119–127 Marylebone Road, London NW1 5PU. Tel: (071) 723 7276.

BRITISH EXPORT HOUSES ASSOCIATION, 69 Cannon Street, London EC4N 5AB. Tel: (071) 248 4444. This is also the address of the London Chamber of Commerce and Industry who provide additional services in terms of education and help to exporters.

BRITISH DIRECT MAIL ASSOCIATION, 1 New Burlington Street, London TW10 6TH. Tel: (081) 948 4151.

BRITISH FRANCHISE ASSOCIATION, Thames View, Newton Road, Henley-on-Thames, Oxon. RG9 1HG. Tel: (0491) 578050.

CHARTERED INSTITUTE OF MARKETING, Moor Hall, Cookham, Maidenhead, Berks SL6 9QH. Tel: (06285) 24922. The examining and professional body for the marketing and selling professions.

INDUSTRIAL MARKETING RESEARCH ASSOCIATION, 11 Bird Street, Lichfield, Staffs. WS13 6PW. Tel: (05432) 23448.

INSTITUTE OF ADVERTISING PRACTITIONERS IN IRELAND, 35 Upper Fitzwilliam Street, Dublin 2. Tel: Dublin 785685.

INSTITUTE OF EXPORT, Export House, 64 Clifton Street, London EC2A 4HB. Tel: (071) 247 9812. The examining and professional body for export.

INSTITUTE OF PRACTITIONERS IN ADVERTISING, 44 Belgrave Square, London SW1X 8QS. Tel: (071) 235 7020. The examining and professional body for personnel in their member agencies.

INSTITUTE OF PUBLIC RELATIONS, 1 Great James Street, London WC1N 3DA. Tel: (071) 405 5505. The professional body for public relations practitioners.

INSTITUTE OF SALES PROMOTION, Arena House, 66/8 Pentonville Road, London N1 9HS. Tel: (071) 837 5340.

IRISH EXPORTERS ASSOCIATION, 17 Merchants' Quay, Dublin 8. Tel: Dublin 770285.

IRISH COMMERCIAL TRAVELLERS' FEDERATION, Gillabbey House, Connaught Avenue, Cork. Tel: Cork 23319.

MARKETING INSTITUTE OF IRELAND, Confederation House, Kildare Street, Dublin 2.

PUBLIC RELATIONS INSTITUTE OF IRELAND, 50 Waterloo Road, Dublin 4. Tel: Dublin 689169.

THE ADVERTISING ASSOCIATION, Abford House, 15 Wilton Road, London SW1V 1NJ. Tel: (071) 828 2771. The professional body for advertising, except agency, personnel.

THE COMMUNICATIONS, ADVERTISING AND MARKETING EDUCATION FOUNDATION (CAM), Abford House, 15 Wilton Road, London SW1V 1NJ. Tel: (071) 828 2777. The examining and educational body of the advertising industry, excluding advertising agencies.

THE MARKET RESEARCH SOCIETY, 15 Belgrave Square, London SW1X 8PF. Tel: (071) 235 4709. The examining and professional body for marketing research.

Bibliographical References

BAKER, K., GERMINGHAM, J., AND MACDONALD, C. (1979) 'The utility to market research of the classification of residential neighbourhoods', Market Research Society Conference.

BISS, A. (1985) 'The Narrowcasting Naturals', *Campaign*, 31 May.

BOWMAN, P. AND ELLIS, E. (1982) *Manual of Public Relations*.

CARDOZO, R.N. (1980) 'Situational segmentation of industrial markets', *European Journal of Marketing*, 14, 5/6.

CHURCHILL, D. (1986) 'Cracks Appear in the Image', *Financial Times*, 27 February.

CLINE, C.E., AND SHAPIRO, B.P., *Cumberland Metal Industries (A)*, case study, Harvard Business School.

COREY, E.R. (1983) *Industrial Marketing: Cases and Concepts*, 3rd edition, Prentice-Hall.

COULAUX, C., AND JOBBER, D. (1989) 'Motivation of consumer salespeople'. University of Bradford Management Centre Working Paper.

DECORMIER, R., AND JOBBER, D. (1989) 'The Counsellor Selling Method: Concepts, constructs and effectiveness'. University of Bradford Management Centre Working Paper.

DESSLER, G. (1979) *Human Behaviour: Improving Performance at Work*, Prentice-Hall.

DOYLE, P., AND HUTCHISON, J. (1973) 'Individual differences in family decision making', *Journal of the Market Research Society*, 15, 4.

ENGEL, J.F., AND BLACKWELL, R.D. (1982) *Consumer Behaviour*, Dryden Press.

FESTINGER, L. (1957) *A Theory of Cognitive Dissonance*, Row & Peterson.

FISHER, L. (1976) *Industrial Marketing*, 2nd edition, Business Books.

GREENBERG, G., AND GREENBERG, H.M. (1976) 'Predicting sales success – myths and reality', *Personnel Journal*, Dec., p. 61.

HERZBERG, F., MAUSNER, B., AND BLOCH SNYDERMAN, B. (1959) *The Motivation to Work*, 2nd edition, Wiley.

HOWARD, J.A., AND SHETH, J.N. (1969) *The Theory of Buyer Behaviour*, Wiley.

JAPANESE EXTERNAL TRADE ORGANISATION (1976) 'Selling to Japan: know the business customs', *International Trade Forum*, 12.

JEFKINS, F. (1989) *Jefkins School of Public Relations – A Broadsheet*.

JOBBER, D., AND MILLAR, S. (1984) 'The use of psychological tests in the selection of salesmen: a UK survey', *Journal of Sales Management*, 1, 1.

JOBBER, D., HOOLEY, G., AND SHIPLEY, D. (1989) 'The effects of organisational size on salesforce evaluation practices'. University of Bradford Management Centre Working Paper.

KENNEDY, G., BENSON, J., AND MACMILLAN, J. (1980) *Managing Negotiations*, Business Books.

KENT, C. (1985) 'Outgunning the Sloane Ranger'. *C & E International*, July.

KOTLER, P. (1980) *Marketing Management: Analysis, Planning and Control*, 4th edition, Prentice-Hall.

LANCASTER, G.A., AND BARON, H. (1977) 'Exhibiting for profit', *Industrial Management*, November.

LANCASTER, G.A., AND WRIGHT, G. (1983) 'Forecasting the future of video using a diffusion model', *European Journal of Marketing*, 17, 2.

LEARNING INTERNATIONAL ORGANIZATION (1988) 'Selling Strategies for the 1990s'. *Training and Development Journal*. March.

LEE, A. (1984) 'Sizing up the buyers', *Marketing*, 29 March.

LEVITT, T. (1962) *The Marketing Mode*, McGraw-Hill.

LIDSTONE, J., AND MELKMAN, A. (1977) 'Make marketing plans for major customers', *Marketing*, Oct.

LIKERT, R. (1961) *New Patterns of Sales Management*, McGraw-Hill.

LODISH, L.M. (1974) 'Vaguely right approach to sales force allocations', *Harvard Business Review*, 52, Jan–Feb.

LUTHANS, F. (1981) *Organisational Behaviour*, McGraw-Hill.

MCCARTHY, E. JEROME (1960) *Basic Marketing: A Managerial Approach*, 1st edition, Irwin.

MASLOW, A.H. (1943) 'A theory of human motivation', *Psychological Review*, July.

MAYER, M., AND GREENBERG, G. (1964) 'What makes a good salesman', *Harvard Business Review*, 42, July–August.

MEIDAN, A. (1982) 'Optimising the number of industrial sales persons', *Industrial Marketing Management*, 11, 1.

MOSS, C.D. (1979) 'Industrial salesmen as a source of marketing intelligence', *European Journal of Marketing*, 13, 3.

PA CONSULTANTS (1979) *Sales Force Practice Today: A Basis for Improving Performance*, Institute of Marketing.

PAUL, W.J., ROBERTSON, K.G., AND HERZBERG, F. (1969) 'Job enrichment pays off', *Harvard Business Review*, March–April.

RANDALL, G. (1975) 'The use of tests and scored questionnaires in salesmen selection', in Millar, K.M. (ed.) *Psychological Testing in Personnel Assessment*, Gower.

REED, J. (1983) 'How Perkins changed gear', *Marketing*, 27 Oct.

ROBINSON, P.J., FARIS, C.W., AND WIND, Y. (1967) *Industrial Buying and Creative Marketing*, Allyn & Bacon and the Marketing Science Institute.

SAUNDERS, J.A., AND HON-CHUNG, T. (1984) 'Selling to Japan', *Journal of Sales Management*, 1, 1.

SEMLOW, J. (1959) 'How many salesmen do you need?', *Harvard Business Review*, 37, 3, May/June.

SHIPLEY, D., AND KIELY, J. (1988) 'Motivation and dissatisfaction of industrial salespeople − how relevant is Herzberg's theory?' *European Journal of Marketing*, 22, 1.

STAMFORD-BEWLEY, C., AND JOBBER, D. (1989) 'A study of the training of salespeople in the UK'. University of Bradford Management Centre Working Paper.

TALLEY, W.J. (1961) 'How to design sales territories', *Journal of Marketing*, 25, 3, Jan.

VROOM, V.H. (1964) *Work and Motivation*, Wiley.

WEBSTER, F.E. (1979) *Industrial Marketing Strategy*, Roland.

WILSON, M. (1983) *Managing a Sales Force*, Gower.

WINKLER, J. (1981) *Bargaining for Results*, Heinemann.

WORCESTER, R. M., AND ENGLISH, P. (1985) 'Time for PR to Mature?' *PR Week*, 1 November.

Further Reading

ADAMS, T. (1985) *The Secret of Successful Selling*, Heinemann.
ALLEN, P. (1979) *Sales and Sales Management*, 2nd edition, Macdonald & Evans.
ANDERSON, R.E., AND HAIR, J.F. (1983) *Sales Management: Text with Cases*, Random House.
ATTWOOD, C. (1969) *The Sales Representative's Handbook*, Business Books.
BROWNSTONE, D.M. (1979) *Sell Your Way to Success*, Wiley.
CUMMINGS, R. (1979) *Contemporary Selling*, 2nd edition, Macmillan.
DALRYMPLE, D.J. (1988) *Sales Management: Concepts and cases*, Wiley.
DODD, T.F. (1974) *Sales Forecasting: How to Prepare and Use Market Data and Sales Forecasts in Profit Planning*, Gower.
ELSBY, F.H. (1969) *Marketing and the Sales Manager*, Pergamon.
ELVY, B.H. (1978) *Salesmanship Made Simple*, 3rd edition, Heinemann.
FENTON, J. (1979) *The A–Z of Sales Management*, Heinemann.
FUTRELL, C.M. (1984) *Fundamentals of Selling*, Irwin.
GILLAM, A. (1982) *The Principles and Practice of Selling*, Heinemann.
GORMAN, W. (1979) *Selling: Personality, Persuasion, Strategy*, Random House.
HUDSON, C.L. (1967) *Professional Salesmanship*, Staples.
KOSSEN, S. (1982) *Creative Selling Today*, Harper & Row.
LANCASTER, G.A., AND LOMAS, R.A. (1985) *Forecasting for Sales and Materials Management*, Macmillan.
LANCASTER, G.A., SEEKINGS, D., WILLIS, G. AND KOZUBSKA, J. (1985) *Maximising Industrial Sales*, MCB University Press.
LUND, P.R. (1979) *Compelling Selling*, 2nd edition, Macmillan.
MAGNUS-HANNAFORD, R. (1964) *Selling and Salesmanship*, Pan.
MANNING, G.L., AND REECE, B.L. (1984) *Selling Today: A Personal Approach*, Brown.
MILLER, R.B., HEIMAN, S.E., AND TULEJA, T. (1988) *Strategic Selling*, Kogan Page.

NOONAN, C. (1986) *Sales Management: the complete marketer's guide*, Allen & Unwin.

PEDERSON, C.A., WRIGHT. M.D., AND WEITZ, B.A. (1981) *Selling – Principles and Practice*, 3rd edition, Irwin.

SELTZ, D.D. (1982) *Handbook of Effective Sales Prospecting Techniques*, Addison Wesley.

SENTON, D., AND KIRKBY, P. (1985) *Organising for Improved Sales and Materials Management*, Macmillan.

SLIJPER, M.T. (1972) *Assessing Export Potential*, Gower.

SMALLBONE, D.W. (1968) *An Introduction to Sales Management*, Staples.

STILL, R.R., CUNDIFF, E.W., AND GOVONI, N.A.P. (1981) *Sales Management: Decisions, Strategies and Cases*, Prentice-Hall.

TACK, A. (1989) *Increase Your Sales the Tack Way*, Gower.

WILSON, M. (1968) *Managing and Sales Force*, Gower.

FOR EXAMINATION STUDENTS

LEADER, W.G. (1984) *How to Pass Exams*, Macdonald & Evans.

Index

M&E Handbook

Selling: Management and Practice

Peter Allen

This popular introductory handbook recognises selling as the cutting edge of business.

The book emphasises pro-active selling: customer creation, understanding the buyer, the need for product knowledge, selling techniques, communications. Traditional sales management functions of forecasting, planning organisation, training and appraisal are also included.

Suitable for all studying for business and marketing examinations . . .
Marketing

1989   288pp   Paper   0 7121 1900 0

How to Sell To Europe

Peter Danton de Rouffignac

After 1992 British firms will have unrestricted access to at least 320 million consumers in the new domestic market of Europe, yet many business people remain uncertain and uninformed as to the new opportunities this offers. *How to Sell to Europe* is a highly practical, comprehensive, step-by-step guide to the changes, threats and challenges of this new Common Market.

Any owner/manager of a small sized firm wanting to export to Europe for the first time would find this book useful. The book is particularly relevant to manufacturing and service companies.

As a first primer on venturing into Europe this would be invaluable.
Daily Telegraph

1990   256pp   Cased   0 273 03149 X

Practical Sales Management

Gordon J Bolt

This book covers both the theory and practice of sales management and will appeal to students taking a wide variety of degree and professional courses.

Important features include:
- the role of the sales manager, especially in relation to selecting and maintaining a dynamic sales force
- the administrative and support role of sales management
- the crucial issue of credit control.

. . . a comprehensive treatment of the theory and practice of sales management. *Business Executive*

1987   464pp   Paper   0 273 02736 0